Middle East realignment: the Arab upheaval
by Augustus Richard Norton

Jan. 18, 2011: Police form a line in front of demonstrators in downtown Tunis, Tunisia. The protesters are holding a sign urging the police to back down. (HOLLY PICKETT/THE NEW YORK TIMES/REDUX)

THE YEAR 2011 proved extraordinary in the Arab world. Assumptions about the weak appetite for freedom in Muslim societies was discredited as three veteran dictators—Tunisia's Zine al-Abidine Ben Ali, Egypt's Hosni Mubarak and Libya's Muammar Qadhafi—were toppled by popular movements. The fate of autocrats in Syria and Yemen hung in the balance. In other states, notably Bahrain and Saudi Arabia, sitting regimes have been shaken but applications of repression and largesse permit the rulers to continue to reign. In Jordan, Morocco and Oman, skillful political maneuvering has tempered demands for reform. In Iraq and Algeria, the living memory of years of trauma and carnage has dampened the appetite for confrontation and protest.

The Arab world seems to be entering a new historical phase, one in which the contours of political power may be reshaped as more governments face cries for accountability and responsiveness to citizens' demands. Never in the modern history of the Middle East have so many millions demanded the dismantling of their autocratic regimes with such unanimity, perseverance, persistence and peacefulness.

The great political upheaval that began when fruit seller Mohammed Bouazizi set himself alight in a desperate quest for dignity in the Tunisian city of Sidi Bouzid, on December 17, 2010, is likely to continue for some time to come. Since December 2010, thousands of demonstrators have gone to the streets and squares of towns and cities across the Arab

AUGUSTUS RICHARD NORTON *(Ph.D., University of Chicago) is a Professor of International Relations and Anthropology at Boston University, where he is also the Director of the Institute for Iraqi Studies. His books include* Hezbollah *(Princeton University Press, 2009), and* Civil Society in the Middle East *(E. J. Brill, 2 vols., 1995, 1996, 2005). He has done fieldwork in Bahrain, Egypt, Lebanon, Jordan, Syria and the Occupied Palestinian Territories.*

The author wishes to thank Emile Nakhleh for his insights, and Boston University's Layla AlBallooshi for her skilled research assistance.

world to participate in what many Arabs call "the awakening" (al-sahwa) or "the renaissance" (al-nahda), rather than the "Arab Spring" as favored by many Western reporters. (The latter term recalls the Prague Spring of 1968, an exhilarating political and cultural opening in Czechoslovakia that was crushed within months by Soviet tanks.)

Just weeks after Bouazizi died of his burns on January 4, 2011, demonstrations erupted around the Arab world, including Mauritania, Morocco, Algeria, Oman, Iraq, Saudi Arabia and the Sudan, and, of course, Bahrain, Egypt, Libya, Syria and Yemen. In fact, by February at least five men were inspired to imitate Bouazizi and died in public self-immolations in Algeria, Egypt and Saudi Arabia. In mass demonstrations, young people—60% of the Arab world is under 30 years old—were in the lead demanding freedom in a region where public demonstrations have seldom been tolerated and popular efforts to organize politically have been met for decades with repression, economic coercion and fear. In most Arab states, even small-scale gatherings require a permit, which is seldom granted. In 2011, however, growing crowds in Tunis (Tunisia), Cairo (Egypt), Benghazi (Libya), Manama (Bahrain) and elsewhere courageously demanded reform or democracy. The young, in particular, were insisting that they would not tolerate the indignity and disrespect dealt to their fathers and mothers by ensconced autocrats. The regimes responded: in Algiers (Algeria), where the generals keep a steel grip on power, the government ended 19 years of martial law in February 2011 in order to dampen calls for demonstrations.

The welcome news for Washington is that al-Qaeda has to be crestfallen. The terrorist organization preaches violence and hatred in the name of Islam, but Muslim and Arab youths in Cairo's Tahrir Square, Manama's Pearl Square and Tripoli's Green Square endured death and injury in the defense of their peaceful demands for dignity and freedom. They showed astounding discipline in rejecting violence.

Though antigovernment protests

began peacefully in almost every instance, state security forces rejoined with deadly violence—occasionally on a mass scale, as in Libya. In Egypt and Tunisia, where demonstrators showed remarkable fortitude by sticking to mostly peaceful protest, chants of "silmiya, silmiya" ("peaceful, peaceful") would become a trademark of the demonstrators. Even so, over 200 people were killed by security forces in Tunisia, and nearly 900 civilians died in Egypt. These were hardly bloodless transitions. The casualties were much higher in Libya* and Syria, where thousands have died violently in civil war and in government suppression of protests.

Many Arabs have looked for years for exemplary models of reform and responsive government. Among educated Arab publics there was widespread awareness that non-Arab Turkey was demonstrating it was not only feasible to be a vibrant and prosperous democracy, but that an Islamically oriented party could win elections and lead the country. The Justice and Development Party (AKP), which came to power in 2002, has provided a political model that was more culturally authentic and familiar than Western democracies. Across the Arab world, many are now watching Tunisia, Egypt and Libya with combinations of awe and hope. The spectacle of a supine Mubarak caged and on trial in Egypt, Ben Ali fleeing in January to an ignominious exile in Saudi Arabia or the battered carcass of Qadhafi on display prove that the people may finally have the last word.

While Americans may cheer on the reformers, it bears remembering that the inspiration for rebellion grew locally. In marked contrast to recent attempts by the U.S. to promote reform and democracy, notably during the presidency of George W. Bush (2001–2009), the impetus for the upheavals of 2011 has been purely indigenous. The initial demonstrations that gathered momentum in January and February 2011 were publicized aptly as "Days of Rage." The

*The Libyan Interim Health Minister estimates that 30,000 died. Libya has a total population of 6 million.

rage has been pent up for years and decades. It stems not just from government neglect, dishonesty and corruption, but also from the fact that most Arab governments have treated their subjects and citizens with disdain. Across the Arab world, the social contract between the regime and the people promised economic well-being and public services in return for limited freedom and muted political voice. Regimes have been unable to fulfill their side of the bargain as populations have burgeoned and large slices of national wealth have ended up in private hands.

Complaints about greed and malfeasance that for many years were only whispered are now fully aired. Cell phones, satellite television stations and the Internet allowed people to know that so many others shared their rage. Disclosures of classified documents by WikiLeaks in 2010 also fed complaints by leaking diplomatic cables that lent official corroboration to rampant elite corruption in several Arab countries, including Tunisia. The new generation has grown up with cell phones and, increasingly, the Internet. Through millions of text messages, tweets and Facebook posts, restrictions on free speech and assembly have often been deftly skirted. Yet the Arab upheaval has not been a Twitter or Facebook revolution: those are only tools. Nor is it simply an onrush of economic grievances. At the epicenter of the upheaval has been a clamor for respect and dignity.

Different regimes, common patterns

Despite the wide variations in national wealth, quality of life and cultural diversity across the Arab world, there are several common patterns, including severe limits on oppositional activities, limited accountability of the rulers and an absence of effective term limits for those wielding power. Once in power, rulers stay in power—as do the coteries of surrounding elites.

Although secular opposition groups and parties have sometimes been permitted to operate nominally, state surveillance, intimidation and prudent self-policing ensure that the oppositionists

Great Decisions Resources

National Opinion Ballot Report 2011

Since 1955, opinion ballots have been included with *Great Decisions* to enable those interested to make their views known. The Foreign Policy Association produces the annual **NATIONAL OPINION BALLOT REPORT (NOBR)** based on the tabulation of ballots submitted by Great Decisions participants. In 2011, over 20,000 ballots were collected across the eight topics.

Each year, FPA sends the **NOBR** to the White House, the departments of State and Defense, members of Congress, the media and concerned citizens. Free upon request.

NATIONAL OPINION BALLOT REPORT
Results of the Foreign Policy Association's 2011 National Opinion Survey
GREAT DECISIONS 2011

FOREIGN POLICY ASSOCIATION
470 Park Avenue South, 2nd Floor • New York, NY 10016-6819
Phone: (212) 481-8100 • Fax: (212) 481-9275 • www.fpa.org

Teacher's Packet & Classroom Packet 2012

Specially priced packets provide educators with the *Great Decisions* materials they need for their classroom at a significant discount.

The **GREAT DECISIONS TEACHER'S PACKET** contains 1 copy each of the *Great Decisions* briefing book, *Teacher's Guide* and *Great Decisions* Television Series on DVD.

The Teacher's Guide

Written by curriculum experts, the Teacher's Guide provide educators with ideas and lesson plans corresponding to each of the *Great Decisions* topics for the high school level. Available as a PDF.

The **CLASSROOM PACKET** contains 31 copies of the *Great Decisions* briefing book, along with 1 copy of each of the *Teacher's Guide* and *Great Decisions* Television Series on DVD.

Great Decisions Online

GREAT DECISIONS
FOREIGN POLICY ASSOCIATION

UPDATES

Produced each spring and fall, the **Updates** provide concise and pertinent information about the latest developments in each *Great Decisions* topic. Available at **www.fpa.org** and free upon request.

NEWSLETTER

Sign up for the Great Decisions online **newsletter** to receive updates on recently posted resources, quizzes, special features and exclusive offers on *Great Decisions* materials. Sign up today at **www.fpa.org**.

"With all the new vaccines being developed today, hopefully people won't have to suffer like I did."

– Leslie Meigs, meningitis survivor

Leslie was only eight years old when she was rushed to the hospital with meningococcal meningitis. She was in a coma for weeks, in the hospital for months and had to go on dialysis. Still, she was considered lucky. Without a vaccination to prevent it, the disease, although rare, can lead to serious complications and death within 48 hours. Novartis is developing new and innovative vaccines for meningitis, influenza and other infectious diseases. To learn more, visit **ThinkWhatsPossible.com**

GREAT DECISIONS 2012

About the cover

On February 10, 2011, one day before Egyptian President Hosni Mubarak stepped down in the face of overwhelming public demonstrations, an un-identified young woman pauses in the crowd of protesters at Tahrir Square, the epicenter of the protests in Cairo.

Photo Credit:
 XINHUA/CORBIS

About the back cover

The inscription is a quotation Henrik Ibsen's *An Enemy of the People* (1882), Act I, trans-lated by R. Farquharson Sharp.

The image, which depicts the USS *Constitution,* is a repro-duction of a period painting in the collection of the National Archives in College Park, MD.

PRINTED IN THE UNITED STATES OF AMERICA BY DART-MOUTH PRINTING COMPANY, HANOVER, NH.

LIBRARY OF CONGRESS CONTROL NUMBER: 2011934217. **ISBN:** 978-0-87124-238-9.

Researched as of November 18, 2011. The authors are responsible for factual accuracy and for the views expressed.

FPA itself takes no position on issues of U.S. foreign policy.

*T*he late Arthur M. Schlesinger, Jr., a long-time friend and Fellow of the Foreign Policy Association, said it well: "In a world of change, our foreign policy will be effective only as it expresses an America which shows it understands the imperatives of change. And this suggests again that foreign policy has meaning only as an extension, a projection, of what we are at home."

If, as a nation, we look at ourselves in the mirror, what would we like to change? The World Affairs Councils of America recently issued a call to action for higher standards of education for young Americans in the face of the reality of globalization—the emergence of a single global market for goods, labor and capital. Like it or not, American students are in competition with their counterparts around the globe, who are surpassing them. If we fail to raise educational standards, the consequences will be grim. Growing poverty, unprecedented income inequality and social turmoil are not outside the orbit of plausibility.

An unintended consequence of the No Child Left Behind legislation has been the marginalization of core social studies disciplines. Proficiency in these subjects is critical if young Americans are to be prepared for an increasingly competitive, interdependent world. While the Internet, social media and television carry global events, most young Americans lack the background to understand how such events affect them, their communities and their country. And yet, in today's world, any people, who are parochial and construe their interests narrowly, risk being condemned to the margins of the global economy.

For our part, the Foreign Policy Association is committed to working with educators to develop global studies with innovative models that inspire new ways to stimulate curiosity and learning about our ever-changing world. And I could not be more proud of the GREAT DECISIONS outreach program. I commend to you this year's compelling briefing book and the 2012 GREAT DECISIONS Television Series in which former Secretary of State Colin Powell observes: "Foreign policy is not just something for intellectuals and people in government to do, it is something for every American—especially our young Americans—must understand and study...because we are counting on you to tell the leaders of your country what you want to see happen with the foreign policy of the United States of America."

Noel V. Lateef
President and CEO
Foreign Policy Association

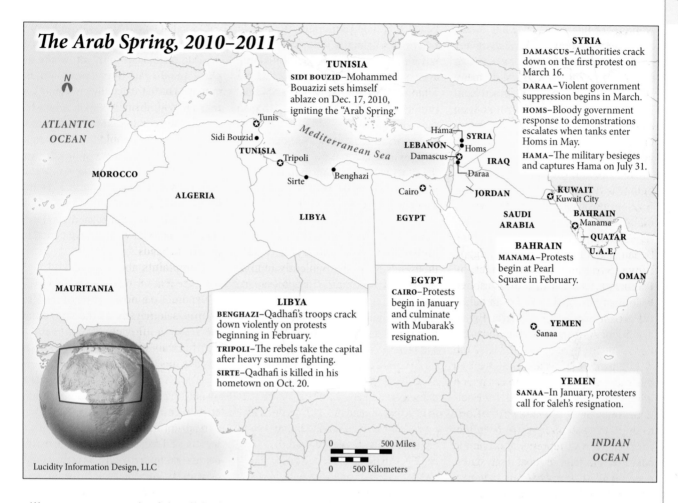

The Arab Spring, 2010–2011

TUNISIA
SIDI BOUZID–Mohammed Bouazizi sets himself ablaze on Dec. 17, 2010, igniting the "Arab Spring."

SYRIA
DAMASCUS–Authorities crack down on the first protest on March 16.
DARAA–Violent government suppression begins in March.
HOMS–Bloody government response to demonstrations escalates when tanks enter Homs in May.
HAMA–The military besieges and captures Hama on July 31.

EGYPT
CAIRO–Protests begin in January and culminate with Mubarak's resignation.

BAHRAIN
MANAMA–Protests begin at Pearl Square in February.

LIBYA
BENGHAZI–Qadhafi's troops crack down violently on protests beginning in February.
TRIPOLI–The rebels take the capital after heavy summer fighting.
SIRTE–Qadhafi is killed in his hometown on Oct. 20.

YEMEN
SANAA–In January, protesters call for Saleh's resignation.

Lucidity Information Design, LLC

0   500 Miles
0   500 Kilometers

will not pose a meaningful political challenge. Islamist groups, such as the venerable Muslim Brotherhood (MB, founded in 1928), have been more robust, but their legal status varies from state to state. In Egypt, the MB was, until 2011, an illegal organization, yet its members were permitted to compete for parliamentary elections while being subjected to intermittent harassment, legal prosecution and arbitrary detention. By comparison, the MB is legally tolerated in Jordan, whereas membership was a capital crime under Emergency Law 49 in Syria, until 2011. Given the long-standing weakness of secular opposition groups, it has been common for observers to describe the Islamists as the only viable opposition group.

It is common to hear Middle Eastern states described as "*mukhabarat*-states." Strictly speaking, the "mukhabarat" are the intelligence-gathering agencies, but the term is often used to refer to all the agencies spawned by the state to control and coerce society and thwart dissent.

The argument was that Arab states used a sophisticated combination of limited political reforms, co-optation, patronage, surveillance and coercion to strengthen the modern authoritarian state.

It became fashionable for scholars and policy experts to express cynicism about the prospects for democratic reform, the activism of a vibrant civil society in the Arab world and the significance of a secular opposition. Predictions were proffered that "broadened authoritarianism" would prevail. Of course, the Arab upheaval has not only upended some regimes, but illustrated that some of them are far less politically durable and far more vulnerable to mass protest and public dissent than many U.S. officials and Middle East scholars recognized.

Reemergence of political discourse

In addition, there is far more political diversity in Arab societies than is often realized. While the Islamic-ori-

ented parties still command broad support, rival secular parties have begun to gain a footing in the newly enlivened political spaces of Egypt and Tunisia. The secular parties will not build a grassroots base overnight, but they are finding constituencies. More important, while there is no doubt that the Islamist parties will win a significant share of the vote, the Islamist milieu is broadly competitive. This is evident on satellite television, where personalities such as Shaykh Yusuf al-Qaradawi and the Egyptian accountant-turned-pious-savant Amr Khaled offer competing commentaries on religion, freedom, capitalism and modernity. Debates have raged for years in Islamist circles about the nature of politics, the application of Islamic norms in society, relations with non-Muslims and secularly oriented Muslims, and the legitimacy of democracy. A variety of views are represented, reflecting generational differences, ideological debates and competing conceptions of piety. While the contours of these debates were known to scholars and other close observers of Muslim societies, the persistence of authoritarianism helped to ensure that the debates remained largely out of view. Moreover, these regimes often played expertly on Western stereotypes of Muslim extremism to discredit moderate Islamist voices.

The opening of political space in countries like Egypt and Tunisia has brought the issues more clearly into view, particularly as Islamists decide to compete for political power. Thus, in Egypt the MB now finds itself challenged not just by secular political forces, but by at least a dozen different religiously oriented groups, including ultraconservative Salafist groups that are intent on imposing Islamic law in

tionalist counterparts rather than with reactionary Islamist groups, which often view such alliances with disdain. Among the fascinating aspects of the ongoing upheaval will be to observe the new patterns of political alliance that emerge.

Scholars, diplomats and journalists with experience on the ground in the Arab world have long been acutely aware of the underlying discontent and seething anger. These sentiments were typically discreetly expressed because of the consequences of overt dissent, but the sentiments were widespread, especially below the ranks of the privileged class. A common refrain was that the government does not treat the people with dignity. When this charge was unpacked it entailed encounters with

cast a ballot were those who were most easily manipulated or bought. This was strikingly apparent in Egypt, where the participation rate in elections was inversely related to socioeconomic status: The better off a person might be, the less likely she was to vote. As a result, in the upper-middle-class neighborhoods of Cairo, the voting rate was often less than 10%. People would say: "why vote? It doesn't matter." Therefore, until recently, the idea that people lived in a democracy was viewed as a ruse intended to fool foreigners. The people were not fooled.

The stirrings of widespread economic discontent were apparent throughout the first decade of the 21st century, especially in the states that were not well-endowed with massive hydrocarbon wealth. After decades of state-centered development, extensive subsidies and the development of massive state bureaucracies, countries like Egypt and Tunisia began to restructure their economies in the 1990s. These countries were often under pressure from international agencies such as the International Monetary Fund (IMF), which conditioned stabilization funding and loans on a reduction in the scale of the state sector of the economy. The restructuring steps included the sale of state companies to well-connected entrepreneurs and the reduction of jobs in the public sector. While these reforms were often acclaimed by economists, the local results included widening income inequality, underemployment and unemployment. Combined with the competitive pressures of globalization, laborers and members of the rank-and-file middle class were caught in a struggle to sustain their standard of living and many felt they were losing headway. The economic discontent is reflected in the countless protests, demonstrations and strikes that occurred in Egypt and Tunisia, as well as in Jordan, Morocco and Lebanon. Therefore, it comes as no surprise that the upheaval of 2011 first gained momentum in Tunisia and Egypt, where economic inequality was widely felt and expressed. ■

Feb. 1, 2011: Protests in Egypt continued with many tens of thousands assembling in Tahrir Square in central Cairo, demanding the ouster of Egyptian President Mubarak. The Egyptian army has said it will not fire on protestors as they gather in large numbers in central Cairo. (PETER MACDIARMID/GETTY IMAGES)

Egypt, and middle-of-the-road Islamic politicians who are intent on building coalitions with secular political forces. Generational differences are striking, especially because the MB is famous for a geriatric leadership, which has reliably proved to be out of step with its youth wings. The divided Islamist milieu necessitates a variety of coalitions and partnerships. Thus, moderate Islamist groups may be prompted to seek alliances with secular and na-

capricious officials who acted above or even outside the law, a sense that the government was not accountable and corruption widespread, and that most people were on the losing side of widening income inequality.

Although elections were held in a variety of Arab countries, including Egypt, Jordan, Syria and Tunisia, the electoral process was blatantly corrupt. Indeed, bribery and coercion were so common that the voters most likely to

The awakening

THE ARAB WORLD is in a state of upheaval, with the "revolutions" in Tunisia, Egypt and Libya and the ongoing struggles for change in Syria, Yemen, Bahrain, Saudi Arabia and the Persian Gulf states. These cases vary widely in several key respects, particularly the relationship between political leaders and the security establishment, especially the military; the extent to which the states are culturally and ethnically diverse; and the financial resources readily accessible to the government. It matters a great deal whether the military institution is a patrimonial vestige of the head of state, as opposed to a corporate institution in which promotions are largely merit-based and the core mission is to protect the state as opposed to protecting a particular ruling elite. It also matters whether the cleavages in society coincide with regional rivalries and whether these divisions are mitigated by patterns of interethnic or interreligious habits of cooperation. Finally, governments with extensive material and financial recourses may succeed in quelling demands or co-opting dissidents, whereas less well-endowed governments have to choose between accommodating or attempting to squash protests.

June 20, 2011: A woman speaks out before the trial of Ben Ali in the Palace of Justice in Tunis. Tunisians are anxious to see faster social and economic improvement in the country following the January Revolution. (SAMUEL ARANDA /CORBIS)

Tunisia: the Jasmine Revolution

Of all the North African countries, Tunisia would seem to enjoy the best chance for a democratic transformation. The population of 10.6 million is generally well-educated and there is a well-established middle class and an impressive civil society. North Africa, known as "the Maghrib" (the West) in the Arab world, is a region of remarkable cultural and political diversity. While the population is predominantly Arab, there are also important ethnic minorities, especially the Berbers, who comprise important and often restive minorities in Algeria and Morocco (with sizable numbers as well in Tunisia and Libya). While this may change, within Tunisia, the Arab-Berber divide has been far less important than it is in either Morocco or

Algeria, where the Berbers have insisted on education in the Berber language, as well as cultural autonomy.

Various sides of the political debate have emerged. The Constitutional Democratic Rally was Ben Ali's political arm and it is now being disassembled. Tunisia's Islamists are led by Rachid Ghannouchi, a moderate. He returned from exile in February 2011 after years of living in London, where he played an important role as a voice for Muslim accommodation in Europe. Ennahda (al-Nadha, or the Renaissance Party), which Ghannouchi founded, managed to survive years of state suppression by maintaining a covert presence in society and cultivating a youthful leadership. As in all the countries of North Africa, Salafist currents exist in Tunisia, but their support is presently not widespread. Tunisia is also blessed with a strong labor union movement, one that is without parallel in the region. Similarly, the small Tunisian military, which includes fewer than 40,000 people under arms, is led by a professional officer corps that has not infiltrated the civil-

ian economy as the behemoth Egyptian military has done.

Time and again since December 2010, Tunisians have rallied to preserve the momentum of the Jasmine Revolution. Many remnants of the oppressive Ben Ali regime have been expunged and the Mediterranean republic was competently led during much of the transition to elections by Prime Minister Beji Caid Essebsi, an octogenarian and former associate of the legendary secularist dictator Habib Bourguiba, who led Tunisia to independence half a century ago. One of Bourguiba's legacies was a commitment to women's rights, which are arguably more respected in Tunisia than in any other North African country. This means that Tunisian women will turn out in significant numbers if their rights are at risk.

Elections for the 217-member national Constituent Assembly were held on October 23, 2011. The assessment of European observers was that balloting was organized and carried out under high standards of integrity and transparency. Each party was required to assemble a party list by governate, with equal numbers of male and female candidates, whose names were alternated on the ballot. Individuals were also allowed to run. The elections were designed to preclude an overwhelming victory by any single party, as happened in Algeria in 1991, with disastrous results. About 30 parties or movements competed, with six winning about three quarters of all seats. The five leading parties were al-Nahda (90 seats); the Congress for the Republic (CPR), a party founded by a respected human rights figure in 1981 (30 seats); Aridha, or the Popular Petition Party, which was established only in March 2011 by a widely known journalist (initially 26 seats, but some were revoked for election finance violations); the center-left Democratic Forum for Labor and Liberties (FDTL, 21 seats); and the Progressive Democratic Party (PDP, 17 seats).

Arabs are watching developments in Tunisia closely. The country is a bellwether for the fate of the Arab Awakening; but the impediments to reform are formidable in every other Arab state, including Egypt.

Egypt: the January 25th revolution

Egyptians had been chafing under the Mubarak dictatorship for years. While opposition activities were often stymied by repression and dampened by fear, labor strikes were increasingly commonplace and political activists highlighted regime abuses. Within some opposition Islamist circles there was much debate and discussion about themes of civil society, democracy and tolerance.

Using word of mouth, cell-phone messaging, and social networking tools, especially Facebook, which had become a locus of opposition communication during the previous autumn, January 25, 2011, was declared a "Day of Rage," inspired by Tunisia. For many, the memory of Khaled Said, a young computer activist who was savagely beaten to death by police the previous summer in Alexandria, Egypt, was vivid. Tens of thousands turned out, especially in Cairo's Tahrir (Liberation) Square, a central site adjacent to Egypt's famous archeological museum, where chants of *"irhal, irhal, irhal!"* (scram, get out, leave) were commonplace. Although the momentum was tenuous, especially when armed thugs were unleashed by the government to foster a climate of lawlessness, the "revolution" succeeded in a mere 18 days to topple Mubarak, who had ruled Egypt since 1981. Mubarak was shown the door by the military—or, more precisely, the cohort of senior generals who have long exercised decisive power in Egypt, but behind tightly drawn curtains.

The old order has been shaken but it seems doubtful that a revolution has occurred in Egypt; what has occurred is better described as the reformation of a regime rather than a revolution. The military holds the reins of power and it was the senior generals who pledged to superintend a transition to elections. Yet, the military has a big stake in the present distribution of resources and privileges and it begs credulity to imagine that the uniformed brass will accept any political arrangement that challenges vested interests. This is one major constraint on reform.

The military is led by a professionally competent and patriotic officer corps that has benefited, especially since 1967, from military education and training, meritocratic promotions and generous funding.* Little is actually known publicly about the internal workings of the military, or about the interaction between senior flag officers and the top tier of the regime. The thwarted ascendancy of Gamal, President Mubarak's younger son, is a case in point—it has been speculated that the military blocked his rise. Mubarak was attentive to diminishing the power of potential military rivals as famously illustrated in 1989 when Field Marshal Abu Ghazala (who was on very good terms with senior U.S. officials) was "promoted" to become an adviser to the president. Mubarak's aversion to naming a vice president was indicative of his motives as well. Yet if the military's power to play kingmaker was diminished, Mubarak seems to have failed to end its veto.

The generals have been content to remain behind the curtain, avoiding a direct hand in politics provided that their corporate interests are safeguarded and the leadership of the state is in trusted hands. The military's aims seem to be to maintain the unity and security of the state; to preclude a return to the egregious policies and practices that fomented the January 25 revolution and its concomitant instability; and to protect the dignity of the military and

Jan. 29, 2011: "Thanks to the People! Thanks Facebook!" on a wall close to Avenue Bourguiba in Tunis, Tunisia. (CAPUCINE BAILLY/REDUX)

*The annual budget for the military is thought to be $6 billion, including $1.3 billion in U.S. military aid.

to ensure that it is adequately funded.

These goals are compatible with the establishment of a reasonably open political system, but not necessarily with the full-fledged democracy that many Egyptian activists seek. It remains to be seen whether the military will seek a constitutional provision to formally declare that the military is the guardian of the political system, but this is the role that it is now playing and is likely to play for some time to come. If the next president is a civilian, will the military accept a civilian as the supreme commander of the armed forces? It is doubtful that the military will tolerate civilian oversight of its budget, whether from the Parliament or the president. To date, military spending has been a taboo topic in Parliament, notwithstanding occasional demands from opposition members. By law (Law 49, 1974), there is no monitoring of military armaments, which applies equally to military hardware and military-owned bakeries. Public scrutiny of the military's use of state land is largely off limits as well. Retired senior military officers have been able to move with ease into public sector agencies and into ministries. This has evoked resentment among civilian officials, but it is an example of the privileges that officers would expect to continue in post-Mubarak Egypt.

The members of the Supreme Council of the Armed Forces (SCAF) have been sometimes sensitive to public opinion, and the pulse of demonstrations seems to have checked some of the autocratic inclinations of the generals. Public demands to hold officials of the former regime accountable for corruption and for serious violations of law may have propelled the generals to permit the detention of Mubarak and his sons Alaa and Gamal, as well as the prosecution of former officials, most notably Habib al-Adly, the former interior minister who has been jailed for 12 years for corruption. He is also being tried for his role in ordering attacks on demonstrators, as well as other abuses of power.

However, the 30-year state of emergency remains in effect and the military has been in no hurry to lift it. These

Feb. 25, 2011: Soldiers pray on top of a tank during antigovernment protests and Friday prayers in Tahrir Square in Cairo, Egypt. (CARSTEN KOALL/GETTY IMAGES)

laws permit the security apparatus to ignore constitutional protections and judicial safeguards and to arrest and jail just about anyone for any reason. The victims of these laws are subjected to military courts from which there is no appeal, as well as routine mistreatment and often torture. (In Algeria the state of emergency was lifted, although the military regime has remained openly hostile to large-scale demonstrations.)

Next steps

The Egyptian military moved firmly against the residual Tahrir demonstrators and cleared the square by April 11, 2011. In a worrying move, an outspoken blogger named Maikel Nabil Sanad was sentenced to three years in prison in April 2011 for insulting the military. The fact that Nabil has declared himself a supporter of Israel has no doubt undermined his public support.

In March, the Egyptians went to the polls and overwhelmingly approved (more than 77% voted "yes") a series of constitutional amendments intended to permit parliamentary and presidential elections. The referendum was transparent and most people were able to vote without intimidation—uncommon conditions for Egyptian elections. Nonetheless, many reformers worried that national elections were being rushed and that there would be little

time to organize credible parliamentary elections. There was also concern that the referendum did not address the many glaring defects of the existing constitution, which they wished to rewrite entirely.

Although the former ruling National Democratic Party (NDP) was legally dissolved in April 2011, many members of the party retain significant bases of support, particularly outside of the large cities, in provincial towns and in the countryside. Half of Egypt's voters live outside of major cities, where the structure of power has hardly been shaken, so the old order is likely to retain a significant base of support and win seats in a new Parliament.

There is considerable worry among Egyptian secularists that the MB will make a deal with the remnants of the toppled ruling party, perhaps with the blessing of the generals. Adding to the concern is the growing vitality of Salafist groups that are generally contemptuous of profane politics, but have proved quite pragmatic in exploiting political opportunity in order to advance their goal of instilling a conservative Islamic order in Egypt. Salafi groups have long been especially active in Alexandria, but are now gaining a national profile. Although Egypt is socially conservative, many Egyptians are suspicious of the MB and they do not embrace the

Feb. 3, 2011: Libyan protesters burning poster of Libyan leader Muammar Qadhafi during a demonstration against him in Benghazi, Libya. (ALFRED/SIPA/AP)

stark Islam promoted by the Salafists.

It is worrying to many Egyptians that SCAF has reneged on a number of its earlier promises to turn over power to an elected government. The full dimensions of the generals' agenda became clear on November 1, 2011, when a conference of 500 intellectuals was convened at Cairo's elegant Opera House. At the meeting, SCAF distributed its "guidelines" for the drafting of a new constitution, including a prohibition on civilian scrutiny of the defense budget, and veto power for the military during the drafting of the new constitution. Two days later, SCAF announced that it would choose 80 of the 100 members of the constituent assembly charged with writing the new constitution. Should any single party win a majority in the Parliament, the new guidelines would obviously dilute their ability to shape the new constitution. The guidelines render the military autonomous from civilian control and increase the prospect that Egypt will fall far short of becoming a full-fledged democracy.

Egypt's first round of parliamentary elections began on November 28, 2011. At press time, presidential elections are not expected until 2013. Amr Moussa, the respected former foreign minister and secretary general of the Arab League is the favorite; there is still room for surprises, especially because SCAF is keeping its cards close to its chest.

Libya: the 'Mukhtar* Revolution'

Qadhafi's strategy of ruling was premised on weak state institutions and alliances with favored tribes. His self-styled *jamahiriya*—a state of the masses—was intended to preclude challenges to his power by diffusing power throughout society. Hence, the Libyan Army was weak and fragmented, particularly the eastern units around the city of Benghazi. The judiciary was fragmented, and the police forces lacked a central authority. As for civil society, any initiative that suggested establishing anything resembling autonomous local actors was suppressed or crushed by the state. The result was a dearth of national institutions.

In Libya, swelling protests began in mid-February. On February 17, 2011, a proclaimed "Day of Rage" inspired by the models of Tunisia and Egypt prompted a deadly response, especially against demonstrators in Tripoli's Green Square. A vindictive Qadhafi promised to tolerate no dissent, declared that his opponents were drug-addled al-Qaeda-led terrorists and called on Libyans to fight the "greasy rats."

In an extraordinary meeting on March 12, the Arab League voted to support international action to protect

Omar Mukhtar was a hero of the Libyan struggle against Italian colonialism in the 1920s. He was hanged by the Italians in 1931.

Libyan civilians, which was followed five days later by United Nations Security Council Resolution 1973. The resolution enabled the U.S.-European intervention to create "no-drive" and "no-fly" zones to stop attacks on Libyan civilians. The North Atlantic Treaty Organization (NATO) effort evolved into a transparent campaign to systematically destroy the military apparatus of the Qadhafi regime in support of opposition forces.

Qadhafi's capture and ignominious end came on October 20, 2011, amid reports not only of government atrocities and mass executions, but scores of summary executions of regime loyalists by opposition militias. The disregard for legal processes and disrespect for fundamental human rights by both sides suggest that rocky days lie ahead in liberated Libya, where many militias will resist or refuse disarming. Deepseated regional animosities suggest the country could be balkanized, even if it is united in principle.

Libya lacks both an established political opposition and established legal institutions other than tribalbased traditions of customary law. In post-Qadhafi Libya, the partners in power will include religious groups and the tribes, and inchoate political parties. The MB does enjoy considerable support, especially in the eastern cities, including Benghazi, and Salafist groups have been picking up wind in recent years. Libya's prospects for enjoying a pluralist and tolerant political system therefore lag well behind the chances of the other North African states. A cooperative effort by the U.S., European and Arab states to repair the ravages of four decades of dictatorship could smooth the transition to democracy in Libya.

The 'Syria Revolution'

In the capital city of Damascus, the regime was smugly confident that Syria would not be affected by the upheaval. Not only were the many agencies of the security apparatus vigilant to control dissent, but President Bashar al-Assad presented himself as a reformer. Assad, a medical doctor, was catapulted to power in 2000 upon the death of his father, Hafez, who had ruled Syria for 30 years.

By March 2011, it became clear that Syria was by no means immune to unrest: A surge of demonstrations began in the Houran region in the south, particularly in the Sunni town of Daraa. The demonstrations were provoked by the arrest and mistreatment of teenagers who had been nabbed by the police for posting antiregime graffiti. The initial protests evoked a bloody response from the regime. The demonstrations spread throughout the southern region, despite widespread arrests and indiscriminate killings by the army and police. By the end of March, Assad had sacked his cabinet and made empty promises of reforms.

By the end of April, Assad declared an end to emergency rule (which had been in force for 48 years), but the harsh regime response continued and the death toll mounted. From the beginning of the protests in Syria, a pattern of response by the government was established: when antigovernment demonstrations were mounted, the military would cordon off the town, arrest hundreds of boys and men and often kill indiscriminately anyone with the temerity to be on the street. Government thugs, known locally as "shabiha" (ghosts) were commonly unleashed as well. The shabiha were originally created by Assad's uncle, Jamil al-Assad, but now they are often simply local criminals and hoodlums given free rein by security forces. By year's end, up to 30,000 people were in custody, and more than 3,500 had been killed by government forces. Prominent supporters of the opposition were singled out for retribution. For example, Ibrahim Qashoush died with his throat cut and his voice box removed in July, and the famous cartoonist Ali Farzat's fingers were broken when he was beaten by shabiha in August.

While the central areas of Syria's two main cities were relatively quiet, Homs, the third-largest city, has become an important center of resistance. Indeed, many provincial cities joined the protests, including Idlib, Banias, Hama, Dair al-Zour and Latakia, as well as many Damascus suburbs. The protests remained largely peaceful for several months, despite official propaganda claiming that it was confronting Islamist extremists, al-Qaeda and other terrorists; however, by the fall of 2011, there were a number of armed clashes. Data on the number of defections from the army is imprecise, but one American official estimated that perhaps 10,000 soldiers have defected to the opposition, and attacks by these renegade elements took a periodic toll on the government forces.

Nonetheless, the bulk of the army remains loyal to the regime. For more than 40 years the Syrian regime has been dominated by the minority 'Alawi community, which accounts for 12% of Syria's population of 22.5 million but controls almost all senior positions in the army. The 'Alawi sect is an offshoot of Shi'i Islam, but the sect is quite unique in its practices and structure. For generations, the 'Alawis were poor and disadvantaged, so their path to influence and power was the military. Unlike either Tunisia or Egypt, where professional army officers broke with the president, this is unlikely to happen in Syria. The two most important army divisions are controlled by Assad's relatives, including the Fourth Armored Division, led by his brother Maher, who has taken the lead in attempting to brutally crush the growing insurrection.

The government continues to enjoy important support in Damascus and Aleppo, notably from Christians, who account for as much as 10% of Syria's population. In addition to other religious and sectarian minorities (including the Druze and the Assyrians), the Christians fear that a new government would disavow the secular stance of the present government, and attempt to impose a Sunni Islamic agenda on minorities.

External powers are divided on how to respond to Syria. The U.S. lost faith in Assad's willingness or ability to promote reform, and in August President Barack Obama said it was time for him to step aside. The U.S. and the European Union (EU), with France playing an important role, have led a campaign to isolate and punish the Syrian regime, but efforts to gain UN support for tougher action have been met by Chinese and Russian vetoes. Turkey, an important trading and diplomatic partner of Syria in recent years, has also urged reform and an end to regime violence, to no avail.

The Arab League, which opened the door to intervention in Libya with a request that a no-fly zone be implemented to protect Libyan civilians, waited until November 2011 to suspend Syria's membership and impose sanctions. Many

July 16, 2011: Demonstrators react during a march through the city center of Hama, Syria. "Come on Bashar, leave," is a song that in the weeks since it was heard in protests in this city has become a symbol of the power of protesters' message to its president, Bashar al-Assad. (MOISES SAMAN/THE NEW YORK TIMES/REDUX)

Arab League members openly detested the erratic and troublesome Qadhafi, but they feared chaos in Syria, including a possible opening to Iran and a contagion of instability that would inevitably affect Lebanon and Iraq, as well as the stability on the Syrian-Israeli border.

In Libya, the army was kept weak by design, but the standing Syrian military, with an active force of 400,000, is no pushover, even if a U.S.-led NATO force had the appetite to intervene militarily, which is certainly not the case. Equally important, the Syrian opposition is a work in progress, although the Turkish government has lent significant support to its coalescence. The Syrian National Council has begun to coordinate between the loosely aligned admixture of secular, nationalist and Islamist elements that comprise the opposition, but it remains unclear what a new Syrian government would look like.

In early November, the Syrian government accepted an Arab League-brokered initiative that called for dialogue and for the withdrawal of Syrian forces from the dissident cities; however, the ink was hardly dry before the government killing continued in Homs, while calling for all Syrians to turn in their weapons. There is no evidence that Assad has any plans to stop short of van-

quishing the opposition, and it is likely that the bloodletting will not only continue, but probably become much worse if the opposition turns to violence.

Fractured Yemen

In contrast to Syria—where change is thwarted by a military establishment that is part and parcel of a ruthless regime bent on survival—in Yemen the military has split into segments that correspond to tribal and regional divisions. Arguably more than in any other Middle Eastern country, the central government, in the capital city of Sanaa, is checked by the provincial forces. The civilian population is heavily armed, and tribal confederations often field formidable military might.

President Ali Abdullah Saleh has ruled in Yemen since 1978, first as the president of North Yemen, and since 1990 as the president of a united Yemen, following the unification of the Yemen Arab Republic and the People's Democratic Republic of Yemen (South Yemen). Inspired by Tunisia and Egypt, Yemenis rallied in late January to call for the end of Saleh's reign.

Saleh's initial response was that he would not seek reelection and that his son Ahmed would not succeed him in a handover that was widely suspected to

be in the works. On February 3, 2011, a "Day of Rage" was launched, with thousands of Yemenis participating.

Despite defections in the military, and despite suffering serious wounds in June—requiring months of medical treatment in Saudi Arabia—Saleh still clung to power. He periodically has promised to step aside and has called for a true and new dialogue, but his opponents argue that he is simply calculating how to stay in power.

The U.S. has urged Saleh to resign, and the Gulf Cooperation Council (GCC) has mediated an exit plan that remains unimplemented, notwithstanding occasional interludes when Saleh seems to be ready to accept the GCC framework for relinquishing his control of the country.

Hence, impoverished Yemen remains at an impasse—with an opposition that lacks the decisive strength necessary to push Saleh and his allies from power, and a government with sufficient strength to cling to power but that is too weak to subdue its opponents. This is a recipe for instability that undermines an already anemic economy and offers opportunity for violent jihadist groups to build local centers of power, precisely as al-Qaeda in the Arabian Peninsula (AQAP) has done in parts of the country.

The Arab states of the Persian Gulf

There have been stirrings of dissent in the Persian Gulf. In the United Arab Emirates (UAE), petitions have called for elections and more equitable sharing of oil wealth. The government responded with the detention of activists. Similarly, in Kuwait there were several small demonstrations, including one in the city of Jahra to demand citizenship rights for stateless Kuwaitis (who number about 100,000). Kuwait boasts the only effective Parliament in the Persian Gulf, and demands for more political freedom were voiced. Compared to the tumultuous changes elsewhere in the region, the developments in Oman, Kuwait and the UAE were quite minor in significance.

In Saudi Arabia, the minority Shi'i

May 7, 2011: Antigovernment protesters demonstrating in Saana, Yemen. Yemen's President Ali Abdullah Saleh had recently told a rally of his supporters that he would remain " steadfast" in resisting his opponents' demand for his immediate ouster. (XINHUA NEWS AGENCY/EYEVINE/REDUX)

Muslim community of the Eastern Province, who may account for 10% of the country's population, mounted a "Day of Rage" on March 11, 2011. Reformers called for respect for the civil rights of the Shi'i, including the end of long-term imprisonment without trial (citing the case of some prisoners who have been held for 14 years without trial). Security forces arrested dozens of protesters in response.

The government in Riyadh was also concerned that restive Sunni citizens would be inspired to protest. By March, several obliging senior clerics in the holy city of Mecca issued a religious opinion forbidding protests on the grounds that they undermined stability. Subjects were also threatened with punishment if they mounted illegal demonstrations (and there is no possibility of "legal" demonstrations). Simultaneously, King Abdullah announced a large stimulus package of $66.7 billion to be spent creating jobs, housing and medical facilities.

In June, a group of reformist women renewed efforts to lift the ban on women driving cars, handed down in a 1991 *fatwa*. Earlier efforts prompted harsh retaliation by the authorities, and though the rejoinder was a bit milder in 2011, the government clings to the view that banning women from driving protects them from vice. From the standpoint of many Saudi women, the ban is hugely inconvenient and expensive because it forces them to hire male drivers or depend on male members of the household to drive them. King Abdullah attempted to offer some solace in September 2011 by promising that women would be permitted to vote and stand for local elections—in 2015.

The tragedy of Bahrain

Many of the complaints coincide with sectarian differences and disparities in privilege that are extraordinary because they are so readily apparent. Although the Shi'i Muslims account for nearly 70% of the small population (excluding expatriate workers, Bahraini citizens number about 600,000), they have typically gotten the short end of the stick in terms of access to government employ-

Mar. 16, 2011: Smoke covers Pearl Square in the Bahraini capital of Manama, as riot police and military troops moved in to clear it of antigovernment protesters. (ANDREA BRUCE/THE NEW YORK TIMES/REDUX)

ment and favors. Unemployment and per capita income data speak volumes about the inequity that defines Bahraini society, and the migrant workers occupy an even more precarious position.

On February 14, 2011, protests were mounted by predominantly Shi'i demonstrators, although they were also joined by some reform-minded Sunnis. Many of the demonstrators gathered around the Pearl Roundabout, a downtown Manama landmark where a white concrete pedestal held aloft a pearl, recalling earlier days when Bahrain was a world center for the harvesting of natural pearls. The demonstrators were overwhelmingly peaceful, and police efforts to dislodge them were largely unsuccessful, despite police violence that killed five protesters on February 18. The government—urged on by the U.S.—sought a negotiated end to the protests. Crown Prince Salman took the lead in negotiations to initiate a serious dialogue about reform, particularly with Wefaq, the main opposition party. Hard-liners on both sides were skeptical of the proposed dialogue and it was stymied.

U.S. efforts to encourage the reform dialogue seemed to be bearing fruit in early March, but any further talk ended on March 14, when Saudi and UAE troops crossed the causeway linking the main island to the mainland to lead a crackdown on the demonstrators. The

Saudi-led incursion was clearly a riposte to the U.S., which King Abdullah felt was much too quick to jump on the bandwagon of reform and far too reticent to support old friends (such as Mubarak).

Within days, the government had demolished the very symbol of the protests, the Pearl monument.

With the government charging that Iran was behind the demonstrators, all talk of reform came to a crashing halt. Hundreds of Shi'i employees were dismissed from state jobs as punishment for having demonstrated, and hundreds were arrested. Health professionals who treated injured demonstrators were accused of trying to overthrow the regime, and were tried by military courts and sentenced to long terms in prisons. Little has been done to address the underlying disparities that gave rise to the protests, which continue periodically. Meanwhile, the risk is that the majority Shi'i population, which has long been surprisingly moderate, especially given the discrimination they face routinely, will be radicalized and that charges of foreign meddling by Iran will prove to be self-fulfilling. The U.S. continues to issue pro forma calls for reform, but the contrast between the U.S. posture in Libya and Syria, on the one hand, and Bahrain, on the other hand, is glaringly obvious and is interpreted as hypocrisy. ■

Changing seasons in the Arab world

IT WOULD BE NAÏVE to expect miraculous political transformations, and in several cases examined here—Syria, Yemen and Bahrain—it is difficult to see a way forward that would meet the core demands of the demonstrators and the agenda of the regime incumbents. The pace of the upheaval, the ideals of the participants and the breadth of mobilization are often breathtaking and inspiring, but the prospects for change vary significantly from one country to another. Wise, prudent leaders may emerge with enhanced popularity in some cases, but those who seek to frustrate and stifle change are likely to find that the year of upheaval never ends.

Even in cases such as Tunisia, where the prospects for a political transformation seem brightest, the pitfalls are massive. Nearly 20% of Tunisians, many of them college-educated, are unemployed. Huge bureaucracies are by no means unmitigated prizes, but in Egypt, Tunisia and Morocco there are potentially effective agencies for responding to public needs and providing services. Where public administration and the delivery of public services are not well institutionalized, then government has to be created from scratch. This is the case in Libya, where Qadhafi extolled the decentralization and fragmentation of government institutions to the point of ineffectualness.

Popular demonstrations provide American policymakers with several lessons and challenges. First, the generation calling for change is generally youthful, inclusive, tolerant and not beholden to the regime. Nor are they controlled or directed by Islamist radicals. In Tunisia, Egypt, Libya and Bahrain, Islamist movements had to play catch-up with the revolt. Second, Islamist leaders quickly realized that they are only one of many voices in the movement and that they must collaborate with emerging centers of power to help chart their countries' future.

Third, imperiled Arab autocracies are now in a rush to clean up their act. Whether the sitting governments survive or not, Western governments that for so long were willing to avert their eyes from human rights offenses and brutality will now find it more embarrassing to do so, and much more difficult to defend if they do.

In the meantime, civil society in several Arab countries is producing new cadres of leaders—youthful, sophisticated, legitimate, inclusive and nonideological. They want their societies to prosper and to join the modern world. The enlightened interest of the U.S. dictates that Washington become more serious about telling regimes that America's backing is contingent on their people's support. If regimes lose their legitimacy, they may no longer count on ready support in Washington. This is the lesson from the historic upheaval that has now begun.

If 2011 marks a new epoch in Arab world politics, as now seems likely, the impact is likely to be every bit as unsettling for non-Arab autocrats as it already has been for Arab potentates. In the U.S., demonstrators on Wall Street and in Wisconsin have already alluded to the inspiration that they drew from the Tahrir demonstrations in Egypt. Reverberations of the upheaval have already been observed in Iran, Azerbaijan, Africa south of the Sahara and in China. Perhaps most important is that the demonstration effect of courageous people standing firm even in the face of deadly violence cannot be unlearned.

Implications for the U.S.

U.S. foreign policy in the Middle East is caught in a web of contradictory interests that became all the more apparent during the tumultuous days of 2011. U.S. officials, including President Obama in his June 2009 speech in Cairo, have embraced political reform and democracy, but in practice the elixir of stability has often proven irresistible. In Egypt, for instance, the now toppled Mubarak was committed to peace with Israel, supported the U.S. in its battle with al-Qaeda and stood against Iran's quest for regional hegemony. After it became apparent that Mubarak could not survive, the U.S. endorsed a democratic transition in Egypt while also continuing close relations with the generals who now dominate the political system. Moreover, the generals seem to have no intention of loosening their ultimate grip on power. Given the balance of U.S. interests, there are no feasible black or white policy choices. Although it will be awkward to watch, expect the U.S. to continue to espouse freedom and reform while still sipping the elixir of stability.

One trademark of the region's repressive dictatorships has been that they only permit anemic opposition forces. This was certainly illustrated in Qadhafi's Libya. Any U.S. decision to intervene militarily has to take into account not only U.S. and allied military capabilities, but the likelihood that the bumpy transition to a new government will require extensive external support. While a cooperative NATO campaign, preceded by an Arab League request and an enabling UN Security Council resolution, toppled Qadhafi, the Libyan model of intervention is unlikely to be replicated elsewhere in the Middle East.

Despite the slaughter of thousands of civilians at the hands of Syrian security forces, intervention there poses much more difficult military problems than Libya did. Yet, Syria is the closest regional ally of Iran, so a change of regime in Damascus might have profound geopolitical consequences. In August, Obama called for Syrian President Assad to step aside, and the U.S. is now using a combination of sanctions, opprobrium and intense diplomacy to achieve that end. Neighboring non-Arab Turkey, a major trade partner of Syria, is closely coordinating with Washington and has increasingly taken a lead in nurturing the external Syrian opposition. The November decision of the heretofore quiescent Arab League to hold Syria accountable makes it ever more unlikely that Assad and his relatives and cronies will continue to wield power, but the opposition is still finding its political feet.

U.S. options are particularly constrained on the Arabian Peninsula. In Yemen, until 2011, President Saleh skillfully manipulated his cooperation with the U.S. against al-Qaeda to gain significant financial and military assistance. He has also clung to power, despite U.S. and GCC efforts to ease him out. His heavily armed opponents, including some army units, will not succumb to Saleh's iron fist but they also lack the capability to push Saleh and the bulk of the army out of power. Under these conditions of stalemate, U.S. policy in Yemen will continue to juggle its contradictory interests in ensuring that remote terrorist havens in Yemen do not grow while also facilitating the installation of a free and less corrupt government that better meets the aspirations of the population.

The Kingdom of Saudi Arabia is a key interlocutor for the U.S. in Yemen, and particularly in the Persian Gulf region. The U.S.-Saudi relationship underlines the checkered policies that the U.S. is likely to continue to pursue in the Middle East. On the one hand, the Saudi government represses many of its own people, not least the minority Shi'i Muslim population that lives in the oil-rich Eastern Province. On the other hand the Saudis, with wide financial investments in the U.S., have their hand on a spigot through which flow 9 million barrels of oil daily. While the U.S. and Saudi Arabia find common ground on the security front, the monarchy has been critical, even contemptuous, of U.S. policy for withdrawing support from Mubarak in Egypt. In Bahrain, the Saudis moved decisively to thwart U.S. reform efforts. Following the Saudi-led intervention in March to support its satrap, King Hamad, the change of tone in Washington about Bahraini reform was pitifully obvious. Therefore, even when the U.S. embraces significant reforms, it may find not only its foes but its allies working to sabotage its efforts.

The U.S. enjoys a singular relationship with Israel, and the Israelis have watched 2011 unfold with dismay

and apprehension. Key among Israeli concerns is the fate of its peace treaty with Egypt. If the Egyptian commitment to sustaining the treaty and the military coordination that accompanies it wanes, Israel will find that the keystone of its regional strategy is disappearing. This will have a massive impact on its defense budget, the size of its army and its economic health. The Obama Administration has urged Israel to understand that in a changing geopolitical context a resolution of the Israel-Palestine conflict is imperative, but the hard-line Israeli government has rejected the counsel.

The year 2011 was a watershed in the Middle East, and many of the key changes are going to take many years to play out. There is little reason to doubt that U.S. policymaking toward the region will grow in complexity as newly empowered citizens gain voices in their political systems. Key challenges will include the following:

● It will be increasingly costly for the U.S. to be cozy with governments that rule through repression.

● In key regional conflicts, especially the Israeli-Palestinian conflict, U.S. efforts to shield an unpopular party from condemnation will feed anti-American impulses that will jeopardize rela-

tions with democratizing governments.

● Free elections in the Arab world will necessarily bring Islamic-oriented parties greater political power, whether in partnership with secular or nationalist parties, or alone. While some of these parties have increasingly embraced pluralism, tolerance and protection for minorities, they will be far less susceptible to U.S. influence than the dictators they replaced.

● The widespread underlying discontent in the Arab world stems in significant part from government failures to meet economic needs. Those needs will be all the more urgent as new political institutions come into place. This means that the U.S. and its regional and global allies will need to stand ready to support development strategies that are likely to be short of resources and indigenous expertise.

The Middle East is in the midst of a transformation that may make at least parts of the region almost unrecognizable in the years to come. This is a period that is laden with potential for the growth of freedom, but it is also a period heavy with risks and challenges for the U.S. ∎

Opinion Ballots
after page 32

discussion questions

1. Compare the different U.S. responses to protests in Egypt, Tunisia, Libya, Syria, Bahrain, Saudi Arabia and Yemen. Why has the U.S. response not been uniform? What do you make of the criticism that the U.S. has been too slow to switch allegiances from old allies to protesters? What are the interests that are most salient to the U.S. response in each case?

2. The removal of authoritarian rulers has allowed Islamist organizations, such as the Muslim Brotherhood in Egypt, to enjoy a resurgence. Are these groups compatible with U.S. interests in the region? What would it mean for the U.S. if Islamist governments came to power? What should govern U.S. relations with these new regimes?

3. The U.S. is committed to human rights, women's rights and democratic values. What does the "Arab Spring" mean for these interests? How has the upheaval affected regional security and the war on terror? Going forward, how should

the U.S. partner with the new governments of the Middle East on these issues? With these agendas in mind, should the U.S. reassess its ties with semidemoratic regimes like Bahrain and Saudi Arabia?

4. The U.S. contributed to, but did not lead, NATO's intervention in Libya, which significantly assisted the rebels' ouster of Qadhafi. Would a similar international intervention be appropriate in Syria or Yemen? How should the international community respond? Should regional organizations, like the African Union or the Arab League, take the lead, or the UN? What are the advantages and disadvantages of the U.S.'s scaled-down participation? What are the larger implications for the U.S.'s position on the global stage?

5. The new government in Egypt and the unrest in Syria, among other shifting conditions, have destabilized the position of Israel, a staunch U.S. ally in the region. What are the implications of the upheaval for the Middle East peace process? How will these new partners for peace affect the U.S. strategy in pursuing a resolution?

suggested readings

al Aswany, Alaa, **On the State of Egypt: What made the revolution inevitable**. New York, Vintage Books, 2011. 192 pp. $15 (paper). Translated from the Arabic, this collection of essays provides penetrating insights into Mubarak's Egypt. The author is a dentist turned novelist (renowned for The Yacoubian Building) and political activist.

"The Middle East," **Current History**, December 2011. Available online at: <http://www.currenthistory.com/> (requires subscription). Timely articles on the "Arab Spring" by an impressive collection of scholars and experts covering Libya, Syria, Palestine, Iran, Islamic movements, and regional issues.

"North Africa: The Political Economy of Revolt," **Middle East Report**, Summer 2011. Available online at: <http://www.merip.org> (requires subscription). Incisive and critical accounts of political and social life in the Middle East, as well as critical assessments of policy issues. The Summer 2011 issue includes seven readable essays by experts, which are particularly valuable for assessing citizens' complaints.

Matar, Hisham, **In the Country of Men**. New York, Dial Press, 2008. 256 pp. $15.00 (paper). The author is the son of a Libyan opposition figure who disappeared into Qadhafi's dungeons. His novel, which was shortlisted for the

Man Booker Prize, offers a haunting portrait of life in an authoritarian state obsessed with security and in a society where even banal acts of dissent could spell danger.

Wright, Robin, **Rocking the Casbah: Rage and Rebellion across the Islamic World.** New York, Simon & Schuster, 2012. 320 pp. $17.00 (paper). Wright is a veteran foreign correspondent who knows the Middle East well. She offers compelling glimpses of a youthful region hungry for change.

For up-to-date news and analysis of this time-sensitive topic, we recommend the following Internet resources:

Arab Reform Initiative, <http://www.arab-reform.net>. This Web site provides analysis in English and in Arabic from experts, including staff on the ground in the Middle East.

Center for Strategic and International Studies, <http://www.csis.org>. Expert assessments of strategic options for U.S. policy.

International Crisis Group, <http://www.crisisgroup.org>. Features detailed and valuable assessment of crisis spots around the globe, including expertise on Syria, Egypt and Libya.

Visit **WWW.GREATDECISIONS.ORG** *for quizzes, seasonal topic updates and other resources to further your understanding*

18

Promoting democracy: foreign policy imperative?
by Larry Diamond

March 1965: U.S. Marines wade ashore at Da Nang, Vietnam, to defend the coastal airbase against Communist attack. (AP)

SINCE THE FOUNDING of the American Republic, the U.S. has been torn between two quite different visions of how it should relate to other countries. One approach sees the world as it is, not as the U.S. would like it to be—an intrinsically anarchic and amoral collection of states seeking to expand their power and influence in the world. In this unsentimental conception of a dangerous, conflictual world—where (to paraphrase the 19th century English statesman Lord Palmerston) nations have no permanent friends or allies, only permanent interests—the guiding foreign policy priorities for the U.S. are the safety of its citizens, the security of its borders, the extension of its power and the advancement of its economic interests in trade, investment and natural resources. Not surprisingly, this approach to foreign policy has come broadly to be known as the "realist" school, though realism has contained within it sharply different tendencies, from isolationism to a strong propensity for interest-driven intervention. In the early decades of American independence, when the U.S. was still a relatively new and fragile nation, its basic tenet was caution about alliances and "foreign entanglements." Thus, in 1821, President John Quincy Adams proclaimed that America's

principal "gift to mankind" was its repeated affirmation of democratic principles. The U.S., he said, had been wise to abstain from "interference in the concerns of others, even when conflict has been for principles to which she clings." He added, in terms that would have a deep impact on 20th-century advocates of realist restraint in global affairs, like Hans P. Morgenthau and George F. Kennan:

> *Wherever the standard of freedom and Independence has been or shall be unfurled, there will [America's] heart, her benedictions and her prayers be. But she goes not abroad, in search of monsters to destroy. She is the well-wisher to the freedom and independence of all. She is the champion and vindicator only of her own.*

An alternative strain of thinking in American foreign policy

LARRY DIAMOND *is senior fellow at the Hoover Institution and the Freeman Spogli Institute for International Studies, Stanford University. He also directs Stanford's Center on Democracy, Development, and the Rule of Law (CDDRL), and coedits the* Journal of Democracy. *He is the author and editor of more than 30 books on democratic development worldwide, including* The Spirit of Democracy: The Struggle to Build Free Societies Throughout the World.

On left, July 24, 1973: President Richard M. Nixon in the White House with the shah of Iran, Mohammad Reza Pahlavi, when he made a state visit to the U.S. (AP) *On right, Nov. 1979: A bound and blindfolded hostage is held at the U.S. embassy in Tehran, Iran.* (ALAIN MINGAM/GAMMA-RAPHO/GETTY)

has insisted that the ideals of the American Revolution and its founding declaration must somehow shape and inform the way the U.S. relates to other countries in the world. Its first full expression came in the presidency of Woodrow Wilson (1913–21), who believed that it was America's moral obligation and vital interest to shape the rest of the world in the image of its own values of freedom and democracy—that (as the historian of American foreign policy Walter Russell Mead has characterized it), "the U.S. has the right and the duty to change the rest of the world's behavior." Out of this Wilsonian conception sprang not only America's military engagement in World War I, and Wilson's pursuit of a League of Nations, but a recurrent American concern with the nature of government in other countries around the world that would find prominent expression in the presidencies of FDR, Truman, Kennedy, Carter and Reagan. This approach became labeled the "idealist" school in American foreign policy, though idealism always coexisted with (and not infrequently was trumped by) frequent concessions to geostrategic realities.

If the early American realists were isolationists in their caution about foreign entanglements, their more modern-day successors understood that America's territorial expansion and economic rise inevitably gave it global interests that required robust alliances, partnerships of convenience, coercive actions, and even long-term military deployments around the world. This more muscular and ambitious worldview first emerged full-blown in

the foreign policy of President Theodore Roosevelt (1901–09) and then reached its apogee during the cold-war struggle to check Soviet expansionism and Communist revolutions. Its most consummate practitioners were Secretary of State Henry Kissinger (1973–77) and President Richard Nixon (1969–74). Other American Presidents during this era, including Dwight D. Eisenhower and Lyndon B. Johnson, also privileged the defense of American power over the advancement of American ideals, and were even willing to use American power to oust elected leaders or block popular aspirations when they seemed to conflict with American interests. After each of these periods of foreign policy realism, however, there came a correction. President John F. Kennedy's Alliance for Progress in 1961, and his rhetorical embrace of freedom and socioeconomic reform, reinjected idealism after President Eisenhower and his secretary of state, John Foster Dulles, had emphasized containing communism and advancing American economic interests. After the supremely "realist" years of the Nixon-Ford era, President Jimmy Carter (1977–81) launched a new and lasting emphasis on human rights in American foreign policy. It succeeded in pressuring a number of Latin American dictatorships to return power to elected civilians, but critics charged that it also paved the way for anti-American revolutions in Iran and Nicaragua.

President Ronald Reagan (1981–89) came into power criticizing Jimmy Carter's naïveté in undermining American allies and interests, yet he wound up go-

ing much further, making the promotion of democracy an elevating purpose of American foreign policy. Reagan not only challenged communism as a system, but he ultimately pressed for democratic transitions among American allies—the Philippines, Korea and Chile. Both Carter and Reagan permanently changed American foreign policy by establishing new and lasting institutions to press for democracy and human rights. Although he was considered a realist, President George Herbert Walker Bush (1989–93) then further institutionalized democracy promotion by making it a major purpose in American foreign aid, and by crafting an ambitious strategy of diplomacy and aid to solidify the emerging democracies of Central and Eastern Europe. During the subsequent presidencies of Bill Clinton, George W. Bush and Barack Obama, the weight given to democracy promotion in American foreign policy has shifted back and forth, in rhetoric and in practice. But these shifts have always occurred within the boundaries of broad agreement among foreign policy elites that the U.S. should spend at least some resources and diplomatic capital working to advance and defend democracy around the world. And strikingly, each of the last five American Presidents, from Reagan to Obama, has over the course of his presidency given more emphasis to democracy promotion than he did in the early stages of his presidency.

If the polls are to be believed, however, the American people are much more skeptical about the value of promoting democracy abroad than are the country's elected leaders and foreign policy practitioners. Since 2001, Pew Research Center polls have found democracy promotion finishing last in the public's list of priorities for American foreign policy, well behind such "realist" concerns as protecting American jobs, defending the U.S. from terrorism, and reducing dependence on imported energy (though in reality, the first and last are much more the province of domestic than foreign policy). Between September 2001 and May 2011, the percentage of Americans listing democracy promotion as a foreign policy priority fell steadily from 29% to 13%, and the proportion listing promotion of human rights also slipped from 29% to 24%. ■

Democracy promotion: in America's national interest?

June 23, 1987: Students burn effigies of President Chun Doo-Hwan, left, and his designated successor Roh Tae-woo during demonstrations in Seoul, South Korea. The students wrapped the effigies in American flags in denouncement of the U.S., contending it has helped keep Chun in power. (ITSUO INOUYE/AP/CORBIS)

So is it in the national interest of the U.S. to promote freedom and democracy in other countries? Any answer to this question must first raise several others: What is meant by "promoting" democracy—what methods count, and are all methods equally acceptable? Should there be a distinction among countries, or different types of countries? Is it possible that promoting democracy may be more in the American interest in some places—and at some times—than in others? And if it is an interest of the U.S. to promote democracy, does this mean it must be the central interest, trumping other items on the agenda or diffusely shaping every aspect of policy? Moreover, how does one factor in the temporal dimension to thinking about the national interest? If Americans have a long-term interest in fostering democracy, but doing so carries risks in the short run, which point on the time horizon should prevail?

There are many reasons to think that the U.S. should "keep its nose out of other people's business," at least in terms of how states are governed internally. To begin with, a strict reading of the norms of sovereignty, as codified by the Peace of Westphalia, which ended the Thirty Years War in 1648, grants each state not only territorial integrity but also the exclusive right to determine its own policies and governmental structures within its territory. From this has come the principle of "nonintervention" in the internal affairs of other states, which was elevated to a nearly sacred status during the immediate post-World War II era of decolonization and has been written into the charter of the World Bank's International Bank for Reconstruction and Development (IBRD) and other international structures. When states invite international assistance for their efforts to administer free and fair elections, build independent judiciaries, and construct and deepen other structures of democracy, that is one thing. But when other democracies provide assistance to independent organizations, human rights activists, critical media and opposition movements that are trying to change a state's form of government from authoritarianism to democracy, this is a form of intervention, however peaceful the means and idealistic the motivation.

There are, of course, possible real costs to the U.S. of promoting democracy, including financial costs. But the entire budget for "core," nonsecurity U.S. international affairs—in essence, diplomacy and aid (outside of elevated contingency operations in places like Iraq and Afghanistan), as well as all U.S. support for international organizations like the United Nations—is only slightly over $50 billion. That is just 1.7% of the entire federal budget (far exceeded by the $671 billion requested for the Pentagon in fiscal year 2012), and total funding for all democracy and governance assistance programs (not including economic assistance) probably does not exceed $2 billion—considerably less than a tenth of a percent of the overall budget. In short, if a case is to be made for not promoting democracy, it is difficult to make it on fiscal grounds.

Neither is it convincing to argue any longer that democracy is mainly a "Western" concept, unsuitable for and largely unwanted by non-Western peoples and cultures. Since the "third wave" of global democratization began in 1974, the percentage of states that meet the minimal test of electoral democracy (that all the people of a society can participate in choosing and replacing their leaders in regular, free and fair multiparty elections) has gone from barely a quarter to roughly 60%. Today, there is at least a critical mass of democracies in every region of the world except the Middle East. Democracy has become the predominant form of government in all of Europe, as well as in Latin America, and has a substantial presence in Africa and Asia. Many of the third-wave democracies—including all the new members of the 27-nation European Union (EU), many in Latin America (such as Chile, Argentina and Brazil), as well as Korea and Taiwan—can be considered "consolidated," in that political elites and the mass public do not want and cannot really imagine any other form of government. A number of Muslim-majority countries—including Turkey, Indonesia, Bangladesh and Mali—are democracies. Moreover, public opinion surveys show clear majorities of the public in each cultural zone and in most countries preferring democracy as the best form of government and wanting their leaders to be accountable to them. In short, democracy has become

a universal value, in the sense that it has broad appeal within every region of the world and essentially no global rival as an ideal form of government.

The more sophisticated objections come in two forms. One is that the world is still a dangerous and essentially anarchic place, where "real" security and economic interests must trump the moral concern to see the triumph of democracy and human rights. It would be nice if Saudi Arabia and China were democracies, but securing trade and financial relationships with these countries is more important. Similarly, the U.S. needs Russian cooperation on strategic arms reduction, and in containing nuclear arms proliferation, Islamic terrorism and the spread of Iranian influence, more than it needs Russia to be a democracy. By the same token, moderate and friendly Arab autocracies, the argument goes, have kept at least a cold peace with Israel and a broader stability in the Middle East region, which supplies up to 40% of the world's oil exports. Moreover, they have been reliable sources of cooperation in the war on terror, even if the U.S. has had to look the other way while they torture suspects handed over to them.

A second objection asserts a bias for modesty and restraint in the conduct of foreign affairs, doubting that the U.S. knows enough—about other countries

or the underlying dynamics of development—to intervene intelligently and responsibly to advance democracy, and suggesting that such intervention often is clumsy, ill-considered and resented for its pretentious and overbearing moralism. Too often, these realists insist, an initial intention to do political "good" in places like Vietnam and Iraq ends up in horrific miscalculation and costly and debilitating (if not downright immoral) entanglements. When arms are taken up in the cause of advancing freedom, the line between democracy promotion and imperialism can become blurry—or crossed. Thus, in making the case for "ethical realism," political scientists Anatol Lieven and John Hulsman lean heavily on the writings of Morgenthau and Kennan to urge a foreign policy based on prudence, caution and humility—"including humility concerning our ability to understand the outside world, foresee the future, and plan accordingly." By this realist reckoning, democracy is a difficult thing to achieve; each country must find its own path and pace; and America should instead pursue more limited "ethical" goals of peace and development while also privileging its security and economic interests. Some realist critics often add that inordinate amounts of money and manpower get devoted to building democracy and peace in the world's hardest cases, like Afghanistan, Iraq, Haiti and Somalia, which are likely to remain mired in conflict and autocracy no matter what the U.S. does.

The case for promoting democracy is in part moral—that democracies do a much better job of protecting human rights, and that peoples have a right to determine their own future democratically—but it proceeds as well on fiercely practical grounds. Democracies do not fight wars with one another; in fact, no two genuine, liberal democracies have ever done so, and all of America's enemies in war have been highly authoritarian regimes. Today, the principal threats to American security—whether from terrorism or from potential military adventurism or cyberwarfare—all come from the world's remaining authoritarian regimes, such as Iran, North Korea, Russia and China,

KAL

KAL
THE ECONOMIST
London
ENGLAND

GOOD NEWS!!
CHINA IS ACQUIRING
A TASTE FOR
DEMOCRACY!!!

THE BAD
NEWS IS..
I'M
THE
DEMOCRACY

TAIWAN

or from states like Somalia and Yemen that have collapsed or decayed because of authoritarian rule. Democracies make better trading partners because they are more likely to prosper and to play by fair rules, as they are more "likely over time to develop fair and effective legal systems." This same regard for law makes democracies better bets to honor their international treaty obligations. And they make more reliable allies because their commitments are grounded in and ultimately sustained by public opinion; "democracies are like pyramids standing on their bases." By contrast, the international posture of autocracies rests on the personal interests of the autocrat, and when he dies, changes course, or is overthrown, American interests can get burned. Much of the cold-war history of America's engagement with the Third World is a story of heavy investments in authoritarian client regimes—in places like China, Vietnam, Iran, Nicaragua, Haiti and Zaire—eventually going down the drain into revolution or state collapse. Moreover, once democracy takes root in a country, the U.S. is relieved from having to worry about responding to famine, genocide and humanitarian emergency (though certainly not poverty). Both famine and genocide are uniquely phenomena of authoritarian regimes, and state failure is also the product of authoritarian abuse. As the spread of democracy in Europe and Latin America has demonstrated over the last two decades, a zone of democracy is also a zone of peace and security.

Short-term vs. long-term interests

To argue that every country can and should immediately become a democracy flies in the face of history and evidence. Numerous transitions have floundered because of a rush to hold national elections too quickly. And in other instances, if there is not time for an array of new political forces to organize, establish support bases, and generate a pluralistic and tolerant political landscape, the sudden downfall of a tyrant can unleash civil war or a new form of tyranny. Depending on the social order and recent historical circumstances, it can take time to build a

Members of the Nicaraguan resistance brandish the newspaper La Prensa *declaring Violeta Chamorro president after winning the general election on Feb. 25, 1990. These fighters, while on patrol in mountainous northern Nicaragua, said they will put down their arms when the Sandinista Army does the same.* (PETER NORTHALL/AFP/GETTY IMAGES)

viable democracy. But that time is probably measured in years, not decades. The opposite argument—that it took the U.S. 200 years to become a democracy and so Uganda or Azerbaijan needs the same amount of time—is equally silly, and a transparent excuse for indefinite, predatory autocracy. Even many poor countries with few of the presumed developmental requisites for democracy, such as a strong middle class and high levels of education and income, have managed to implement at least the rudiments of democracy rather quickly and sustainably. ∎

Means and instruments

MUCH OF THE DEBATE about "democracy promotion" in American foreign policy involves those with opposing views making assumptions and talking past one another. When many Americans—including even some who work on or in international affairs—see the words "promoting democracy" they think "imposing democracy." Yet many of the actual actors who work to promote the spread and stability of democracy around the world think of "democracy promotion" mainly as "democracy assistance," and understand that to be effective it must be done in partnership with local actors and in response to their stated needs. In truth, there is a very wide range of instruments available to the U.S. to extend democracy as a form of government in the world

and help it become more effective and viable. Whether one thinks democracy promotion is a worthwhile purpose for American foreign policy may depend not only on the priority one thinks it should be given in competition with other foreign policy goals but also on the means that are used.

Forced imposition

At the extreme end of the range of instruments for promoting democracy is imposing it by force. Particularly in the wake of the 2003 U.S. military invasion of Iraq, followed by a quasi-colonial, U.S.-led, foreign occupation of the country, many Americans imagine coercion and imposition when they think of democracy promotion. President George W. Bush made the decision to invade Iraq on the basis of national security concerns (believing that Iraqi President Saddam Hussein was hiding weapons of mass destruction [WMDs] that constituted a major, long-term security threat to the region and the U.S.). However, in the run-up to the war, and even more so in its aftermath (when WMDs were not found), many hawks inside and outside the Bush Administration also justified the intervention by insisting that it could enable Iraq to emerge as a free (and pro-American) democracy, and a source of democratic diffusion throughout the Arab world.

For more than a year, from May 2003 to June 2004 (the period of formal occupation under the Coalition Provisional Authority [CPA], the transitional government in Iraq), the U.S. led a complex and extremely ambitious "nation-building" effort that had as one of its principal aims developing the political institutions, civic structures and values of democracy. Promoting a democratic transformation of Iraq was not only embraced as a means of legitimating the American occupation. It also reflected deeply held convictions on the part of President Bush and many in his Administration, as expressed most memorably in Bush's second inaugural address:

America's vital interests and our deepest beliefs are now one…. So it is the policy of the U.S. to seek and support the growth of democratic movements and institutions in every nation and culture, with the ultimate goal of ending tyranny in our world.

To be sure, President Bush went on to add immediately:

This is not primarily the task of arms…. America will not impose our own style of government on the unwilling. Our goal instead is to help others find their own voice, attain their own freedom, and make their own way.

But the far-reaching mission that was the CPA, and the enormous, high-profile investment of American lives, talent, and treasure, along with the rapid emergence of a virulent anti-American and antidemocratic insurgency, gave credence to the view that the American

project of transforming Iraq into a democracy had a good bit of the character of imposition.

In recent decades, no major current of American foreign policy thinking has advocated using force in order to promote democracy as the main or highest objective. From Iraq and Afghanistan in the last decade back to the most ambitious American ventures in democratic transformation—in Germany and Japan—at the end of World War II, national security has always been the principal driver of American decisions to wage all-out war. To be sure, some other American military interventions—Somalia, Haiti and Bosnia in the 1990s, and Libya (with European states in the lead) in early 2011—were motivated by humanitarian imperatives (or the intersection of humanitarian and geopolitical concerns) rather than by "hard" security calculations of imminent danger or harm to the U.S. But in virtually all of these interventions, the effort to stand up and strengthen democratic institutions became an important part of the postwar nation-building effort. Moreover, this has not just been an American impulse to make democracy the form of government left behind. Increasingly, democratization has been a major theme of UN nation-building missions in war-torn countries like El Salvador, Mozambique, Sierra Leone and East Timor. And despite the legendary tensions between the American administrator of the CPA in Iraq, Ambassador L. Paul Bremer III, and the UN mission there, the goal of reconstructing the Iraqi state on democratic foundations was one that the UN and the U.S. shared.

Post-conflict democracy

Post-conflict states present some of the most challenging circumstances for promoting democracy, because they lack many of the conditions that make democracy sustainable. For one thing, these states all have experienced violent conflict and the shattering of the central state. No country can have a democratic state without first having a state—a legitimate administrative apparatus that commands a relative monopoly over the

means of violence in a country and is capable of mobilizing collective resources to generate public goods. Also, these states have typically also suffered a meltdown of the economy, and without means of livelihood for the people and revenue for the state, no form of political order can be stable. Moreover, viable democracy requires a range of other political institutions—political parties, legislatures, courts, local governments, and a competent, neutral electoral administration—as well as some degree of understanding of democracy, tolerance for opposition, and independent organizations and media in civil society. All of these institutions and norms must gradually be built or reconstructed, often from scratch, while also stabilizing and reviving the economy and rebuilding the military and police forces. Typically in "post"-conflict states, ethnic or religious divisions, violent resistance, aspirations for vengeance against past abuses and endemic corruption pose continuing formidable challenges.

Thus, nation building is an immensely challenging, expensive and protracted exercise. If they are to have any reasonable hope of success at reconstructing an effective state—not to mention a democratic one—international intervening actors (not least the U.S.) must carefully assess the circumstances, prepare the mission and ensure that the goals they establish are matched by the time and resources they are willing to commit. The structure, strategy and sequence for reviving effective governance can also make a big difference. Often it makes sense to defer multiparty national elections for a few years until a country has had time to assemble a viable transitional administration, revive public services, create representative local governments, and generate the administrative and political elements for meaningful, free and fair elections. Yet the experience of countries like El Salvador, Mozambique, Liberia, Sierra Leone and East Timor shows that international assistance (with the U.S. as a major actor and donor) can be effective in helping countries move from civil war and state failure to democracy. And once political order is restored and foreign military forces draw down, the specific means for assisting them overlap quite a lot with those deployed in countries not traumatized by recent violent conflict.

Diplomacy

American power and influence is in decline, but the U.S. is still by far the most powerful country in the world. Beyond its military, it has numerous other instruments—diplomacy, aid conditionality and sanctions—to pressure states to democratize, to respect human rights or to govern more democratically. These instruments are also available to other democracies, and some of them can be most effectively applied by regional or international democratic coalitions or international organizations.

Diplomacy is the most common and conventional means by which states try to influence other states. But even when a powerful state like the U.S. appeals privately to a foreign government or leader to enact democratic reforms, or issues a diplomatic démarche formally protesting the undemocratic actions or stances of the foreign government and requesting specific democratic reforms or guarantees, autocratic leaders do not yield simply because they are persuaded by the moral or practical logic. Rather, underlying the diplomatic message is at least the implication that relations with the U.S. could be damaged if the regime clings to its repressive ways. When threats of consequences become explicit, then the diplomatic effort to nudge a regime toward democratic reform has escalated from pure diplomacy to the use of aid conditionality and the possible implementation of sanctions.

Diplomatic pressure works to open up autocratic regimes or to edge them forward to democracy when the U.S. and other democracies have leverage over those regimes because of the density of economic, social and cultural ties. Linkages that render authoritarian states vulnerable to external pressure include economic ties (trade, investment and credit), security ties (treaties and guarantees), and social ties (tourism, immigration, overseas education, elite exchanges, international nongov-

Dozens of Haitians on a boat moored in Port-au-Prince, Haiti, wave to a U.S. helicopter as it approaches the docks in order to land U.S. troops, who arrived in September 1994 as part of the international effort to restore democracy in Haiti. (PEDRO UGARTE/AFP/GETTY IMAGES)

ernmental organizations (NGOs) and church networks, and Western media penetration). Strong linkages forge cultural bonds that help rally democratic societies and parliaments to lobby for the defense of human rights and democracy, as seen with the pressure on the Clinton Administration to move against the Haitian military dictatorship in 1994 and the "extensive Hungarian lobbying" of the EU to press Romania and Slovakia to improve the treatment of their Hungarian minorities.

At the same time, international linkages can make critical social and political constituencies within authoritarian countries either more committed to democracy or more sensitive to Western pressures, generating a more subtle form of democracy promotion. Ties to the West induced elites both "to reform authoritarian parties from within (as in Croatia, Mexico and Taiwan)" and "to defect to the opposition (as in Slovakia and, to a lesser extent, in Romania during the mid-1990s)." After Western countries "forced severance of [Taiwan's] formal ties" and revoked Taiwan's UN membership in order to warm relations with mainland China, Taiwan's elites saw that democratic reform might provide a means to renew the sympathy and support of the American public and other Western

democracies. The desire to be accepted as a partner among industrial nations also contributed to the democratic transitions in South Korea as it prepared to host and risked losing the 1988 Olympics and in Chile as it prepared for the 1988 plebiscite on whether to extend Pinochet's dictatorship. In these contexts, U.S. and international criticism of authoritarian rule bred a sense of isolation and a desire to be regarded with respect by the industrialized democracies. But where ties are less intimate, for example in the former Soviet Union and much of Africa, Western pressure to democratize has been less consequential.

Leverage, too, depends on the power of the authoritarian state, and thus, mighty states like China and the Soviet Union (and subsequently, Russia) have found it easy to slough off American criticisms of their repressive practices. Moreover, successive U.S. Administrations have backed away from an initial impulse to confront China on its human rights record, realizing how little leverage the U.S. has and worrying about the consequences for American efforts to obtain China's cooperation on other foreign policy goals. Many authoritarian regimes in the world—Saudi Arabia, Nigeria under military rule, Iran, Azerbaijan, Kazakhstan and Venezuela—are relatively immune from international democratic pressure because oil gives them an independent source of steady, or even staggering, revenue. And geopolitics may also powerfully affect foreign policy calculations. The U.S. has historically been nearly silent about the highly undemocratic nature of Saudi Arabia because of the latter's pivotal importance as a counter to Iran in the Persian Gulf region and as the largest reserve supplier of oil on world markets. Thus, when Saudi Arabia made it clear earlier this year that the preservation of Bahrain's embattled al-Khalifa monarchy was one of its vital interests, and then deployed its own troops to help crush pro-democracy demonstrators in that small neighboring island state, the Obama Administration meekly muted its criticisms and focused its energies on supporting democratic change elsewhere in the region. Similarly, Kazakhstan's oil and gas wealth, its long border with Russia, and its value as part of the Northern Distribution Network providing an alternate route of supply for American military forces in Afghanistan have all given that former Soviet Republic significant leverage with the U.S., again leading to a muting of American criticisms of political repression.

As noted earlier, strategic interests often led the U.S. to compromise its democratic principles in order to forge mutually supportive relations with dictatorships during the cold war. This realist practice subsided following the fall of the Soviet Union but resumed after the September 11 terrorist attacks, when a new group of authoritarian "frontline" states in the war on terror—Pakistan, Egypt, Saudi Arabia, Kazakhstan, Kyrgyzstan and Uzbekistan—became more critical to U.S. strategic interests. Even before September 11, "Pakistan's status as a nuclear power hostile to India, with ties to the Taliban regime in Afghanistan and fundamentalist factions gaining ground at home," led the Clinton Administration to temper its response to the October 1999 military coup. In recognition of Peruvian President Alberto Fujimori's support for the war on drugs, the Clinton Administration maintained military cooperation and attended his third-term inauguration despite describing Fujimori's fraud-ridden 2000 election as "invalid." In the fall of 2005, the U.S. backed away from its appeals for free and fair parliamentary elections in Azerbaijan and accepted a blatantly fraudulent outcome. Six months later, in April 2006, Bush granted President Ilham Aliyev an official White House visit. So much for the promise in his second inaugural address to "all who live in tyranny": "When you stand for your liberty, we will stand with you."

Yet when the U.S. is motivated to exert diplomatic pressure on authoritarian allies, it can make a difference, either in helping to generate space for political opposition and dissent, or in tipping the balance at a critical transitional moment. By publicly documenting and denouncing human rights abuses in Latin America, and then coupling these denunciations with reductions in military and economic aid, the Carter Administration contained repression, narrowed the options for military autocrats and accelerated momentum for democratic change in the region. When the Dominican military stopped the presidential election vote count in 1978 in the face of an apparent opposition victory, swift and vigorous warnings from President Carter, Secretary of State Cyrus Vance, American embassy officials and the commander in chief of the U.S. Southern Command succeeded in pressuring the Dominican military to allow the opposition candidate to take office, thus effecting a transition to democracy. Vigorous, explicit diplomatic messages from the Reagan Administration, artfully coordinating public actions and private appeals, dissuaded Ferdinand Marcos in the Philippines in 1986 and Chun Doo Hwan in South Korea in 1987 from forcibly suppressing pro-democracy protests and helped induce them to allow a democratic transition to unfold. And a more extended strategy succeeded in encouraging a process of democratic change in Chile and discouraging military dictator August Pinochet from thwarting the electoral process. Although President Bush in his final two years backed away from pressuring Arab authoritarian regimes, after Islamist parties and movements made alarming gains in Egypt, Lebanon and Palestine, his public appeals for democracy in the Middle East encouraged opposition movements and helped persuade Egyptian President Hosni Mubarak to open up political space and allow a contested presidential election in 2005. The resulting political liberalization was partial and short-lived, but it stimulated political aspirations and the growth of opposition networks and skills in ways that would ultimately contribute to the downfall of Mubarak in the February 2011 revolution.

Diplomats on the ground, from the U.S. (and other democracies), also have many tools at their disposal to support and advance struggles for democracy.

July 28, 2000: Opponents of Peru's President Alberto Fujimori march through the streets of Lima, Peru. Riot police fired tear gas into crowds of demonstrators, as pitched street battles and fires marred Fujimori's inauguration for an unprecedented third term. (ANIBAL SOLIMANO/NEWSMAKERS/GETTY IMAGES)

Their reporting back to Washington (or their other capitals) may help to catalyze the use of stronger tools to pressure for democracy, as described, for example, in *A Diplomat's Handbook for Democratic Development*. U.S. embassy officials may extend their cloak of diplomatic immunity to prevent punitive state violence against dissidents by merely showing up at the scene of protests, demonstrations and imminent arrests. Or they may give hope, inspiration and legitimacy to democratic opposition forces by publicly meeting with them and hearing their concerns, monitoring their trials and imprisonments, observing elections, speaking out for democratic principles and visiting communities victimized by state violence (as U.S. Ambassador Robert Ford did in Syria until he had to be evacuated). They may save dissidents from arrest by granting them asylum. The expanding practice of public diplomacy represents American society to the host society through a variety of public appeals, exchanges and programs that project democratic models, values and experiences and give ideas and moral support to democratic forces. And increasingly, U.S. diplomats may help to provide or facilitate more concrete forms of democracy assistance and technical advice.

Sanctions and aid

When efforts at moral or rational persuasion fail, democracies can increase the pressure by manipulating harder interests. This involves threatening or actually moving to impose costs on a country—and/or its key ruling elites—for violations of international norms of democracy and human rights. The range of tools here includes economic sanctions—reduction or suspension of aid and trade ties; diplomatic sanctions, such as the downgrading of diplomatic, cultural and symbolic ties; military sanctions, such as the suspension of military aid, cooperation and weapons sales, pursuit of a wider ban on arms sales to the country, and cutoffs of access to military-related technology; and aid conditionality. Whereas sanctions are punitive—imposing penalties for bad conduct—aid conditionality offers

Anti-apartheid demonstrators in 1986 hold a vigil in London, England, for a Commonwealth decision in favor of economic sanctions for South Africa. (SAHM DOHERTY/TIME LIFE PICTURES/GETTY IMAGES)

positive inducements of new flows of economic assistance if a country meets objective standards of democracy and good governance.

The academic literature is generally skeptical on the efficacy of international sanctions as a tool for inducing changes in the behavior of states. Sanctions only work when they can generate significant pain on the target country. The realization that trade sanctions just were not going to move a country as big and powerful as China to liberalize politically persuaded the Clinton Administration to lift its conditioning of "most-favored-nation" trading status on human rights in 1994. Typically, sanctioned and isolated states find ways to adapt by developing home-grown alternatives to products they can no longer buy, by simply passing off the costs of sanctions on to their long-suffering populations while blaming the international community for national hardships, and by cultivating or deepening alternative ties and suppliers of resources, technology and geopolitical support. This explains why pariah regimes like North Korea, Myanmar (Burma), Zimbabwe and Iran have been able to survive tough international sanctions imposed by the U.S. and other democracies. In these cases, the relative dearth of linkages to the U.S. has greatly limited American leverage in inflicting pain on the regimes and reshaping behavior.

And the regimes have been sustained by the tolerance or support of friendly neighbors, like China and Russia, and in some cases by their own sources of mineral wealth. Yet, historical experience shows the corrosive impact of poor economic performance on authoritarian regimes may be cumulative, generating a growing vulnerability that may not be visibly apparent.

On the other hand, where ties to the U.S. have been strong, sanctions have had an effect in moving regimes toward democratic concessions. Carter's human rights policy toward Latin America had an effect precisely because it coupled moral denunciations with reductions in economic and military aid. Years of stiffening economic sanctions from the U.S. and Europe, as well as disinvestment by private corporations and institutions, gradually ratcheted up the pressure on the apartheid regime and the white population in South Africa during the 1980s. For some time, South Africa adapted by becoming more self-sufficient, but when gold prices declined and domestic debt and inflation escalated, the result was a "protracted recession, capital flight and a profound sense of isolation.... Whites began to realize that unless they came to terms with the political demands of the black population, the economic noose would not loosen." In the early

Supporters of Ferdinand Marcos hold a poster at a political rally during the presidential campaign against Corazon Aquino with the words, "Bring Back Our Legal President Ferdinand Edralin Marcos," underneath a photograph of U.S. President Ronald Reagan shaking hands with Marcos. (GREG SMITH/CORBIS)

1990s, the freezing or suspension of Western aid forced countries like Benin, Kenya and Malawi to open up and hold competitive, multiparty elections. In short, country-specific sanctions can work, when major powers cooperate, when there is extensive linkage and when domestic pressures converge.

Increasingly, as the sanctions weapon gets refined from a blunt instrument to a range of more targeted and precise tools of punishment, stigmatization and deterrence, sanctions are becoming more credible and effective in shaping the behavior of authoritarian elites. Targeted sanctions on regime elites, including travel bans and asset freezes, can get the attention of venal rulers who may be more prepared to see their countries suffer than themselves. "The warning by senior U.S. diplomats that the U.S. government would freeze personal offshore assets of Ukrainian officials in the event of government repression had considerable restraining impact on potentially violent behavior."

The logic of conditioning economic assistance on democracy (or progress toward it) is relatively recent. While there had been individual country episodes of conditionality, prior to 2000, these generally were much more often linked (by World Bank and International Monetary Fund [IMF] negotiating teams) to a country's economic reform policies, and typically were tied to promises of future reforms rather than offered as rewards for prior behavior. With the initiation in 2002 of a new development assistance vehicle, the Millennium Challenge Account (MCA), the Bush Administration brought the principle of conditionality to a new level. The semi-autonomous implementing agency, the Millenium Challenge Corporation (MCC), rewards developing countries for demonstrated performance in democracy, just governance and economic freedom and entrepreneurship, ranking countries on a set of 22 indicators. Countries that rank highly qualify for substantial new grants of aid, which must be negotiated with the MCC in contracts for specific development programs. While the MCA has only been funded at a fraction of its promise (falling well short of the anticipated goal of $5 billion annually), it has negotiated quite significant compacts for developmental assistance with a number of developing democracies, such as El Salvador, Mongolia, the Philippines, Ghana and Malawi. The amounts of the compacts typically run into the hundreds of millions of dollars, providing a tangible incentive to achieve and maintain standards of democracy and good governance. And the willingness to suspend countries, such as Nicaragua, when they veer away from democracy also reinforces the conditionality mechanism. Unfortunately, some of the recipients, like Armenia and Jordan, are clearly not democracies, while others, like Tanzania and Senegal, are at best ambiguous in their adherence to democratic norms. However, in 2011 the MCC, which administers the grants and judges eligibility, modified the conditions to require that eligible countries score above an absolute threshold on either political rights or civil liberties (as measured annually by Freedom House, an international organization that conducts research on democracy). Whether this most ambitious experiment to date in aid conditionality succeeds over time in promotiong democracy will depend, first, on whether democracies like Ghana achieve more vigorous economic development with this and other aid flows; second, to what extent the political conditions are sufficiently well-monitored and enforced so that elected leaders perceive real costs in trying to diminish or undermine democracy; and third, whether the selection criteria are in fact tightened so that obviously authoritarian regimes do not continue to be selected. One encouraging trend is that several of the countries that have recently been granted more limited aid under the "threshold program" in an effort to raise them up to qualifying standards are emerging democracies, like Liberia and East Timor, where a sizable flow of politically conditional aid might help to lock in democratic commitments while advancing the economic conditions for sustainable democracy.

Democracy assistance

One reason that so many Americans question whether they should be promoting democracy abroad is that they do not realize that high-profile military interventions in Iraq and Afghanistan or humanitarian interventions in places like Haiti and Somalia are the exception rather than the rule. In most countries where democracy is absent or insecure, American efforts to encourage it proceed quietly and incrementally, far out of the glare of major media attention, through quotidian efforts of assistance to strengthen democratic institutions, reform governance, develop independent organizations and media, build democratic culture, monitor democratic elections, and, in authoritarian circumstances, train and support democratic forces in civil society.

Since 1983, the lead American organization for providing this assistance has been the National Endowment for Democracy (NED) and its four core grantees: the international institutes of the two main U.S. political parties (the National Democratic Institute, NDI, and the International Republican Institute, IRI, the Center for International Private Enterprise, CIPE, and the Free Trade Union Institute, FTUI, now the Solidarity Center). These five organizations are publicly funded in their grants and programs by annual congressional appropriations, supplemented in the latter four cases with significant grants and contracts from the U.S. Agency for International Development (USAID). Although it began with very small annual budgets (under $20 million), NED gave critical aid to democratic movements in Poland, Nicaragua and Chile. Probably its greatest success story was in Poland, where FTUI transferred substantial assistance to the Solidarity trade union to support its education, publishing and human rights projects. NED and its affiliates also contributed to peaceful democracy transitions in the Philippines, Namibia, Haiti, Zambia and South Africa, in part by funding election-monitoring efforts and helping to organize international election-observing teams. In retrospect, each of these efforts has an air of inevitability to it, but at the time the odds against successful transitions were long, and the combined assistance efforts of NED, other American donors, and in some cases the NGOs or aid organizations of other democracies crucially helped to make political breakthroughs possible.

Repeatedly over the last two decades, U.S. and international assistance for independent media, free elections and civic organizations have made significant, if not always immediate, contributions to democratic change. For example:

International election-observer missions—with American NGOs like NDI, IRI and the Carter Center playing leading roles—have helped to enhance the credibility and legitimacy of elections in many new and tense circumstances, such as South Korea in 1987, Bulgaria in 1990, and Ghana and the Dominican Republic in 1996; to mediate bitter disputes over the electoral process in countries like Nicaragua, El Salvador, Albania, and Cambodia.

Political parties reflecting diverse societal interests have received training and advice on how to develop membership bases, volunteer networks, campaign organizations, local branches, fund-raising, public opinion polling, issue research, policy platforms, media messages, constituency relations, and democratic methods of choosing their leaders and candidates and involving members. Some of this has come during election campaigns, but much of it is ongoing organization building, helping parties to govern and legislate, to recruit and campaign, and to involve women and youth.

Not all of this aid is effective. Some recipients are weakly commited or openly corrupt opportunists who set up BRINGOS ("briefcase NGOs") and GONGOS ("government organized NGOs," that is, fronts and apologists for authoritarian regimes). Others are simply wasteful or ineffectual. Critics of this aid worry that civil society becomes too dependent on foreign donors—without explaining how independent pro-democracy groups and media could raise the funds to function viably in relatively poor countries, or those where an autocratic state dominates and co-opts the private business sector. Strategic calculations may lead international election observers to pull their punches before declaring that a fraudulent election has been stolen and illegitimate. They may

May 7, 1989: Former Polish President and Solidarity founding leader Lech Walesa shows the victory sign in front of a Solidarity poster during his presidential campaign. The first first free trade union of the Soviet bloc, Solidarity won a sweeping victory in the partially free vote in 1989 and paved the way to the dismantling of communism in Eastern Europe, the fall of the Berlin Wall and the bloody removal of Romanian leader Nicolae Ceausescu. (LESZEK WDOWINSKI/REUTERS/CORBIS)

also soften the U.S. government's resolve to support democratic opposition forces challenging pro-American autocrats, but NED makes its grants entirely independent of the State Department or White House. And large amounts of aid to modernize parliaments, courts and other government agencies may amount to little if political leaders lack the will to allow these institutions to function democratically and check the abuse of power. Even where these forms of political assistance crucially contribute to democratic breakthroughs or tangibly help fledgling democratic institutions to gain strength and credibility, they always do so in a supporting role.

There is general consensus among scholars and practitioners that democracy assistance cannot substitute for the "courage, energy, skills and legitimacy" of a country's own pro-democracy advocates. The most careful and dispassionate scholar of U.S. democracy assistance efforts, Thomas Carothers, concludes (not surprisingly) that these forms of aid have the most visibly positive effects where

there are already present at least moderately favorable conditions for democratic change, such as sincere and effective democrats, divided autocrats, and higher levels of economic and educational development. Nevertheless, where democracy assistance is "properly designed and implemented," where it proceeds from sensitive knowledge of the local political terrain and then endeavors to monitor grants carefully over time, it can "help broaden and deepen democratic reforms" in new democracies and sustain civic awareness, democratic hope, and independent information and organization in authoritarian regimes. Thus, if democracy assistance does not in itself work miracles, it does occasionally help amazing democratic breakthroughs to occur, and over time it helps to build the civic and political foundations of enduringly free societies. Given the relatively modest total amounts the U.S. government spends on these forms of assistance annually (something over $1.5 billion, mainly through USAID, for aid to civil society, political parties, representative institutions, corruption control,

representative and judicial institutions and other elements of democratic governance), this is no small achievement. In fact, when these political aid flows were assessed (for the years 1990 to 2003) by an independent team of social scientists a few years ago, they found the effects were clearly and consistently positive, but only modest because individual country levels of assistance were modest (about $2 million–4 million on average). Larger levels of democracy assistance appear to yield larger impacts. They found that each additional $1 million of democracy assistance increases the "normal" rate of expected improvement in democracy scores by 50%.

The findings—unprecedented for their empirical depth and statistical precision and sophistication—fully justify the authors' conclusions that overall levels of democracy assistance should be increased and that democracy assistance should be sustained in countries even after they have reached what has heretofore been considered a "satisfactory" stage of democratic development. ∎

What is the U.S. agenda in promoting democracy?

A COMPELLING CASE can be made that a more democratic world is not just an intrinsically better and more humane world, but also a safer, less stressful, and more predictable and secure world for the U.S. But even if that is so, how does one get from here to there? The U.S. might well be more secure if democracy really took hold in Egypt and Pakistan, but what about the risks and costs along the way? How much short-term stability is the U.S. willing to sacrifice for long-term gain, and how grave are the transitional risks—not just of a hostile government coming to power, but of political order imploding altogether? And even if these risks are tolerable in many places, what about others—like Saudi Arabia—where the stakes are enormous and so are the dangers

of a rapid rush to popular sovereignty? Then there are the questions of means. If America has the interest, does it have the capacity and means? Or should it draw the line at certain types of means?

Promoting democracy can never be the sole purpose of American foreign policy, and at times it will clearly recede in priority as the U.S. pursues urgent and palpable competing national security concerns. But too often the U.S. has traded short-term gains in stability or economic advantage at the price of long-term costs to its national interest, once autocrats like the shah of Iran, Somoza in Nicaragua, Duvalier in Haiti, Mobutu in Zaire and Siad Barre in Somalia fell from power, leaving chaos or anti-American revolutions in their wake. Pressing for open, accountable, responsive and legitimate government—in other words, democracy—is in the American national interest, even if the means, volume and pace must vary.

One of the attractions of democracy assistance is that it offers some scope for the U.S. to square the difficult circle and have its relations with autocracies proceed on dual tracks when necessary. On one track (the most visible), formal dip-

PETT, USA TODAY, ARLINGTON, VA, USA

lomatic ties and aid flows—at the extreme, the nearly $2 billion dollars a year ($1.7 billion in recent years) that went to the authoritarian regime of Egyptian President Mubarak—can sustain cooperative relations with autocrats the U.S. may not like but judges it needs strategically. On the other track, democracy assistance can provide hope, training and resources to pro-democracy forces in civil society and the political opposition, while American diplomats can monitor and protest the worst abuses and reaffirm American values. The problem with this approach, however, is that when the U.S. perceives a strategic need to embrace a dictator, it gives the latter leverage. And since autocrats under challenge are locked in an existential struggle for survival—where failure could mean not simply retreat into a plush retirement, but sudden death, humiliating exile, or imprisonment and prosecution for past crimes—they will fight furiously to remain in power. Historically, the U.S. has retreated too quickly from this authoritarian counterpressure, underestimating its own leverage and overestimating the leverage and options of autocratic actors like Mubarak or the Pakistani military. Getting the balance right is a delicate and high-stakes challenge, in which American foreign policymakers must wrestle not only with the conflict between ideals and interests, but with a conflict between competing interests and rival scenarios of disaster for the American interest. Moreover, one of the things that recipients of democracy assistance most often and loudly complain about is precisely the lack of coordination and consistency between the civic aid they receive from the U.S.—which they appreciate and even depend upon—and the "high politics" of diplomacy and government-to-government aid, which too often rewards and reinforces the very authoritarian regime they are trying to displace.

Much more can and should also be done to reorganize foreign aid around the incentive-based approach of the MCA. Indeed, the entire U.S. foreign assistance program has become a hopeless jumble of congressional earmarks and partial objectives that rob aid administrators of the flexibility they need to look at countries

Feb. 6, 2006: A UN peacekeeper patrols near a polling station as Haiti prepares for national elections in Port-au-Prince, Haiti. (JOE RAEDLE/GETTY IMAGES)

holistically and with fresh eyes. The most important question that should be asked in allocating aid and designing country strategies is, "How can the U.S. encourage coherent and sustained progress toward just development?" That means not just economic growth or better health for the next year or two, but more open, accountable and effective institutions in the state and civil society, for the long run.

Finally, the U.S. can gain a lot in terms of legitimacy and effectiveness by working to defend and advance democracy as often as possible through regional organizations like the North Atlantic Treaty Organization (NATO) and the Organization of American States (OAS), through international organizations like the UN, and through broad multilateral networks like the Community of Democracies (CD), spearheaded by U.S. Secretary of State Madeleine Albright. Over the last two decades, the UN has emerged as a significant player in democracy promotion, assuming critical roles in assisting the organization of democratic elections and in helping to resolve violent conflict through democratic mechanisms. Today, the UN Development Program (UNDP) is one of the largest international providers of democratic governance assistance, with a budget of about $1.4 billion for that purpose in 2005, including support for about a third of the parliaments in the developing world. While the Community of Democracies has been mainly

a symbolic gathering of states since its founding in Poland in 2000, it is now beginning to develop a more effective governing structure, and means (such as through cooperative democracy partnerships) to provide tangible forms of governance assistance to new and troubled democracies. Having not just other established democracies, like Canada, Japan and the EU nations, but emerging democracies like India, Korea, Mongolia, Mexico, Chile, Mali and South Africa, sharing membership on the Governing Council of the CD, in itself sends a significant message about the growing global legitimacy of democracy.

In a world of ongoing security threats—terrorism, narco-trafficking and proliferation of WMDs, to name a few—and of new threats such as cyberwarfare and China's expanding military power and strategic ambitions, promoting freedom and democracy will sometimes fade from view as an objective. But it should never be lost from view. The states that present these threats to the U.S. are all autocracies, or at least illiberal and weak democracies urgently in need of strengthening. Ultimately, nothing will advance the security and prosperity of the U.S. more than the gradual movement of the world toward more and better democracy. ■

**Opinion Ballots
after page 32**

discussion questions

1. Why might the U.S. have an interest in seeing the spread of democracy? What are the benefits of global democratization? Are there negative consequences? Is the U.S. interest in democratization material, philosophical, or both?

2. How might the U.S. government increase public support for its democracy promotion programs? Has democracy promotion been misunderstood? How would you argue for or against the value of democracy promotion?

3. What are the advantages and disadvantages of the decentralized democracy promotion programs carried out by various U.S. agencies, other nations, NGOs and multilateral organizations? Which actor is best equipped to promote democracy?

4. Why do you think that the "realist" school of international relations has waned in significance? Why has the idealist school gained momentum in the 20th century, especially with Presidents Reagan to Obama?

5. How would you evaluate the U.S. democracy promotion efforts carried out in the last 50 years? Which ones have been successes, and which have been failures? What factors contribute to the success or failure of a democracy promotion effort? Which method or combination of methods is most effective?

6. Democracies now enjoy a majority, and the "Arab Spring" has demonstrated that indigenous democracy movements can achieve success against entrenched regimes. In the future, do you see democracy promotion as a U.S. interest that will grow or decline in relevance? Do democratic movements have more legitimacy if they succeed without intervention?

7. Many vital U.S. allies are semi-democratic nations, such as Saudi Arabia and Bahrain. Does the U.S. have an interest in not pursuing a democracy promotion agenda in these countries? What strategic interests take precedence over democratic values? Under what circumstances should democracy promotion be the U.S.'s overriding interest?

---

suggested readings

Carothers, Thomas, **Aiding Democracy Abroad: The Learning Curve**. Washington, D.C., Carnegie Endowment, 1999. 412 pp. $19.95 (paper). Carothers, one of the world's foremost experts on democracy promotion, brings research and careful analysis together in this text.

Council for a Community of Democracies, **A Diplomat's Handbook for Democracy Development Support**, 2nd ed. Washington, D.C., Council for a Community of Democracies, 2010. 249 pp. Available free online at: <http://www.diplomatshandbook.org>. This volume, with a foreword by the first president of the Czech Republic, Vaclav Havel, provides case studies drawing on the experiences of diplomats engaged in democracy promotion around the world. Available in English, Spanish and Arabic.

Diamond, Larry, **The Spirit of Democracy: The Struggle to Build Free Societies Throughout the World.** 464 pp. $17.99 (paper). New York, St. Martin's Griffin, 2009. This authoritative volume surveys the results of various democracy promotion efforts and examines the factors that contribute to democratization.

Dobbins, James, Jones, Seth G., Crane, Keith, Rathmell, Andrew, Steele, Brett, Teltschik, Richard, and Timilsina, Anga, **The UN's Role in Nation-Building: From the Congo to Iraq.** Santa Monica, CA, RAND Corporation, 2005. 319 pp. Available free online at: <http://www.rand.org/content/dam/rand/pubs/monographs/2005/RAND_MG304.pdf>. In this exhaustive report, the authors examine UN nation-building efforts and discuss the elements necessary for success.

McFaul, Michael, **Advancing Democracy Abroad: Why We Should and How We Can.** Lanham, MD, Rowman and Littlefield, 2009. 304 pp. $27.95 (hardcover). McFaul, a Stanford University professor and Obama Administration adviser, makes an argument for reviving democracy promotion as a cornerstone of U.S. policy.

Mead, Walter Russell, **Special Providence: American Foreign Policy and How It Changed the World.** New York, Routledge, 2002. 400 pp. $51.95 (paper). Mead chronicles the four schools of foreign policy in a historical context and discusses their contributions to U.S. foreign policy.

Visit **WWW.GREATDECISIONS.ORG** *for quizzes, seasonal topic updates and other resources to further your understanding*

ARCTIC OCEAN

Beaufort Sea

Queen Elizabeth Islands

Ellesmere Island

GREENLAND (DENMARK)

Victoria Island

Baffin Bay

Baffin Island

Davis Strait

Denmark Strait

Reykjavik

ARCTIC CIRCLE (66°33')

ALASKA (U.S.)

Anchorage

Gulf of Alaska

Juneau

Aleutian Islands

Great Bear Lake

Great Slave Lake

Churchill

Hudson Bay

Labrador Sea

CANADA

NORTH AMERICA

Lake Winnipeg

Great Lakes

Montréal

Québec

Ottawa

Toronto

Vancouver

Seattle

UNITED STATES

Chicago

New York

NORTH PACIFIC OCEAN

Denver

St. Louis

Washington, D.C.

NORTH ATLANTIC OCEAN

San Francisco

Atlanta

AZORES (PORTUGAL)

Los Angeles

Dallas

BERMUDA (U.K.)

CANARY ISLANDS (SPAIN)

TROPIC OF CANCER (23°27')

Monterrey

Gulf of Mexico

Miami

Nassau

THE BAHAMAS

WESTERN SAHARA (ADMINISTERED BY MOROCCO)

HAWAII (U.S.)

Honolulu

MEXICO

Mexico City

Veracruz

Havana

CUBA

HAITI

DOMINICAN REPUBLIC

VIRGIN ISLS. (U.S.)

BRITISH VIRGIN ISLS. (U.K.)

ANGUILLA (U.K.)

ST. KITTS AND NEVIS

ANTIGUA AND BARBUDA

Nouakchott

ATOLL

Port-au-Prince

Santo Domingo

PUERTO RICO (U.S.)

GUADELOUPE (FR.)

DOMINICA

CAPE VERDE

Praia

Dakar

SENE

BELIZE

GUATEMALA

Guatemala City

Belmopan

JAMAICA

Kingston

Caribbean Sea

MONTSERRAT (U.K.)

MARTINIQUE (FR.)

ST. LUCIA

BARBADOS

THE GAMBIA

Banjul

BISSAU

REEF

HONDURAS

San Salvador

Tegucigalpa

ST. VINCENT AND THE GRENADINES

GRENADA

GUINEA-BISSAU

EL SALVADOR

Managua

ARUBA (NETH.)

NETHERLANDS ANTILLES (NETH.)

Port-of-Spain

TRINIDAD AND TOBAGO

Conakry

Freetown

PALMYRA ATOLL (U.S.)

NICARAGUA

COSTA RICA

San José

Caracas

VENEZUELA

SIERRA LEONE

Mon

KIRITIMATI (CHRISTMAS ISLAND)

PANAMA

Panama

Medellín

Bogotá

Georgetown

Paramaribo

Cayenne

EQUATOR

Cali

COLOMBIA

GUYANA

SURINAME

FRENCH GUIANA (FR.)

VIS ISLAND (U.S.)

GALAPAGOS ISLANDS (ECUADOR)

Quito

ECUADOR

Iquitos

Manaus

Belém

MARQUESAS ISLAND (FR. POLYNESIA)

BRAZIL

Recife

FRENCH POLYNESIA (FRANCE)

PERU

Lima

Cusco

SOUTH AMERICA

Brasília

ANDS

TUAMOTU ARCHIPELAGO (FR. POLYNESIA)

La Paz

BOLIVIA

Sucre

Rio de Janeiro

SOCIETY ISLANDS (FR. POLYNESIA)

TROPIC OF CAPRICORN (23°27')

Paraguay

São Paulo

SOUTH ATLANTIC OCEAN

TUBUAI ISLANDS (FR. POLYNESIA)

PITCAIRN ISLANDS (U.K.)

Antofagasta

Asunción

EASTER ISLAND (CHILE)

ISLA SALA Y GÓMEZ (CHILE)

CHILE

URUGUAY

JUAN FERNÁNDEZ ISLANDS (CHILE)

Santiago

Buenos Aires

La Plata

Montevideo

SOUTH PACIFIC OCEAN

ARGENTINA

Bahía Blanca

FALKLAND ISLANDS (ADMINISTERED BY U.K. CLAIMED BY ARGENTINA)

SOUTH GEORGIA AND THE SOUTH SANDWICH ISLANDS (ADMINISTERED BY U.K. CLAIMED BY ARGENTINA)

Punta Arenas

Stanley

Scotia Sea

Drake Passage

SOUTH ORKNEY ISLANDS (B.A.T.)

SOUTHERN OCEAN

Amundsen Sea

Bellingshausen Sea

Weddell Sea

Ross Sea

Ronne Ice Shelf

Ross Ice Shelf

VENEZUELA Independent state

GUADELOUPE (FRANCE) Dependent territory

Ottawa ✹ Capital

Bangalore ● Major city

Scale 1:35,000,000

Robinson Projection with standard parallels 38°N and 38°S
Source: CIA World Factbook

The Foreign Policy Association, the nation's oldest civic-education organization, was founded nearly a century ago. With the motto "An informed public is an educated public," and the belief that America must possess a citizenry knowledgeable in international affairs, FPA has grown into a national educational institution. FPA produces Great Decisions, a discussion program that takes place annually in communities across the country; the Headline Series, a periodic publication that addresses essential topics in foreign policy; and lectures by experts of all stripes. World dignitaries such as Indira Gandhi, Margaret Thatcher, Bill Clinton and Ban Ki-moon have taken the podium at FPA events.

Mexico: transborder crime and governance
by George Grayson

A body sprawled in an alley in a run-down area in Ciudad Juarez, Mexico, is an all too familiar crime scene. In recent years, drug violence and the economic recession in the city have reshaped the city's character and demographics. (KATIE ORLINSKY/NEW YORK TIMES/REDUX)

O N AUGUST 24, 2010, Mexican Navy personnel found a jumble of decaying, blindfolded and bound corpses slumped against a wall in a remote farm in San Fernando, Tamaulipas, 90 miles from Brownsville, Texas. The 58 men and 14 women, who had endured savage torture before being killed, marked the largest mass slaying to that date in Mexico's version of the "war on drugs." The discovery followed a shootout between marines—an arm of the Mexican Navy—and Los Zetas—a bloodthirsty, sadistic cartel founded by deserters from Mexico's Special Forces.

Initially focusing on drug transactions, Los Zetas have branched into murder for hire, kidnapping, extortion, contraband, human trafficking and a score of other criminal exploits. The desperados had sought to recruit as foot soldiers and extract money from the San Fernando victims, most of whom were Central Americans who had furtively crossed the mountainous, jungle-covered 600-mile Mexico-Guate-

mala border, which is as porous as a sieve blasted by buckshot. Their goal was to use Mexico as a pathway to the U.S.

"We have firmly asked the Mexican authorities to conduct an exhaustive investigation to find those responsible for this abominable event," harrumphed Hugo Martínez, foreign minister of El Salvador, where officials found a suspected Zeta training facility and $14.5 million in drug monies buried in plastic barrels. In the aftermath of this unspeakable disaster, Mexican President Felipe Calderón accepted the

GEORGE GRAYSON *teaches Government at the College of William & Mary. He is a senior associate at the Center for Strategic & International Studies and an associate scholar at the Foreign Policy Research Institute. He has written* The Executioner's Men: Inside Los Zetas *(with Sam Logan) (Transaction, 2012) and* Mexico: Narco-Violence and a Failed State? *(Transaction, 2010). He holds a Ph.D. from Johns Hopkins University and a JD from William & Mary.*

resignation of the head of the notoriously venal National Migration Institute (INM), while promising a radical overhaul of his approach to the epidemic of kidnappings and execution of Central American migrants. Following the jailing of seven Zetas for the San Fernando massacre, one of his top spokesmen declared that these arrests "constitute a significant step toward ending the impunity surrounding assaults on migrants by organized crime." Such rhetoric lost credibility in April and May 2011, when Mexican officials uncovered 47 clandestine graves containing 193 decomposing bodies, some believed to be

then Guatemala's president, responded to this "totally barbaric" act by declaring a state of emergency in the remote, impoverished northern Petén province, twice the size of Hawaii, which borders Mexico and functions as a vital base and training ground for Mexican drug squads, especially Los Zetas.

The following month, dozens of migrants attempting to reach the U.S. were reportedly abducted while clinging to the top and sides of a freight train—commonly called "The Beast"—in southern Mexico. Rubén Figueroa, a human rights activist who runs a shelter for the poor in Mexico's southeastern

Just as Uncle Sam influences Mexico's economic, social, cultural and political milieu, Central Americans tend to regard Mexico as their "big brother" to the north. They read books published in Mexico's capital, the Federal District (DF); sob and laugh at the plots of Mexican soap operas; seek and savor Mexican cuisine; and wheel and deal with Mexican entrepreneurs to sell them goods and construct projects in their countries.

Mass killings have exacerbated tensions between Calderón and his counterparts to the south. While by no means naïve about hazards in Mexico,

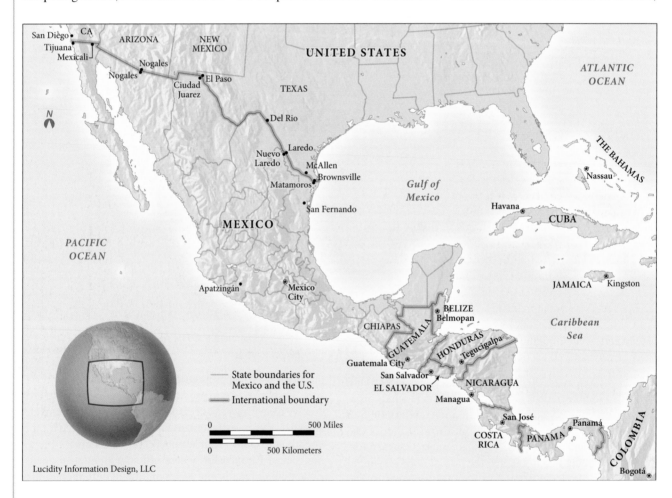

State boundaries for Mexico and the U.S.

International boundary

0   500 Miles

0   500 Kilometers

Lucidity Information Design, LLC

Central Americans. Los Zetas, who had snatched their quarry from buses traveling through San Fernando, later bashed in their heads with sledgehammers or similar blunt instruments. These attacks have spread outside of Mexico as well. Los Zetas allegedly beheaded 26 of 27 Guatemalan workers on a coconut farm in mid-May 2011. Álvaro Colom,

Tabasco state, labeled the perils facing illegal aliens "a humanitarian tragedy, a holocaust, and a genuine hell." The events in Tamaulipas, Petén and Mexico's south represent only a sample of the many atrocities that Mexican drug trafficking organizations (DTOs) have visited on Central Americans at home and abroad.

the region's leaders are aghast that drug smugglers have converted the Central American isthmus into a freeway for moving cocaine and other drugs from the Andes, even as these cutthroats wantonly execute their citizens. The major issues concern not only attacks on Central Americans and other foreigners in Mexico, but also the lethal penetration of Los Zetas and the Sinaloa Cartel into the region, where they work hand in glove with entrenched local Mafias.

What is the status of Mexico's version of the "war on drugs" launched by Calderón after his December 1, 2006, inauguration? Why have the Mexican DTOs cut such a broad swath through Central America? Will Mexico's next chief executive have greater success in thwarting the extremely violent, rich-as-Croesus cartels? Has the U.S.'s vaunted Mérida Initiative crippled organized crime in Mexico and the seven countries of the isthmus? What policies should Washington consider, especially in light of Guatemala's newly elected hard-liner president, and considering the selection of Calderón's successor on July 1, 2012? ■

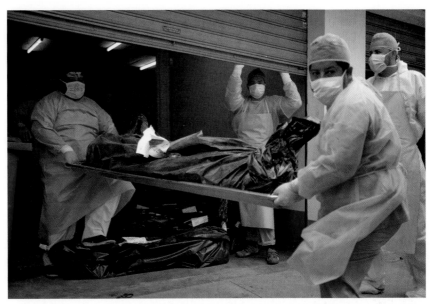

Forensic workers move one of the 28 bodies found decapitated on a farm in San Andres, in northern Guatemala on the Mexican border. Police officials say the killings could be linked to drug gangs operating in the area. (JOHAN ORDONEZ/AFP/GETTY IMAGES)

Mexico's war on drugs

FROM THE COLONIAL ERA to the present, Mexico has never had honest, professional police. The Institutional Revolutionary Party (PRI), which held a vise-like grip on the presidency from 1929 to 2000, spawned some 3,000 police agencies, with 350,000 officers, at the municipal, state and federal levels. In most cases these officers reaped rewards for advancing the political, social and economic agenda of the party. Although the authoritarian regime preferred to co-opt foes, it did not hesitate to coerce or even assassinate opponents. The current number of policemen stands at 427,354, with 61% earning less than $350 per month.

When Vicente Fox (2000–2006) and Calderón (2006–present), stalwarts of the center-right National Action Party (PAN), ousted the PRI from Los Pinos presidential residence, they encountered heavily armed, well-financed drug syndicates that had colonized enclaves such as the "Golden Triangle," where the states of Sinaloa, Chihuahua and Durango converge. The PAN chief executives quickly learned the futility of engaging these culprits with cops who might wear a badge during the day and

Los Angeles Police Chief William Bratton holds a news conference to announce the indictment of 24 leaders, members and associates of MS-13, part of the Mara Salvatrucha gang affiliated with the Mexican Mafia prison gang. (NICK UT/AP)

do the bidding of drug lords at night.

In contrast to the PRI's approach— hammering out "live-and-let-live" pacts with capos—PAN executives endeavored to confront these kingpins. In the absence of reliable police, though, Fox—and especially Calderón—directed the armed forces to spearhead the anti-DTO crusade.

In particular, Calderón bent over back-

ward to ingratiate himself with the armed forces. Soon after donning the red, white and green presidential sash, the new chief executive visited the 43rd Military Zone in Apatzingán, a no-man's land of narco-turbulence in Michoacán, his home state. He showed up in an oversized military jacket and wore an olive-green field hat adorned with five stars and the national emblem to stress his role as commander

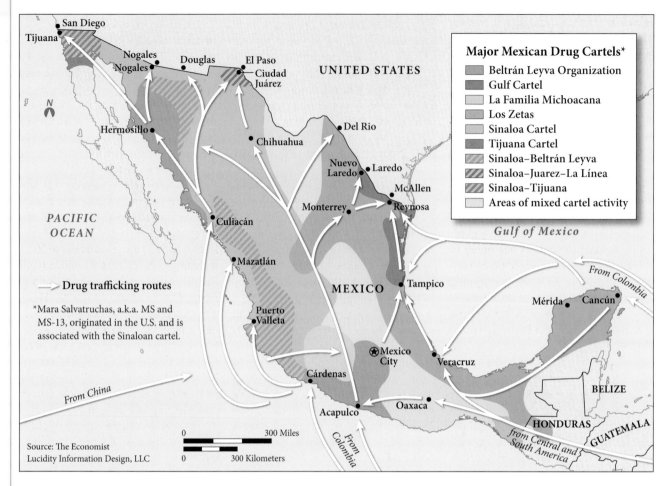

Major Mexican Drug Cartels*

- Beltrán Leyva Organization
- Gulf Cartel
- La Familia Michoacana
- Los Zetas
- Sinaloa Cartel
- Tijuana Cartel
- Sinaloa–Beltrán Leyva
- Sinaloa–Juarez–La Línea
- Sinaloa–Tijuana
- Areas of mixed cartel activity

→ Drug trafficking routes

*Mara Salvatruchas, a.k.a. MS and MS-13, originated in the U.S. and is associated with the Sinaloan cartel.

Source: The Economist
Lucidity Information Design, LLC

in chief. He sought to underscore his solidarity with troops preparing to engage drug barons and their vicious janissaries. At the same time, the government lauded the armed forces in television commercials. For its part, the brass committed themselves to challenging the enemy because of their respect for the president, their nationalistic ethos and the loss of sovereignty over areas under siege by drug barons. Even though many soldiers and sailors live in garrisons, they have found themselves vulnerable to deadly attacks, especially when staffing isolated highway check points.

During his first State of the Nation address, Calderón alluded to austerity but promised to grow the budgets of the military, intelligence agencies and law-enforcement institutions. The nearly $11.4 billion requested for security in 2012 marks a 75.4% upswing over similar funding in 2007, Calderón's first year in office. A surge in personnel accompanied the sharp expansion of resources. The government also boosted salaries of men and women in uniform to reward them for laying their lives on the line, to encourage re-enlistments and to address rampant desertion. Between 2000 and 2006, approximately 100,000 soldiers, including 1,680 Special Forces, fled the barracks. Some made it to "El Norte" (the U.S.), others joined private security firms and a few cast their lot with the Tamaulipas-

Omar Estrada Luna, aka "El Kilo," of the Los Zetas drug cartel, is presented to the press at the Mexican Navy headquarters in Mexico City. Estrada Luna is accused of having planned and ordered the killing of more than 145 people. (STR/AFP/GETTY IMAGES)

based Gulf Cartel, for which Los Zetas became the Praetorian Guard in 1999. Although the desertion toll has dropped compared with previous years, almost 50,000 soldiers and sailors have gone AWOL since Calderón's inauguration.

Calderón is not the first chief executive to deploy the armed forces against drug cartels. In the 1970s, Mexican officials turned to the military to help drive marijuana and heroin-poppy producers from their sanctuaries in the rugged folds of the western Sierra Madres. "Operation Condor," Mexico's campaign against the cartels beginning in 1976, temporarily dislodged the Sinaloan drug lords and gave rise to assigning some 10,000 soldiers to eradicate drugs. Destroying narcotics in the countryside is quite different than battling the nation's current cartels, many of which operate in urban neighborhoods. By and large, soldiers learned to pursue, capture, and, if necessary, kill adversaries. Unlike professional policemen, they were not trained to negotiate, bargain or cajole citizens who enmeshed in community disputes, family quarrels, public drunkenness, fistfights and other antisocial behavior. American politicians have often relied on public schools to tackle intractable social problems such as drug addiction, alcoholism, teenage pregnancies, malnutrition, afterschool idleness and adult illiteracy. In the same vein, their Mexican counterparts have continually passed the buck to the armed forces to perform myriad tasks other than clash with cartels. Civilian authorities have placed troops in charge of prisons, where wardens, other administrators and guards cannot curtail drug use, violence and escapes. In the wake of the fire-bombing of the Casino Royale in Monterrey, authorities dispatched the army to guard this shadowy gambling parlor in which 52 people perished on August 25, 2011. Three weeks later the defense ministry announced formation of a brigade of firefighters. Meanwhile, more than one half of Mexico's 31 states and one third of major violence-torn municipalities have replaced civilian secretaries of public safety with retired or active-duty military officers. There is

no evidence that these officers in *mufti* are more proficient than their civilian counterparts. Still, their presence offers a way for governors—the new viceroys of Mexico's political system—to appear to raise a clenched fist against the malefactors. Regretfully, many state executives are either joined at the hip with the narcos or close their eyes to their behavior. Other retired generals now head security units in corporations beset by bombings, murders, abductions and extortion. Reassignment of the military to wage urban warfare against criminal organizations has impelled a surge in Mexico's output of marijuana and opium poppy. As the acreage of poppy plants destroyed has plummeted, production has boomed—from 8 metric tons in 2005 to 50 metric tons in 2009.

Although not without its critics, the 50,000-member Mexican Navy, which includes 20,000 marines, has registered relatively more gains against criminals than the army, which has been accused by detractors of trampling on human rights. The militarized Federal Police Support Forces (GOPES), a 3,500-member elite detachment within the Public Safety Ministry, has also won praise for skillfully capturing underworld figures. Compared with the army, the navy and GOPES benefit from better intelligence, less corruption, a readiness to act rather than dither and ever-closer links to the U.S. Drug Enforcement Administration (DEA) and sister agencies.

In addition to crooked cops and improperly trained soldiers, several factors have impeded Calderón's offensive: the cartels' success in infiltrating security agencies, the reluctance of federal and state agencies to share intelligence, the army's weariness of playing a role that engenders criticism and the failure of elites outside the north to commit themselves to assailing crime syndicates.

Still, cooperation between U.S. law enforcement agencies and some of their Mexican counterparts has contributed to the capture or death of 21 of 37 drug lords named by the government in 2009, including Osiel Cárdenas Guillén (Gulf Cartel), Arturo Beltrán Leyva (Beltrán Leyva Organization), Jaime "El Hummer" González Durán (Los Zetas), Eduardo Arellano Félix (Tijuana Cartel), Vicente "El Vicentillo" Zambada Niebla (Sinaloa Cartel) and Jesús "El Chango" Méndez (La Familia Michoacana). By mid-2011, Mexico had extradited more than 379 alleged criminals to the U.S.

Yet, the elimination of big shots under Calderón's "Kingpin Strategy" has often proved counterproductive. Takedowns sparked severe violence as younger, less effective lieutenants vied for the top spots, rival cartels encroached on fallen *jefes'* turf and gangs recruited by the capos for protection acted more boldly. For example, Los Zetas began as guardians of the boss of the Tamaulipas-based Gulf Cartel, and La Línea (with units in Ciudad Juárez and

A demonstrator speaks at an anti-violence protest in Mexico City. The sign reads in Spanish, "One minute for no more blood." (EDUARDO VERDUGGO/AP)

its twin city, El Paso, Texas) assumed the same role for the Juárez Cartel. Now Los Zetas are engaged in a vicious war with their former patron, and La Línea decides when, where and how it will cooperate with the badly weakened Juárez Cartel. When the government turned up the heat on the more powerful domestic cartels, they made a beeline for Central America, where the police are egregiously corrupt, judges can be bought or rented and inmates frequently run the prisons. In Guatemala, for example, only one murder in 20 is punished; and, in September 2011, Washington added Belize and El Salvador to the list of 22 "major" drug-producing and transit countries whose role in the drug trade "significantly affect the U.S." Calderón's popularity has declined apace with mounting disenchantment over his strategy against DTOs. Although surveys differ and inconsistent answers abound, most reliable pollsters indicated that the president's approval hovered around 50% in late 2011, while 39%—compared with 45% earlier in the year—concluded the country was on the wrong course. Only one quarter of respondents characterized the nation's situation as good. More Mexicans believed traffickers, not government forces, were winning the drug war, and, for the first time in recent memory, those questioned ranked public safety above the economy as the country's worst problem.

The impact of poet Javier Sicilia's protests on public sentiment has yet to be determined. On March 28, 2011, authorities discovered the 59-year old poet's son, Juan Francisco, and six companions dead in Morelos, a violence-convulsed state contiguous to the DF. Beside the bodies, which bore marks of torture, lay a note signed by the Gulf Cartel. Sicilia organized the Movement

Mexican President Felipe Calderon, center, rides on a military vehicle beside the Secretary of Defense, Gen. Guillermo Galvan Galvan, left, and Secretary of the Navy, Adm. Mariano Francisco Saynez Mendoza, at the start of the traditional Independence Day military parade in Mexico City. (ALEXANDRE MENEGHINI/AP)

for a Peace with Justice and Dignity, which ignited well-attended demonstrations throughout Mexico. His crusade included a march to Guatemala to apologize for Mexico's treatment of its citizens like "animals." Sicilia and his tens of thousands of sympathizers called for the president to end the "stupid" drug war and to resign, and for the return of the military to barracks and the legalization of drugs. "We need a national pact because this is an emergency, and we have to rebuild the tissue of this nation—if we do not, we are going to enter hell," he warned. Although he has met several times with Sicilia, Calderón did not mention him in his September 1, 2011, annual speech to the nation and defended his anticrime efforts as having attained "tangible results."

How Central America became a drug route

Two decades ago, the Coast Guard, the DEA, and allied U.S. agencies cracked down on cocaine shipments into Florida and other southeast states. The export-

ers quickly chose Central America as the new avenue for sending drugs to Mexico en route to the U.S.—with Guatemala suffering the worst ravages of criminal activity.

Its wide-open frontier with Mexico—more of a surveyor's line than a border—made Guatemala an ideal pathway for Mexican syndicates. There, they found a sanctuary to stockpile drugs before moving them to Mexico's north and, ultimately, across the Rio Grande. Mexican syndicates—notably, Los Zetas and their nemesis, the Sinaloa Cartel led by the redoubtable Joaquín "El Chapo" Gúzman Loera—deployed superior force against local criminal bands. Until late 2007, the Lorenzana, Mendoza and León families dominated the nation's crime scene. These clans soon found it expedient either to strike deals with the Mexican invaders or burrow underground. The newcomers took advantage of existing sales networks, relationships and know-how accumulated by local Mafias. In addition, Los Zetas also penetrated Belize, Honduras, El Salvador and Nicaragua.

Guatemala teetered on the brink of a failed state when Álvaro Colom swore the presidential oath on January 14, 2008. A wave of criminality slammed his regime before the new leader completed 100 days in office. To make matters worse, he struggled with a crooked law-enforcement apparatus, which had neither the resources nor the incentives to stand up to foreign and domestic DTOs. Interior Minister Vinicio Gómez lamented that it was "humanly impossible" to protect the nation's 13 million inhabitants with only 18,744 national policemen, the equivalent of one officer for every 2,400 civilians. By comparison, the U.S. has 5.8 policemen for every 2,400 inhabitants. In terms of homicides per 100,000 inhabitants, Guatemala (42) comes in third after Honduras (78), El Salvador (65), followed by Belize (41.7), Panama (22), Mexico (18) and Nicaragua (13). In 2010, the U.S. Department of State observed that "the influence of nonstate criminal actors rivals or exceeds that of the [Guatemalan] government in up to 40% of the country."

Before Colom came to power, analysts considered that less than 1% of the 600 to 700 tons of cocaine trafficked north from Colombia to Mexico passed through Central America. Over the course of his four-year rule, cocaine trafficking by truck, plane or ship gave the impulse to violence that spiraled out of control. In March 2011, U.S. authorities estimated that 84% of the narcotics entering Mexico came through, over or around Guatemala.

The danger posed by Mexico's cartels precipitated meetings among Calderón and his Central American counterparts. In June 2011, the seven Central American nations convened an International Conference in Support of the Central American Security Strategy in Guatemala City. Colombia, Mexico, relevant international organizations, the U.S. and other donor nations sent representatives. The conclave cited 22 initiatives, involving crimes against women

Guatemalan President Álvaro Colom, center, speaks next to Belize's Deputy Prime Minister Gaspar Vega, left, and the Deputy Vice Foreign Minister of Nicaragua, Manuel Coronel, in Antigua, Guatemala after an OAS meeting. (JOHAN ORDONEZ/AFP/GETTY IMAGES)

and children, judicial and penal reform, and arms trafficking. At this gathering, rhetoric seemed to eclipse specific plans by extremely disparate ministates to forge an effective front against DTOs.

Policy on migrants

In addition to the spread of the DTOs through the region, the treatment of migrants has been a source of contention in Mexican-U.S. affairs as well as Mexican-Central American relations. Mexican chief executives have long demanded that Washington provide amnesty to illegal aliens, expand guest-worker programs and issue more visas to their people. They have also excoriated the U.S. over the deaths of Mexican citizens who attempt to cross into the U.S. through the Sonora Desert. The number of such fatalities totaled 132 through July 31, 2011, a 38% drop compared with the 212 migrant deaths logged during the same 10-month period in the previous fiscal year.

As President Fox's first foreign secretary (2000–2003), scholar-diplomat Jorge Castañeda averred: "We think that the broad immigration and labor agenda includes humane, civil, and adequate treatment for Mexicans: Mexicans here, going there; Mexicans as they cross the border; Mexicans when they start work and Mexicans who have already been in the U.S. for a long time."

Though the U.S. has faced Mexican criticism for the treatment of Mexican nationals, Mexico has followed a double standard vis-à-vis its southern neighbor. For decades, Central American ambassadors have complained of abuses heaped on their citizens in general and temporary laborers in Chiapas, in particular. Mexican functionaries vowed

Drug War-Related Deaths in Mexico: 2006 to late 2011

Year / Number of Drug-Related Deaths

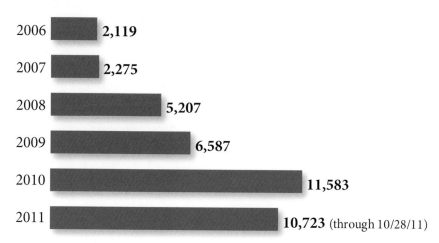

2006 **2,119**
2007 **2,275**
2008 **5,207**
2009 **6,587**
2010 **11,583**
2011 **10,723** (through 10/28/11)

Source: Reforma, a leading Mexican newspaper, publishes a weekly "Execution Meter," which tallies narco-related deaths.

Central American migrants inside the San Juan Diego Migrant House in Lecheria, Mexico, after neighbors prevented a demonstration in memory of Julio Fernando Cardona Agustin, a murdered Guatemalan member of the "Step by Step" caravan for peace. (YURI CORTEZ/ AFP/GETTY IMAGES)

to investigate charges, form working groups, convene additional meetings and sign bilateral agreements. Such promises and legalisms aside, the Mexican government moved very slowly in configuring new policies, except when Washington pressured the INM to increase deportations. Central American countries lack in Mexico the plethora of effective social, political and ethnic advocates that Fox, and now Calderón, count on in the U.S.

Even the Guatemalan community in Mexico, which numbers 500,000 or more according to some estimates, lacks a cohesive structure and lobbyists. El Salvador, a Massachusetts-sized country bursting at the seams with 6 million people, exercises even less clout. Indeed, its officials turn a blind eye as tens of thousands of Salvadorians have sought opportunities outside their poverty-stricken nation each year. So numerous are the émigrés that the country celebrates the "Week of the Migrant" in early September. Amid this event, a critical poster read: "Men and women would not exchange their homeland for a foreign land if their country would give them the possibility to live decently."

This exodus diminished demands on social services at home, while remittances—the monies wired home by

expatriates—enriched El Salvador's sputtering economy by $3.5 billion in 2010 and $2.7 billion from January to September of 2011. Amid official neglect of migrants' issues and the shocking number of deaths, nongovernmental organizations (NGOs) began to inveigh against the trampling of human rights in Mexico. They homed in on the 200,000-member army, as well as the government's indifference with respect to the approximately 140,000 migrants apprehended at the country's

border in 2010, not to mention the tens of thousands who avoided capture. The zealous Mexican Human Rights Commission claimed to have received 5,055 complaints, many against the military, during Calderón's tenure. The same group asserted that 5,300 people disappeared in this period.

A statement by the Washington Office on Latin America (WOLA) epitomized the ever more caustic invective: "For years, organizations and shelters in Mexico have documented the abuses suffered by migrants traveling through the country. Every day along the principal transit routes, migrants, primarily Central Americans, are beaten, extorted, sexually abused and/or kidnapped by criminal groups, at times with the direct participation or acquiescence of Mexican authorities."

The drumbeat of international outrage finally galvanized Mexican lawmakers, who in 2011 approved a new statute that guarantees the rights of migrants, regardless of their immigration status. The legislation, whose purpose was to prevent mistreatment of foreigners, created a 180-day visa for illegal aliens. The law also called for a border-police force to fight crime and conduct surveillance at airports, ports, bus terminals and frontier areas. The effectiveness of the statute remains to be seen. ■

Honduran migrants travel north on a freight train in Mexico, between the towns of Tenosique and Palenque, in 2007. (ALEX WEBB/MAGNUM PHOTOS)

The presidential campaign

MEXICO HAS MADE remarkable strides in the last 20 years, and federal elections are as transparent, if not more so, than those in the U.S. There exists a single national voter registry, difficult-to-forge identification credentials, and party and citizen observers at polling places. Still, fair elections by themselves do not signify democracy unless office-holders exhibit the tolerance to collaborate to address the people's basic needs.

Incumbents in Mexico act with impunity thanks to prohibitions on (1) independent candidacies, (2) advertising by NGOs during campaigns, (3) reelection of presidents and (4) the immediate re-election of deputies and senators. Additionally, governors run their states like fiefdoms, party bigwigs select nominees for office, and the Federal Electoral Institute (IFE) lavishes money on political parties, to the tune of $3 billion in 2011.

"My question, when watching all the violence in Mexico has been 'Where is the outrage?'" asked Joy Olson, WO-LA's executive director. "We see it here. [Sicilia's] march is channeling the outrage." Public safety now trumps unemployment as the number-one concern of Mexican voters, who will select their next chief executive on July 1, 2012.

In 2011, leading up to the election, the PRI's Enrique Peña Nieto, former governor of Mexico State, boasted a double-digit lead over likely candidates of the PAN (former Federal Deputy Josefina Vázquez Mota or ex-Finance Secretary Ernesto Cordero) and the leftist-nationalist Democratic Revolutionary Party and its allies (Mexico City Mayor Marcelo Ebrard or his predecessor, Andrés Manuel López Obrador).

In light of protracted warfare and high unemployment, the public thirsts for change. In the latest Latinobarómetro study, which surveys attitudes toward government in 19 Latin American and Caribbean nations, only 23% of Mexicans approved of "the functioning of democracy" in their country, while 73% disapproved—the lowest in the region. The PRI has lambasted Calderón's anti-cartel strategy. They allege over-reliance

Satisfaction with Democracy in Mexico and Selected Countries in the Region

Percent Dissatisfied with Function of Democracy	Country	Percent Satisfied
42%	Panama	54%
51%	Costa Rica	44%
55%	Nicaragua	38%
63%	El Salvador	35%
64%	Dom. Rep.	33%
68%	Honduras	29%
66%	Guatemala	23%
73%	Mexico	23%

Source: "Encuesta/Reprueba México en Democracia," Reforma, October 29, 2011; based on the Latinbarómetro survey of 20,204 respondents in 19 Latin American countries; conducted between July 15 and August 16, 2011; +/- 3% margin of error. www.latinobarometro.org

on the military has driven up the body count. Peña Nieto has confined himself to generalities, affirming that "all of us must fight organized crime with everything at our disposal," insisting on "applying the law [to felons]," earmarking "more resources" for law enforcement, and spurning "accords with organized crime."

Attention to Mexico has overshadowed Guatemalans' selection of a new chief executive. Retired General Otto Pérez Molina, 61, the army's tough-as-nails intelligence director during a 36-year civil war that ended in 1996, captured the presidency on November 6, 2011, the same date that Nicaraguans reelected Sandinista leader President Daniel Ortega. Pérez Molina's vow to wield a "strong hand" against escalating lawlessness resonated with the public.

Impact of the Mérida Initiative

The U.S. Departments of State, Defense and Homeland Security and other agencies have extolled the Mérida Initiative, a $1.6 billion U.S. program conceived

in 2007 to counter drug-fueled mayhem that endangers citizens on both sides of the border. This project emphasized the "Four Pillars": (1) disrupt the capacity of organized crime by furnishing equipment, technology and training—with a view to tracking down DTO chieftains, curbing drug output and impeding money laundering; (2) institutionalize the sustained rule of law by professionalizing the military and police, while improving the judicial and penal systems; (3) create a 21st century border by curtailing the illicit flow of drugs, people, arms and cash, even as new technologies enhance security at entry portals; and (4) configure strong and resilient communities by fostering a culture of lawfulness, spurring job creation, engaging youth in sports and other neighborhood activities, expanding social safety nets and instilling confidence in public institutions. The U.S. embassy has pointed out that under the Mérida Initiative, the U.S. has furnished 11 helicopters to Mexico, including three Black Hawks delivered to the navy in mid-September 2011. The plan has also financed $612 million in equipment, instruction, and development programs; and training for 8,500 federal police, 2,600 prosecutors and judicial personnel, and 1,800 prison officials.

The venture exemplifies an exceedingly optimistic worldview, consistent with President Woodrow Wilson's quest after World War I to create the League of Nations and actuate democracy throughout the world.

Expanded U.S. efforts

Even as President Barack Obama and members of his Cabinet lauded Calderón's anticrime initiatives, there were rumblings behind the scene. In cables to Washington, U.S. Ambassador Carlos Pascual called the Mexican Army "risk averse" and indicated efforts to play Mexican agencies off against each other.

Calderón was livid at such statements, publicized by WikiLeaks, the disseminator of classified documents. As a result, the 23-year veteran diplomat was replaced by E. Antony Wayne, a State Department luminary who, among other posts, had served as envoy to Argentina and the No. 2 man in the Kabul, Afghanistan, embassy, where he oversaw security and antidrug efforts.

One of Wayne's early tasks was to smooth over the controversy whirling around the "Fast and Furious" project, conceived by the U.S. Bureau of Alcohol, Tobacco, Firearms and Explosives (ATF). This early 2010 mission involved "walking" 2,000 or more weapons from Phoenix to Mexico in hopes of tracing and arresting their purchasers. Much to the ATF's chagrin, they lost track of the firearms, at least one of which was used to kill a U.S. Border Patrol agent. Mexico's Foreign Minister Patricia Espinosa called the ATF's anti-gun trafficking gambit "unacceptable" and demanded that the U.S. punish to the fullest extent of the law the perpetrators of the failed operation. Attorney General Eric Holder demoted the bureau's acting director, and the U.S. attorney in Phoenix, who was immersed in the scheme, resigned. A congressional investigation may lead to other sanctions.

In addition to the Mérida Initiative, the Pentagon is flying unarmed drones through Mexican skies to help locate DTOs. Beside these surveillance flights, Presidents Obama and Calderón agreed to open a second "fusion" center to enhance information sharing between U.S. and Mexican counternarcotics specialists. Moreover, the DEA has a growing, low-key presence.

"It wasn't that long ago when there was no way the DEA could conduct the kinds of activities they are doing now," said a retired chief of the agency's international operations. "And the only way they're going to be able to keep doing them is by allowing Mexico to have plausible deniability." ∎

Policy options

MUTUAL INTERESTS dictate U.S. cooperation with Mexico and Central America against the merchants of death. Criminality has already affected the U.S.; the National Drug Intelligence Center reported that Mexican cartels operate in 48 U.S. states and 195 cities. The Mara Salvatruchas (MS or MS-13), a Salvadoran criminal band that originated in Los Angeles in the 1980s, has evolved from an effective street gang to ultra violent, well-equipped paramilitaries. The thugs pose a menace in the Washington, D.C., area, as well as in other metropolitan and rural areas where violence and organized crime might take root. Los Zetas have provided instruction to 40 MS-13 stalwarts from El Salvador, Honduras and Guatemala.

Trade agreements

As a member of the North American Free Trade Agreement (NAFTA), Mexico is America's third-largest trading partner, a major target for U.S. capital and the second-largest supplier of crude oil to the U.S.'s refineries. The Obama Administration will continue to promote the bilateral flow of goods and services to Mexico. Even though NAFTA provided for unhindered movement of commercial vehicles across North America, the Teamsters Union and environmental groups blocked implementation of the provision. Only on October 21, 2011— almost 18 years after the tripartite accord took effect—did a tractor trailer hauling a large steel drilling structure make an unfettered crossing from Nuevo Laredo, Mexico, to Garland, Texas, without changing cabs and drivers at the border. In return, the Mexican government removed $2 billion in retaliatory tariffs on Christmas trees, onions, toothpaste, sunglasses and other U.S. imports.

Washington is also attentive to broadening the free-trade accord that it signed with five Central American nations (Costa Rica, El Salvador, Guatemala, Honduras and Nicaragua) and the Dominican Republic on August 5, 2004. If grouped together, the CAFTA-DR countries constitute the U.S.'s 12th-largest trading partner, with $38.8 billion in two-way commerce in 2009.

Weapons control

Some critics believe that U.S. officials should stop patronizing Mexico and speak frankly to its representatives. Calderón and his cabinet continually demand "mutual respect" and bemoan any "outside interference" in their nation's affairs. Such shibboleths do not prevent Mexico's leader from coming to the U.S. and blasting the expansive interpretation by some of the Second Amendment that facilitates the flow of weapons into Mexico. He called for restoring the ban on 19 types of military-style, semiautomatic rifles, which George W. Bush's Administration allowed to lapse in 2004.

For his part, Obama avers that he has "not backed off at all" on reinstating this prohibition, and a plurality of Americans agree. In reality, though, neither federal nor state legislators will deep-six the restriction because of the enormous power of the National Rifle

Association of America and its satellites. Even if the bar were reinstated, however, Mexico's cartels could purchase fire-power on the international arms market.

'Eligible entrepreneurs'

U.S. policies also siphon investment from Mexico and Central America. The U.S. Citizenship and Immigration Services will grant "conditional permanent residence," better known as a Green Card, to "eligible entrepreneurs" from Mexico, Central America and other lands. To qualify, a foreigner must create or preserve 10 "permanent jobs" by either investing $500,000 in rural (or high unemployment zones) or $1 million elsewhere. While the program is marginally beneficial to Texas and other states, policymakers should consider whether this policy is beneficial to capital formation in a country where poverty and unemployment pervade.

Economic challenges

Several of the Mérida Initiative "pillars" will remain will-o'-the-wisps unless privileged segments of the population give them real support as opposed to lip service. Colombia is quite different from Mexico and Central America; yet protecting the populations of Bogotá, Medellín and other cities became possible only when the establishment committed itself to fighting organized crime. Elites in Monterrey and other northern cities have awakened to their stake in combating cartels and gangs. The same cannot be said for many of their confreres in the DF, Guadalajara, Cuernavaca and other centrally located population centers. The same applies to the well-to-do in Central America.

Even more than Americans, Mexicans indulge in the illusion that if a statute is enacted, a pact signed or a program announced, the problem at hand will be resolved. For instance, Calderón promised an honest, effective police force by the time he left office in late 2012. The sad truth is that even if commanders vetted cadets, trained them in modern crime-fighting techniques, clothed them in attractive uniforms,

U.S. Customs and Border Protection officers watch cargo trucks enter the U.S from Mexico through the Otay Mesa Port of Entry in San Diego, California. (DAVID MAUNG/BLOOMBERG/ GETTY IMAGES)

provided them a decent salary, and offered low-interest mortgages and other fringe benefits, these men and women would become part of law-enforcement agencies bathed in corruption. If the newcomers refused to accept bribes or resisted intimidation from colleagues and hitmen, they would risk their lives and the well-being of their loved ones: an ultimatum known as "*plata o plomo*"—silver or lead.

Thus, to ensure legitimacy amid widespread criminality, Mexico's establishment might shore up its social programs: for instance, improving educational, health-care and employment opportunities for the third of its 114 million people who live as rag pickers in fetid slums or on unproductive, sunbaked communal farms.

Reformers might also consider breaking the back of the extremely corrupt Mexican National Educational Workers Union (SNTE). Petróleos Mexicanos (Pemex) presents another barrier to the nation's economic advancement. The state oil monopoly, which an enormously powerful union has colonized, is a poster child for corruption, inefficiency, featherbedding and resistance to change. As a result, Mexican reserves of crude oil and natural gas have fallen from 4.43 billion barrels to 3.79 billion barrels in recent years, giving rise to a doubling of gasoline imports from

the U.S. during the first eight months of 2011, boosting tax collections (now only about 17.5% of gross domestic product [GDP], compared with nearly 40% in Brazil), rationalizing the provision of healthcare, now spread among a half dozen or more state agencies, smashing monopolies and bottlenecks in petroleum, electricity, telecommunications and cement.

It is also crucial to launch employment and regional development programs, and, above all, to adopt re-election—at least at the municipal level—and to allow the now powerless citizenry an opportunity to influence public policy, at least at the grass-roots level. The affluent enjoy state-of-the-art security systems, bodyguards, skilled drivers and opportunities for their children to study abroad. In fact, a growing number of Mexicans are either operating their businesses from the U.S. or opening new enterprises in Texas and other states. Rather than expecting deliverance from Washington, however, Mexico's leaders must recognize that the future of their resource-rich country lies in their hands. The powerful in Central America must also spearhead a better life for their citizens. ∎

Opinion Ballots after page 32

discussion questions

1. Mexico faces a choice in its upcoming election: continue the direct military confrontation of the drug cartels, or return to the pre-Calderón practice of tacit agreements in exchange for a reduction of violence. Which is more important, security or sovereignty? What are the potential benefits to reducing military confrontation in the "drug war"? Could there be a return to normalcy after six years of conflict?

2. What social, economic and political factors have contributed to the rise of the drug cartels and the development of international drug routes? How should U.S. policymakers respond to these concerns? Are existing U.S. initiatives, such as the use of drones, the Mérida Initiative or the "Fast and Furious" weapons project, appropriate? Is development aid an effective response?

3. Do you agree with the author's assessment that the U.S. has limited capacity to effect political change in Mexican or Central American domestic politics? If the author is correct that the labeling of Mexico as a democracy is flawed, how should U.S. foreign policy toward the region be calibrated?

4. Mexican domestic pressure on cartels has, in some cases, pushed them south into Central America. What are the obligations of countries to ensure that security problems are not exported to neighboring states? To what extent does the U.S. bear a responsibility for violence within Mexico's borders, or Mexico for increased insecurity in the Central American isthmus?

5. Is there a point at which other countries should intervene, in the interest of regional security and stability, in areas that are otherwise domestic responsibilities? What means, if any, should be used? Through what institutions and policies can these responsibilities be upheld?

6. Is the widespread mistreatment of Central American migrants in Mexico a result of political policy, a problem of social ideas, or both? In what ways are social norms and political actions connected? Do social ideas dictate policy? Can policy alter social realities?

suggested readings

Astorga, Luis, and Shirk, David H., **Drug Trafficking Organizations and Counter-Drug Strategies in the U.S.-Mexican Context**. Center for U.S.-Mexican Studies, University of California at San Diego. Available free online at: <http://www.escholarship.org/uc/item/8j647429.pdf;origin=repeccitec>. Explores the continuing public security crisis, examines the surge in violence among drug trafficking organizations, evaluates strategies available to counternarco-networks; evaluates three approaches: complicity with capos, confronting them, or moving toward decriminalization of drugs.

Booth, John A., Walker, Thomas W., and Wade, Christine J., **Understanding Central America: Global Forces, Rebellion, and Change**. 5th ed. Boulder, CO, Westview Press, 2010. 360 pp. $35 (paper). Experts stress the impact of globalization on the region, progress toward democratic consolidation, and the relationship between Central America and the Obama Administration.

Grayson, George W., **Mexico: Narco Violence and a Failed State?** New Brunswick, NJ, Transaction Publishers, 2010. 339 pp. $35 (hardcover). An overview of Mexico's major drug cartels and of President Calderón's strategy to combat them. Includes policy recommendations for managing these DTOs.

Rubio, Luis, "Decentralization and its Consequences." **Center for Hemispheric Studies,** University of Miami, Coral Gables, FL, August 4, 2011. 8 pp. Available free online at: <https://www6.miami.edu/hemispheric-policy/Perspectives_on_the_Americas/Rubio-Decentralization_and_its_Consequences-FINAL.pdf>. A gem of a paper by Mexico's foremost political/economic scholar, who examines the impact of power migrating from his central government to the states whose governors have become the nation's new viceroys.

Seelke, Clare Ribando, and Beittel, June S., "Mérida Initative for Mexico and Central America: Funding and Policy Initiatives." **Congressional Research Service**, June 1, 2009. 29 pp. Available free online at: <http://fpc.state.gov/documents/organization/127288.pdf>. A comprehensive report prepared by careful analysts of the background, objectives, and funding of the major U.S. initiative to combat narco-trafficking in Mexico and Central America; contains excellent material on individual elements of the initiative and specifics about funding.

Wilson Center on Demand. Available free online at: <http://legacy.wilsoncenter.org/ondemand/index.cfm?fuseaction=home.play&mediaid=1BB9831E-0EDB-7842-1B734DC23488D6FA>. A Web site devoted to videos of speakers and panels on Mexican affairs sponsored by the Mexico Institute, Woodrow Wilson Center for International Scholars.

Visit **WWW.GREATDECISIONS.ORG** *for quizzes, seasonal topic updates and other resources to further your understanding*

Cybersecurity: the new frontier
by Ronald Deibert

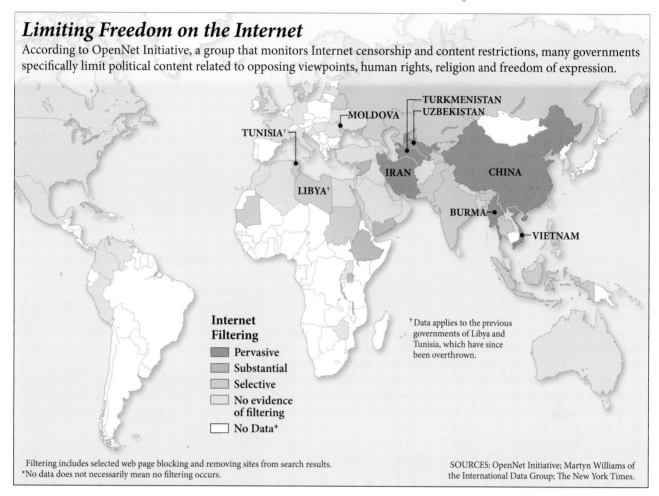

Limiting Freedom on the Internet

According to OpenNet Initiative, a group that monitors Internet censorship and content restrictions, many governments specifically limit political content related to opposing viewpoints, human rights, religion and freedom of expression.

Internet Filtering

- Pervasive
- Substantial
- Selective
- No evidence of filtering
- No Data*

† Data applies to the previous governments of Libya and Tunisia, which have since been overthrown.

Filtering includes selected web page blocking and removing sites from search results.
*No data does not necessarily mean no filtering occurs.

SOURCES: OpenNet Initiative; Martyn Williams of the International Data Group; The New York Times.

CYBERSPACE is the domain of global digital electronic telecommunications. Broader than the "Internet," it includes the entire spectrum of networked information and communication systems worldwide. As cyberspace permeates all aspects of society, economics and politics, it is now widely recognized as "critical infrastructure" by governments and the private sector. Downtime of a telecommunications network, even for a few minutes, can trigger huge financial losses for customers and clients.

At the same time, cyberspace is entering into a period of intense contestation and potential chaos, as a multitude of different actors (states, civil society, businesses, militants and organized criminal groups) struggle to shape the domain in their strategic interests. Many governments are now grappling with a wide range of new threats that have emerged, including cybercrime, espionage and warfare. Major U.S. and European corporations have experienced data breaches, some of which trace back to the network spaces of adversaries like China. For its part, China has faced challenges from technology-enhanced dissidents and ethnic-nationalist movements seeking greater autonomy.

The securitization of cyberspace—a transformation of the domain into a matter of national security—is perhaps the most important force shaping global communications today. Cybersecurity is the field of practice that covers both threats *to* and *through* cyberspace, around which there is significant political tension and national variation. Policymakers around the world are rushing to develop strategies to deal with what they perceive as a growing range of cyber-related threats. Some are following the lead of the U.S., setting up dedicated cyber commands within their armed forces and laying out formal doctrines for cyberspace foreign policy

RONALD DEIBERT *is Professor of Political Science and Director of the Canada Centre for Global Security Studies and the Citizen Lab at the University of Toronto. He is a cofounder and a principal investigator of the OpenNet Initiative and Information Warfare Monitor. He has published extensively on the geopolitics of cyberspace, was an author of the* Tracking Ghostnet *report, and edited* Access Contested: Security, Identity, and Resistance in Asian Cyberspace *(MIT Press, 2011).*

and security. Others appear to be adopting unconventional security strategies in cyberspace, including providing tacit support for nationalist groups to engage in offensive cyber attacks, as has been documented in Iran, Syria and Burma. Generally speaking, states are asserting power in and through cyberspace. Growing cybersecurity concerns reflect a sea change the world over in the way governments approach cyberspace. Whereas 10 years ago, states were either oblivious to the Internet or took a laissez-faire approach, today they are moving swiftly to assert their power and shape the domain in ways that suit their strategic domestic and foreign policy interests. Whether the intent is copyright control or antiterrorism, or to shore up regimes against meddlesome human rights and opposition networks, governments are developing more refined cyberspace controls, ranging from filtering and surveillance to computer network exploitation.

The growing assertion of state power into cyberspace is happening at the same time as information and communication technologies are continuing to deeply permeate social, political and economic life, and merge together into a single ecosystem of communications. A recent International Telecommunication Union (ITU) report noted that Information and Communication Technologies (ICTs) are continuing to expand at an astonishing rate as the costs associated with access to bandwidth decrease. The way in which societies use information and communicate, with the rise of social networking, cloud computing and mobile connectivity, has also undergone a radical shift in recent years. This shift toward social, mobile and cloud-based forms of communicating has amplified the importance of the private sector that owns and operates the vast majority of cyberspace. Many states looking to control cyberspace are now downloading the policing of the domain to these private sector "intermediaries" of communications.

The next decade will be critical for the future of cyberspace. There are several trajectories of possible development, depending on how

the domain is secured and in whose interests. Cyberspace is entering into a period of potential chaos and instability, as cybercrime grows, an arms race in cyberspace escalates and new, potentially lethal weapons are developed to target critical infrastructures. There are countervailing forces, however, that may mitigate some dangerous outcomes: Major stakeholders across governments, the private sector, and civil society recognize the value of developing norms of mutual restraint that protect and preserve cyberspace as a "global commons." Many are actively working on norms, rules, principles and technological infrastructure to support

open networking from the local to the global levels. At the same time, the trends toward a greater degree of nationalized controls are deep and powerful and will be difficult to reverse.

There is no consensus as to whether cyberspace governance should be primarily driven by governments, led by the private sector that owns, operates and leads the development of the technology, or controlled by some combination of governments and private actors that also includes the vast multitude of users. How the norms, rules and principles of cyberspace are developed and made applicable across borders is presently an open question. ∎

Cyberspace and the state

Government perceptions vary widely in terms of what they consider to be the "objects" of cybersecurity (that which is to be protected) and the scope and nature of the threats. These variations in perceptions and policies on cybersecurity have generated significant global tensions. The U.S. and other liberal democracies tend to favor open communication networks, favor the projection of ideas, and see cyberspace (with some exceptions) primarily as a global common pool resource; China, Russia and other authoritarian or democratically challenged countries, on the other hand, speak more often about "information security," which is largely equated with regime and cultural security, and are more comfortable asserting territorialized controls. Their concerns about the control of information extend to the communications of antiregime and even some prodemocracy social move-

ments, especially in the wake of the "Arab Spring," which demonstrated the

A protester in Tahrir Square, Cairo, holds a sign invoking Facebook and Twitter, two tools of the revolution that toppled Egyptian President Hosni Mubarak's government in February 2011. (JESS HURT/REPORT DIGITAL/REA/REDUX)

revolutionary potential of new technologies like Facebook and Twitter. These countries also tend to see an imbalance biased toward the U.S. and its allies' interests in existing cyberspace governance and ownership arrangements and hope to have the United Nations take a more prominent role in cyberspace governance.

Perceptions of threats that are enabled *through* cyberspace also vary widely depending on the country concerned, and include everything from anonymous hacktivists, content deemed offensive (like pornography) or illegal (such as that which violates copyright), the virtual activities of organized militant groups and anti-regime popular mobilization. Governments also vary in terms of how they propose to deal with perceived threats through cyberspace, with less open and authoritarian regimes taking increasingly strong measures to control the services, tools and platforms used by adversaries. In addition to new laws and regulations, filtering, surveillance, disruption and disabling of infrastructure and services have become more common. For their part, democratic countries have mostly avoided overt content filtering, with the exception of pornography and copyright violations,

INTO THE CLOUD

STRICTLY speaking, cloud computing refers to the delivery of software and other services as a utility over computer networks. But the cloud has become a metaphor for the way digital lives have been turned inside out and dispersed into a global web.

Whereas the Internet used to be largely a self-segmented network distinct from other means of communication, such as television, telephone and radio, now all of these media have been integrated into a single system of planetary communications called cyberspace. The integration of these media into a common space has happened at the same time that business models and service delivery mechanisms for information and communications have changed fundamentally, with the rise of social networking, mobile connectivity and cloud computing (referred to together here as "the cloud").

The logic and attraction of the cloud is obvious and pervasive. For large organizations, like businesses and governments, the cloud provides a major cost-cutting solution. For individuals, it is convenient, reliable and fun. For the companies that support the cloud and the various products, services and devices that connect to it, it is an attractive source of growing revenue and innovation.

But there are dark sides to the cloud. The shift to the cloud represents a major paradigm shift in communications, which has upset the principles, norms and rules of what used to be just the "Internet." Under the Internet's operating paradigm, the companies that ran the infrastructure took a "hands-off" approach to the content that flowed through their networks, a principle known as "network neutrality." Today, data is entrusted to vast transnational information empires, like Google and Facebook and Amazon, that act as gatekeepers of what gets communicated and what information is accessible or not. In such circumstances, market considerations can easily outweigh privacy and other rights concerns.

The rapid shift to an entirely new ecosystem has also opened up unforeseen insecurities that are being systematically harvested by a wide range of opportunistic actors, including criminals, unethical businesses, and military and intelligence agencies. Whereas data once was only as secure as the place where it was stored—offices and filing cabinets—today it is only as secure as the companies that host it. In principle, entrusting data to third parties should actually enhance security because security is being delegated to professionals who have the time and knowledge to keep up with the latest threats. But studies have shown that cloud computing companies themselves are far less concerned with security than the bottom line. Not surprisingly, there has been a rash of major security breaches across governments and the private sector.

The shift to the cloud has also created an entirely new set of governance issues. It is important to understand that while the notion of the cloud may seem ephemeral and be experienced by users as some kind of virtual mirage, the infrastructure in which it is embedded involves a complex material, logistical and regulatory infrastructure that can span multiple political jurisdictions, from the local to the national to the international. While the text, the image and the video all may still seem within reach, on desktops and handheld devices, they are not. Data that is assumed to be in one's possession is in fact transmitted in an instant over cables and through radio waves from arrays of servers, many of which are far away in other political jurisdictions. Most importantly, almost all of it is owned and operated by the private sector. Governments looking to control cyberspace must, therefore, enlist the private sector that owns and operates the cloud to "police the Internet," through laws, regulations, incentives or other types of pressures. Of course, opinion on what is considered "intermediary liability" or a market imperative in Canada and the U.S. differs quite fundamentally from that in Belarus, Iran, Vietnam or China. In nondemocratic countries, Internet Service Providers (ISPs), telecom carriers and mobile operators are being asked to police political content, track dissidents, identify protesters, send threatening messages over their networks and disable certain protocols used by adversaries. ■

May 5, 2010: An Egyptian reporter for Islam Online, *a Qatari-based Web site with offices in Egypt, holds a keyboard outside the Qatari embassy in Cairo during a protest against alleged efforts by the Web site's management in Qatar to assume editorial control.* (KHALED DESOUKI/AFP/GETTY IMAGES)

and have focused instead on implementing regulations around "lawful access" to communications networks that introduce greater forms of "intermediary liability" and mechanisms for close cooperation with state law enforcement and intelligence agencies. In spite of their different aims and methods, in other words, most countries are moving in the same direction toward downloading controls to the private sector, raising questions about

the conditions under which the operators and owners of ICT products and services are empowered or otherwise made responsible to control that which is communicated over their networks.

Filtering and beyond

The worldwide growth of Internet filtering is one of the main characteristics of cyberspace securitization. Early in the Internet's history, it was widely assumed that the Internet was difficult

for governments to manage and would bring about major changes in authoritarian forms of rule. Over time, however, these assumptions have been called into question as governments, often operating in coordination with the private sector, have erected a variety of information controls not only on the Internet, but on other platforms as well. It is now fair to say that there is a growing norm worldwide for national Internet filtering, although the rationale for implementing filtering varies widely from country to country. For example, since 2003 the OpenNet Initiative (ONI) project (a collaboration among the Citizen Lab at the University of Toronto, Harvard University's Berkman Center, and the SecDev Group) has documented the growth of cyberspace controls through testing and research conducted in more than 70 countries worldwide (http://opennet.net/). Its research shows that more than 40 countries engage in Internet content filtering in some manner.

Western democracies justify their Internet filtering to control access to content that violates copyright, concerns the sexual exploitation of children or promotes hatred. In many liberal democratic countries, such as the U.S., Canada and the member states of the European Union (EU), policymakers have argued that such filtering should be extended to cover content that promotes radical militancy, Islamic fundamentalism and terrorism.

Other countries filter access to content related to minority rights, religious movements, political opposition and human rights groups. For example, Pakistan recently required 13 ISPs in the country to block access to the Web site of *Rolling Stone* magazine because of an article that referenced Pakistan's military spending. Countries vary widely in terms of their transparency and accountability around such processes and in terms of the methods by which they carry out filtering. Invari-

The Chinese flag flies outside the Google Inc. office in January 2010. Google withdrew from China shortly thereafter, amid concerns about cyber attacks and China's censorship policy. (NELSON CHING/BLOOMBERG/GETTY IMAGES)

ably, the private sector actors who own and operate the vast majority of cyberspace infrastructure, including Internet search engines, are being compelled or coerced to implement controls on behalf of states. Companies like Google, Microsoft, Yahoo!, Twitter, Facebook and others have all faced these growing pressures as their operations expand worldwide, struggling to balance the desire to penetrate growing and potentially lucrative markets, the need to comply with local law in order to do so, and respect for freedom of speech and access to information.

The Internet and opposition movements

The trajectory of greater government intervention into cyberspace has developed beyond Internet filtering. Governments have shown a greater willingness to employ a broader range of means, including covert and offensive-minded tactics, to shape cyberspace in their strategic interests. These tactics have developed largely as a consequence of the way cyberspace has grown in significance as an organizing and communicating platform for dissidents and activists. The tug-of-war between autocratic states seeking to limit communications and dissidents and activists armed with new technology has led to often dramatic episodes of disruption and counterdisruptions. For example, there has been a growing number of incidents where states have disrupted or tampered with communication networks for political purposes, including around elections and public demonstrations.

Both Egypt and Libya severed all Internet access for brief periods of time during the so-called Arab Spring, a tactic that was also employed in Nepal, China and Myanmar (Burma) at various times. Such a drastic move shows that some governments may be willing to sacrifice a lot to prevent the Internet from being used as a tool for mobilization.

Even though Egypt has a relatively low Internet penetration rate of around 27%, the 34-member Organization for Economic Cooperation and Development (OECD) estimated that the five-day shuttering of the Internet in early 2011 contributed to a loss of $90 million

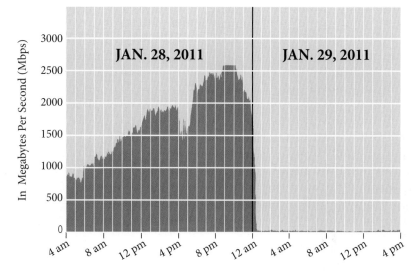

Internet Traffic in Cairo Drops Suddenly

At 12:20 AM on Jan. 28, 2011 (local time), internet traffic to and from Cairo slowed to a crawl as measured by 80 world-wide providers.

SOURCE: Arbor Networks

in direct revenues and a substantially higher amount in secondary economic impacts for which it did not account. It is noteworthy in this respect that the shuttering of the Internet did not initially include the ISP Noor, whose clients include the Egyptian stock exchange, five-star hotels and corporate clients ranging from Coca-Cola to Pfizer.

During the Green Movement, which began in Iran in 2009, the government was suspected of ordering ISPs to tamper or "throttle" bandwidth and using

certain protocols associated with censorship circumvention and anonymity tools as a means to control opposition activities. As an illustration of the cat-and-mouse game that can go on between governments in cyberspace, it is noteworthy that the U.S. government lobbied the microblogging platform Twitter to postpone scheduled maintenance of its servers in order to avoid disruptions for Iranian activists who were using the service during the Green Movement. Cambodia banned

Jan. 31, 2011: People sit outside a building in Cairo with a sign that reads, "We Want Internet," days after the Egyptian authorities effectively shut down the Internet. (DANA SMILLIE/POLARIS)

Aug. 15, 2011: BART police officers stand guard on a train platform during a demonstration by members of the Internet group known as Anonymous in San Francisco. (DAVID PAUL MORRIS/BLOOMBERG/GETTY IMAGES)

all short message service (SMS) operations two days prior to national elections.

These "just-in-time" methods of blocking access to services or Web sites are not exclusive to nondemocratic regimes. During riots in England in 2011, some parliamentarians discussed implementing similar controls on mobile devices and social networking platforms—though these ideas were not implemented. The Bay Area Rapid Transit (BART) authority in San Francisco, CA also disabled cellular networks on its transit system in 2011 to prevent its use by protesters demonstrating against the BART police force.

Role of the private sector

Regimes aiming to control popular uprisings fueled by cyberspace technologies are turning to the private sector to identify, isolate and contain organizers and participants. These actions, in turn, have generated fear, intense scrutiny, widespread condemnation and often very vocal criticism of the companies compelled or encouraged in some manner to collude with the regimes. For example, in 2008, one of Egypt's largest cell phone carriers, Vodafone, turned over information on users who employed the service to organize food protests. Later, in 2011, the company

admitted that it had sent messages on behalf of state security services, encouraging Egyptians to take to the streets to counter the mass uprising in that country. Both cases caused public outrage and calls for boycotts against the company from human rights and privacy advocates. Similarly, in a much-publicized set of squabbles, Research in Motion (RIM), the maker of the popular Blackberry device, has found itself facing demands from governments ranging from the United Arab Emirates (UAE) to India and Indonesia for access to its encrypted data streams. In 2011, RIM agreed to implement content filtering on its Web browser in response to requests made by the Indonesian government to block pornography. The controversy has brought about scrutiny into RIM's mobile architecture that otherwise would have likely never existed, pitted governments against each other and generated criticism of RIM itself by human rights advocates suspicious that the company has made secret deals that violate due process and public accountability. Should RIM comply with such requests for user data, its security would be called into question and users (including large businesses) may lose confidence in the integrity of RIM's service offerings. Not complying, on the other hand, could force RIM out of potentially lucrative markets.

As cyberspace grows exponentially, embedding itself deeper into everyday life through a greater range of connected devices and services, the contests

THE POLITICS OF CIRCUMVENTION TECHNOLOGY

WHILE THE SCOPE and depth of Internet censorship has grown, so too have the means by which citizens attempt to circumvent these controls. "Circumvention technologies" refers to the tools and methods used to bypass Internet filtering and surveillance. These efforts range in sophistication, from avoiding content filtering at a school or library to bypassing national-level Internet backbone filtering in countries like China or Iran.

The technical methods for bypassing censorship can include Web-based proxies, like Psiphon or Ultrasurf, that allow users to access pages in a Web browser as if they were in an uncensored location, to fee-based virtual private network services that let users tunnel all Internet traffic through a proxy machine, such as the popular Hotspot Shield. Other methods include "onion routing," as seen in the Tor project, which attempts to provide anonymity as well as circumvention by passing encrypted traffic through a network of nodes. Users may also rely on less sophisticated means of accessing banned material, such as using cached search engine content or translation services that display and translate blocked text. All of these tools and methods range in effectiveness, ease of use, cost, degree of anonymity offered and resilience against blocking.

Circumvention technologies are highly politicized. The U.S. State Department has developed an "Internet Freedom" agenda that includes funding for circumvention

over the rules and protocols by which such a complex domain is organized naturally intensify as well. Issues such as these bring to the forefront questions concerning the challenges private sector actors have in providing public communications services. How should companies whose operations may span multiple jurisdictions balance public rights with obligations to follow local laws in jurisdictions that may have widely differing due process standards and protections for civil liberties? How should they reconcile the imperatives of profit seeking, national security and human rights when they conflict?

The new generation of cyberspace control techniques appears to include targeted computer network exploitation and other, highly sophisticated attacks on human rights and political opposition groups. The InfoWar Monitor (http://www.infowar-monitor.net) discovered major cyber espionage networks in 2009 and 2010 that were traced back to mainland China, both of which emerged from their investigations of the security of Tibetan-related organizations, including the Office of the Dalai Lama, whose systems were thoroughly infiltrated along with other victims of the espionage network.

These cases show that governments lacking resources or advanced capabilities of their own may instead be turning to the underworld of cybercrime for asymmetrical strategic advantage. The latter offers the benefits of accruing intelligence and achieving other ends

Aug. 17, 2007: (From left) Chinese President Hu Jintao, Russian President Vladimir Putin, Kazakh President Nursultan Nazarbayev and Uzbek President Islam Karimov attend a counterterrorism exercise of the Shanghai Cooperation Organization. (DMITRY ASTAKHOV/ AFP/GETTY IMAGES)

while allowing for plausible deniability.

More recently, the InfoWar Monitor project documented computer network exploitation and Web site defacements conducted by what appear to be pro-patriotic hacker groups based in Iran, Syria and Burma. In these cases, governments appear to be offering tacit support and sometimes vocal encouragement of these attacks while keeping the perpetrators at arm's length. The tolerance of these computer network operations by autocratic regimes that are traditionally averse to new technologies demonstrates an evolution of cyberspace control strategies and a willingness to turn a blind eye to illegal activities when it suits national interests.

Internationalized strategies

Governments with more "territorialized" visions of cyberspace controls are not just exercising their muscles in domestic contexts or through covert means; they are developing ambitious and increasingly internationalized strategies, coordinated through regional venues and standard-setting bodies that were once largely restricted to technical discussions. One example is the Shanghai Cooperation Organization (SCO),

tools. In two well-publicized speeches in 2010 and 2011, Secretary of State Hillary Clinton announced financial support totaling $45 million for the development and distribution of circumvention tools, as well as the provision of training and local language support. This promotion of circumvention tools by the U.S. government has not gone without criticism, both at home and abroad. Critics have portrayed these efforts as a vaguely masked projection of U.S. foreign policy interests. Others suggest that the State Department needs to broaden its efforts beyond circumvention tools because the far-reaching impact of targeted attacks and the chilling effects of restrictive domestic censorship policies present great challenges to users.

Some within the U.S. government have criticized the slow distribution of funds and the initial reluctance of the State Department to fund existing circumvention efforts supported by the Broadcasting Board of Governors (BBG). (The Obama Administration has since redirected $10 million in State Department funding to BBG efforts at circumventing censorship in China to provide access to the Voice of America service.) Political leaders in Iran have also pushed back against these efforts to promote circumvention tools. Iran's Supreme Leader, Ayatollah Khamenei, has portrayed these measures as a plan to impose Western culture and ideas as part of a "soft war" against Iran. As a result, Iran has made it illegal to distribute or use circumvention technologies and has begun development of a "national Internet," promoted as more consistent with Islamic religious practices and free from the influence of Western content and tools. ■

which is a regional organization made up of China, Kyrgyzstan, Kazakhstan, Russia, Tajikistan and Uzbekistan. India, Iran, Mongolia and Pakistan have observer status, and Belarus and Sri Lanka are considered dialogue partners. Iran is engaged in the SCO but prevented from formally joining because of UN sanctions. However, it is considered an active participant in the SCO summits, which have been held regularly throughout the region since the early 2000s.

The SCO aims to share information and coordinate policies around a broad spectrum of cultural, economic and security concerns, among them cyberspace policies. Generally speaking, experts see the SCO as a regional vehicle of "protective integration" against international norms of democracy and regime change, with shared informa-

tion policies being seen as critical to that end. Recently, the SCO issued a statement on "information terrorism," which drew attention to the way in which these countries have a shared and distinct perspective on Internet security policy.

The SCO has also engaged in joint military exercises and missions, described by some observers as simulations of how to reverse color-style revolutions and popular uprisings. Unfortunately, the SCO's meetings tend to be highly secretive affairs and not easily subject to outside scrutiny. But they are likely to become important vehicles of policy coordination, giving unity, normative coherence and strength to the members beyond the sum of their individual parts.

This greater assertion of state power is not going unchallenged. In fact, these growing controls are largely in direct

response to the ways in which new information and technologies have enabled new forms of social mobilization and even regime change, as witnessed in the color revolutions of the countries of the former U.S.S.R. and more recently in the Arab Spring.

Networks of civil society actors, in some cases openly supported by the EU and countries like the U.S., and even by some private sector actors like Google, are developing a vast array of techniques and software tools to circumvent state controls.

The stakes are becoming increasingly acute as governments and civil society struggles in cyberspace spill into physical battles in the streets, as the contests in Tunisia, Egypt, Libya, Yemen and Syria demonstrate (as well as Belarus, Burma, Thailand and Kyrgyzstan before them). ∎

Explosion of cybercrime

RELATED TO THREATS to cyberspace is the growing problem of cybercrime. The underworld of cybercrime has exploded worldwide, with security researchers estimating 80,000 new malicious software samples are being released to the public every day. A recent crime report by Norton, a division of Symantec, suggests that the market for cybercrime is larger than the global black market for marijuana, cocaine and heroin combined ($288 billion) and approaching the value of all global drug trafficking ($411 billion). Norton's report estimates that over 1 million people per day are considered victims of some kind of cybercrime, or approximately 431 million a year. Meanwhile Verizon's 2011 Data Breach Investigations Report noted the growing *industrialization* of cybercrime that includes chains of specialized professionals ranging from coders to attackers to money launderers, all of whom managed themselves as professional businesses or independent contractors in what Verizon describes as a highly competitive arena. Although it is difficult to assess the accuracy of these figures given the

obscure nature of cybercrime and the interests security companies may have in inflating threats, it is clear there is an enormous problem. There have been a series of high-profile data breaches of major businesses, defense contractors and government agencies worldwide in recent years.

Borderless crime, local punishment

Cybercrime is growing at such an accelerated pace for several reasons. First, the number of users coming online—including individuals, businesses, organizations and governments—is growing rapidly, creating an increasing baseline

The Vast Reach of the 'Ghostnet'

Researchers have detected an intelligence operation involving at least 1,295 compromised computers, with the location of 347 of them shown below. Many of the hacked machines were traced to diplomatic and economic government offices of South and Southeast Asian countries.

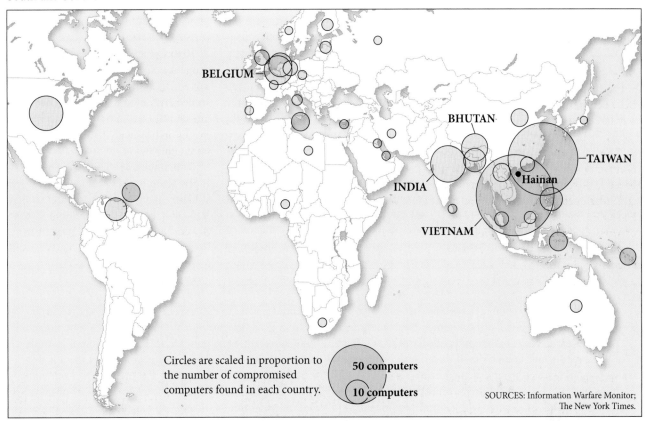

BELGIUM

BHUTAN

TAIWAN

INDIA

Hainan

VIETNAM

Circles are scaled in proportion to the number of compromised computers found in each country.

50 computers

10 computers

SOURCES: Information Warfare Monitor; The New York Times.

of potential targets. Second, the ways of communicating and sharing information online have changed fundamentally over the last several years, with the growth of social networking, cloud computing and mobile forms of connectivity. More data is shared or entrusted to third parties outside of the user's immediate control. An epidemiologist studying this dynamic ecosystem of sharing would not be surprised by the cyber equivalent of disease. But cybercrime also thrives because of the lack of deterrence. Law enforcement agencies tend to operate in national jurisdictions, and numerous constraints exist that prevent coordination across borders. Cybercriminals can act globally, but hide locally in jurisdictions where such activities are tolerated or police lack resources and capabilities.

The worlds of cybercrime are not limited to profit-driven theft; there is an increasing blurring of the techniques of cybercrime, cyber espionage, and cyberwarfare. In 2009, researchers at the InfoWar Monitor discovered a major global cyber espionage network, *Ghostnet*, had infected 1,295 computers in 103 locations, including government agencies, diplomatic missions, embassies and ministries of foreign affairs. Ghostnet and other networks like it are notable for the ways in which the techniques employed by attackers are largely indistinguishable from those of the cybercriminal underworld. In 2010, a German security researcher discovered that a sophisticated computer worm of unknown origin, called Stuxnet, had infiltrated and sabotaged high-security Iranian nuclear enrichment facilities. The code for Stuxnet is now widely available online, and, in spite of its sophistication, it includes several techniques that are known in the cybercriminal underground. Stuxnet-style attacks present a higher-order level of foreign policy and security threat than data breaches or other forms of exploitation

since they target critical infrastructures that could cause significant loss of life. In light of the difficulties with positively identifying the source of these type of attacks, Stuxnet-style acts of sabotage may prove to be tempting for governments and armed militant groups alike.

The combination of enabling conditions, including a lack of law enforcement capabilities and resources, a growing number of victims, more valuable data being placed online and major incentives among state intelligence agencies and illicit actors to expoit the wares of the cybercriminal, means that the underworld of cybercrime can be expected to grow and expand into areas critical to global security worldwide.

The changing face of cyberspace

The values and interests of those who make up cyberspace's user community will affect the security of domain. There is a major demographic shift occurring in cyberspace, as the center of gravity shifts from the North and West of the planet, where it was first developed, to the South and the East. At present, Asia comprises 44% of the world's Internet population (the most by region), but it ranks only sixth with a penetration rate of 23.8%—meaning that there is an enormous population yet to be connected, most of them young. In China, 60% of Internet users are under the age of 30. According to the ITU, among the roughly 5.3 billion mobile subscriptions at the end of 2010, 3.8 billion are in the developing world. Of the top 55 nations with the highest Internet penetration growth rates from 2008 to 2009, 18 are considered by the UN to be the world's least-developed countries, "representing the poorest and weakest segment

of the international community." With these new users will come new ways of using and governing cyberspace, both at home and abroad, which will have far-reaching implications for the world. The demographic shift is bringing the weight of entire national collective identities and state interests hitherto largely absent or irrelevant to cyberspace governance issues. Although English has been the "operating system language" for the Internet since its inception, if present growth rates continue, Chinese will be the dominant language on the Internet in five years. Such a shift alone will have repercussions for how cyberspace is constituted as a global network. But more practically, it has begun to put pressure on the governance of cyberspace routing principles. Already, the desire

to encourage linguistic communities to express themselves online has triggered serious questions about how the systems that support them are managed and resources allocated, particularly around allocation and management of country top-level domains. For example, the 2010 introduction of a Cyrillic top-level domain controlled by Russian authorities and a Chinese language domain controlled by Chinese authorities has been enormously popular in both worlds, but has furthered the division of the Internet along national or linguistic lines. While interoperability is technically unaffected in the short term, the prospects for politically motivated government control is greater since the registration process moves into the hands of government-delegated bodies. ■

CYBERSPACE GOVERNANCE AND SECURITY

CYBERSPACE is a complex domain that encompasses a variety of media (the Internet, telecommunications, cable, satellite and cellular phones). Each of these media has its own site of governance, with overlapping but distinct groups of stakeholders, norms, principles and rules. Cyberspace governance is thus diffuse and heterogeneous. There is no central organization of governance.

The main forum for Internet governance is the Internet Corporation for Assigned Names and Numbers (ICANN) and its subsidiary and related bodies that operate under a renewable contract with the U.S. Department of Commerce. ICANN is under constant scrutiny and pressures from a revolving cast of new interests and authorities. Some governments see this contractual arrangement as a form of U.S. control over the Internet. Some countries are pushing for the UN and the ITU to address governance issues. Russia has urged the ITU to develop a formal delegation of the Government Advisory Committee (GAC) of ICANN that would have veto powers over ICANN decisions, while China has consistently voiced concerns over the need for a more state-based framework that would limit civil society stakeholder participation in, for example, the Internet Governance Forum (IGF).

One area of international governance that may come to have a bearing on cyberspace governance and security issues is international political economy and trade law. For example, the legality of Internet censorship under world trade laws, and in particular China's statutory obligations to the General Agreement on Trade in Services (GATS) agreement of the World Trade Organization (WTO), has become a considerable topic of discussion and an area of

potential impact to cyberspace governance and security.

In at least one prominent white paper, Google argued that China's filtering policies are an infraction of its trade obligations under GATS. Google's main argument is that state-sponsored censorship of the Internet is a relevant trade issue because it denies access to free flow of information which, in the time of an expanding global digital economy, should be treated as a commodity.

Google's case finds support from prominent lawmakers in Congress, the European Commission and several academic think tanks. At the time it was drawn up, GATS's relevancy for cyberspace issues was limited to value-added services around telecommunications (e.g., voice mail). Over time, the GATS has come to be seen as a potential protocol for a broader range of Internet services as well, in the face of radically evolving technology in the telecommunications domain. A decision in the WTO on Internet censorship could have wide-ranging repercussions. One unintended consequence, however, may be to push countries into invoking "national security exceptions" clauses, such as those in GATS Article XIV, which state that "Nothing in this Agreement shall be construed . . . to prevent any Member from taking any action which it considers necessary for the protection of its essential security interests."

China and other countries, if pushed to defend Internet censorship practices in trade-based forums, may use the national security exception to justify their filtering practices. Already many countries—authoritarian and democratic—including China, Iran, Pakistan, India, South Korea, Uzbekistan, Turkmenistan and Belarus, justify Internet censorship policies under the rubric of "national security." ■

The next battleground

CYBERSPACE is emerging as a new domain of waging war. Cyberspace is now explicitly recognized in U.S. strategic doctrine as equal in importance to land, air, sea and space, and a dedicated command has been established. Although estimates vary widely, numerous governments are actively developing military doctrines for cyberspace operations, while others may be employing unconventional cyberspace strategies. There is a looming arms race in cyberspace that suggests a period of intense hostility operating within and through this domain. Questions of whether and how traditional concepts of strategic thought, such as deterrence, apply in the cyber domain are now very much alive in the strategic studies literature.

While the rhetoric of cyberwar is often heated and exaggerated to serve policy ends, there are recent cases of international conflict in which cyberspace has played a prominent role. During the 2006 war in South Lebanon, for example, Hezbollah, the Islamist guerrilla group, was able to dominate the information environment by exploiting the Internet and other technologies as part of its distributed communication infrastructure. Likewise, in 2007, Estonia's banking and public administration systems were brought to a standstill as millions of computers from around the world were hijacked and harnessed together as a botnet to flood the country's servers, crippling the electronic infrastructure of the country. During the Russia-Georgia 2008 war over the disputed territory of South Ossetia, Georgian government ministries came under a massive distributed denial of service (DDoS) attack. These attacks greatly affected the ability of the Georgian government to disseminate information and struck key infrastructure, such as the financial sector. Ironically, the Georgian government's attempts to mitigate these attacks included filtering access to Russian news and information sources. When combined with the DDoS attacks, the filtering had the un-

Employees of the National Security Agency work at the Threat Operations Center. The U.S. Treasury Department and Secret Service are among the agencies whose Web sites have recently been attacked. (EVAN VUCCI/AP)

fortunate consequence of sowing fear and panic in the Georgian capital as citizens were subject to a widespread information blackout of unknown origin. Given the way that information and communication technologies permeate society, economics and politics today, it is impossible to engage in armed conflict separate from cyberspace.

Cyberspace securitization includes a political economy dimension: there is a growing cyber industrial complex around security products and services that both responds to, and also shapes the policy marketplace. Corporate giants of the cold war, like Northrup Grumman, Boeing and General Dynamics, are repositioning themselves for lucrative cybersecurity defense contracts, alongside an array of subterranean niche companies that offer network exploitation products and services. The global cyber arms trade now includes malicious viruses, computer exploits and massive botnets. Many firms that produce these products and services are based in Western countries, but have found a market in authoritarian governments. For example, after the fall of President Hosni Mubarak in February 2011, Egyptian protesters uncov-

ered secret documents of the Egyptian security services among which was a contract for services from a British firm selling offensive computer exploitation capabilities. Likewise, when Libyan rebels permeated Muammar Qadhafi's intelligence facilities, they uncovered contracts between the regime and Narus, a subsidiary of Boeing, providing electronic surveillance equipment. An arms race in cyberspace has been unleashed, with international, ethical and moral implications.

The market for surveillance and offensive computer attack products and services that has emerged in recent years was preceded and is supplemented by a market for Internet filtering technologies. The latter were developed initially to serve business environments but quickly spread to governments looking for solutions for Internet censorship demands. ONI research throughout the 2000s was able to document a growing number of authoritarian countries using U.S.-based commercial filtering products, including Smartfilter in Iran and Tunisia, Websense in Yemen, and Fortinet in Burma. More recent ONI reports document a Canadian company's products being used in Yemen, Qatar and the

SECURING THE CYBER COMMONS?

CYBERSPACE IS OFTEN referred to as a "commons," either as an empirical descriptor, or a desirable organizing principle. However, the concept of the commons is contentious in a number of respects.

The "commons," first articulated in ancient Rome, was meant to distinguish *res publica* (the sphere of the state) and *res privataes* (the private sphere) from the community resources that must be actively protected and managed for the good of all. The commons are inherited or jointly created by the public and are intended to be passed on from one generation to the next. Many see nature, such as air, oceans and wildlife, to be "commons," as well as great public works of invention and sometimes art.

Many hope that cyberspace will come to be seen as such a commons, or is in fact already one in many important ways that need to be preserved and protected. But there are conceptual problems, a lack of shared understanding as to what this would mean in practice, and existing structures and institutions in cyberspace that do not conform to classic definitions of the commons.

It is important to underscore that a commons does not mean the absence of rules; a commons is a social convention or a complex social system that enables us to use common resources in a sustainable and equitable way. It requires a shared understanding of norms, rules, principles and behavior, and the boundaries of what constitutes the commons itself. In some respects, for example with regard to the common routing protocols that provided the original governance of Internet traffic (TCP/IP; end-to-end; network neutrality), the concept seems to provide

UAE. Some of these products appear to have been tailored to meet the unique requirements of authoritarian regimes. A presentation by the company Cisco (the maker of telecommunications routing equipment) surfaced in 2008 in which the argument was made that a market opportunity presented itself for the company working in collusion with China's security services. Commercial solutions such as these can help structure the realm of the possible for governments. Whereas in the past it might have been difficult or even inconceivable to engage in "deep-packet inspection" or keyword-based filtering on a national scale, commercial solutions open up opportunities for policymakers looking to deal with vexing political problems on a fine-grained scale. In doing so, long-standing principles of network governance—such as network neutrality—can be eroded.

Some researchers and policymakers are now debating the merits of "cyber arms control." While it is clear that there is a growing need for mutual restraints on increasing hostilities and threats in cyberspace, not everyone agrees arms control accords apply to the domain. Information—the central ingredient of warfare in cyberspace—is thought to be impossible to control in today's digitally networked and highly distributed environment. Moreover, attackers can hide their tracks and muddy

attribution, making verification of any arms control agreement difficult.

However, lessons can be derived from arms control regimes that do not restrict classes of weapons per se but rather behavior of actors or behavior in entire domains instead (e.g., parts of the Outer Space Treaty of 1967 or the Antarctic Treaty of 1959). Governments may look to some of the principles enshrined in these treaties for to how to conduct themselves in a common resource like cyberspace that benefits all but is owned by no one in particular.

There is also a largely informal and influential cybersecurity "epistemic community" that cuts across public and private sectors. It secures cyberspace in an ad hoc but occasionally very coordinated fashion that could be thought of as a form of cybersecurity "arms control." For example, in April 2011, the Federal Bureau of Investigation (FBI) and Justice Department, working with the nonprofit Internet Systems Consortium, dismantled the Coreflood botnet, a network of compromised computers that had been used to steal user credentials and an estimated $100 million from victims. With a court order permitting them to set up what is known as a "sinkhole," officials replaced the botnet's command and control servers and sent code directly to compromised machines, stopping them from commu-

nicating and effectively disabling the botnet—without the user's permission. Government filings claimed that the commands sent would not cause any damage to compromised machines and would not provide officials with access to any user data.

However, some questioned how certain investigators could be that this approach would not disrupt sensitive equipment, while others questioned whether this would open the floodgates to other requests to disrupt the computers of individuals engaged in questionable activity. The Coreflood takedown, and others like it, may be seen as part of a new form of distributed cybersecurity in which governments, the private sector and civil society work to contain and mitigate unwanted behavior in cyberspace. A critical question will be whether such mitigation is done in a transparent and accountable way or not, and avoids the risk of cyber vigilantism. Already one can discern a growing vigilante atmosphere in cyberspace as represented in the attacks by "Anonymous," and retaliation from their detractors.

Toward "rules of the road" for cyberspace

The next decade will be critical for the future of cyberspace. There are several trajectories of possible development, depending on how the domain

an apt description of the principles and practice. There is also a vibrant community of users across multiple sectors who subscribe to the ideas and principles of the "creative commons" and open source software development models that derive inspiration from the commons.

On many other levels, however, the idea of cyberspace constituting a commons is problematic. For example, how can cyberspace be thought of as a commons when as much as 90% of it is owned and operated by the private sector? The decisions taken by these private actors can have political consequences for cyberspace and its users, though often without public accountability. Private actors build, operate, maintain and own the services through which users communicate and share information online.

Additionally, although the virtual worlds that exist in cyberspace—chats, social networking platforms, games—may seem to be a virtual commons, there is a very real physical infrastructure that supports those virtual spaces and the content that flows through them. How can something be called a commons whose physical infrastructure, from fiber-optic cables to Internet Exchange Points and gateway servers, includes material components located within hundreds of jurisdictions and subject to a huge and growing array of local laws and regulations?

Some believe that the commons continues to hold promise as a normative vision for cyberspace governance as an alternative to pure centralized government or private property ownership regimes. Drawing on the Nobel Prize-winning arguments of the political economist Elinor Ostrom, "adaptive governance systems"—essentially decentralized and distributed pluralist components—can be effective mechanisms of cyberspace governance that would ensure an open and secure system of global communication. ∎

is secured and what contingencies may arise as the future unfolds. Cyberspace is entering a period of potential chaos and instability, as cybercrime continues its growth in an unabated fashion, an arms race in cyberspace escalates—served by a growing cybersecurity industrial complex—and new, potentially lethal weapons are developed to target critical infrastructures. When these factors are considered alongside growing trends of territorialization, the future of cyberspace as an open commons of information may be in peril.

There are countervailing forces, however, that might be marshaled to check and constrain some of the more dangerous possible outcomes while protecting and even furthering the gains in freedom and individual empowerment that have been made over the last decade because of open networks. Major stakeholders across governments, the private sector and civil society recognize the value of constituting cyberspace as a "global commons" and are actively working on norms, rules, principles and technological infrastructure to support it as such. In some respects, a "constitutive" moment for cyberspace is approaching, one that may define the global communications environment for decades to come.

One promising development is that there is now a growing momentum around discussions of "norms of mutual restraint" and "rules of the road" for cyberspace. Several major international conferences and meetings have been held on this topic, attended by Russia, China, the U.S. and Britain, as well as representatives from the private sector and civil society. To be sure, there are significant differences among major stakeholders concerning what should be the substance of those rules of the road, particularly between China, Russia and some other rising powers on the one hand, and the Western democratic countries on the other, led by the U.S. and its allies. Meanwhile, technological change—a constant moving target and central characteristic of cyberspace—presents an unpredictable "wild card" for the future. Just as no one could have predicted the ways platforms like Facebook and Twitter could help unleash social transformation in the Middle East and North Africa, there is no way to predict the consequences of unforeseen technical developments that will come.

Critical to moving forward will be finding ways to secure cyberspace and address all of the vexing threats that exist without undermining the benefits of open networking and democratic principles, such as access to information, freedom of speech and privacy, as well as the enormous gains that have been made in advancing democracy and liberty through open networking. In an urgency to address critical security issues as exemplified in radical plans to build a new Internet or outlaw anonymity online, there is a real risk that the "baby will be thrown out with the bathwater"—thereby undermining the positive social benefits of the Internet and its associated technologies.

Here, democratic governments have a special role to play in this process, ensuring that the same principles that are promoted internationally are respected in domestic settings. When democratic countries download policing functions to the private sector without proper oversight and accountability, stand up within their armed forces capabilities to fight and win wars in cyberspace and allow companies based in their jurisdictions to profit from tools and services that enable widespread censorship and surveillance abroad, authoritarian and other governments find legitimacy for their own policies. A consistent, comprehensive strategy to secure cyberspace in a way that deals with mutually perceived threats while at the same time ensuring that basic human rights, such as freedom of speech, access to information and privacy are bedrock pillars of global cyberspace will be the major challenge for the next decade. ∎

Opinion Ballots after page 32

discussion questions

1. In the formulation of cyberspace policy, two major interests collide: the practical necessity of securing cyberspace to preserve public confidence (which extends to policing, commercial viability, and national security), and the preservation of openness as a global public good that is in line with the norms of liberal democratic societies. How should these competing challenges be balanced? What other interests are at stake?

2. Who should govern cyberspace? Should international efforts be conducted by governments in a centralized, multilateral body—possibly under the auspices of the UN? What are the barriers to international cooperation on efforts to combat cybercrime and to regulate other activity in cyberspace? What should be the role of the private sector?

3. How might a cyberspace "arms race" affect the U.S. in fighting wars "on the ground"? Consider the examples of the cyber attacks that accompanied the Russia-Georgia war in 2008.

4. Western democracies have been willing to use Internet filtering to restrict access to illegal or offensive content, such as pornography or child exploitation. Would governments overstep by extending Internet filtering to content that promotes terrorism and fundamentalism? What about restrictions on social networking during civil unrest? Under what circumstances are governments justified in controlling cyberspace?

5. What considerations should be taken into account in the formulation of U.S. military doctrine for cyberspace operations? What concepts from traditional warfare can be applied to cyberspace?

6. Consider the U.S. State Department's request that Twitter postpone scheduled downtime that would have interfered with mobilization of the Green Movement in Iran. How should the U.S. government interact with private-sector actors that have unique power in implementing or thwarting the U.S. foreign policy agenda? What principles should shape the relationships that the U.S. has with companies like Google, Facebook and Twitter?

---

suggested readings

Axelrod, Robert, "Governing the Cyber Commons." **Perspectives on Politics,** 2010. Available free online at: <http://www-personal.umich.edu/~axe/Ax%20Cyber%20Commons%202010.pdf>. Axelrod examines those characteristics of the Internet that make it a commons, and others that challenge that formulation.

Committee on Deterring Cyberattacks, "Letter Report from the Committee on Deterring Cyberattacks: Informing Strategies and Developing Options for U.S. Policy." **National Research Council**, 2010. This expert panel considers whether and how to defend and deter against computer network attacks on critical infrastructures.

Deibert, Ronald, Palfrey, John G., Rohozinski, Rafal, and Zittrain, Jonathan, eds. **Access Controlled: The Shaping of Power, Rights, and Rule in Cyberspace.** Boston, MIT Press, 2010. This volume presents up-to-date regional reports and country profiles, and documents emerging trends and technologies as governments seek to control the Internet.

Deibert, Ronald, and Rohozinski, Rafal, "Risking Security: Policies and Paradoxes of Cyberspace Security." **International Political Sociology**, 2010. This article addresses the differences between two major types of risks: risks to cyberspace and risks through cyberspace.

"Contesting Cyberspace and the Coming Crisis of Authority," in Deibert, Ronald, John G. Palfrey, Rafal Rohozinski, and Jonathan Zittrain, eds. **Access Contested: Securing, Identity, and Resistance in Asian Cyberspace.** Boston, MIT Press, 2011. 432 pp. $24.00 (paper). This chapter outlines the driving forces that create a "perfect storm" of geopolitical contestation in cyberspace, and the crisis of authority that is ensuing.

Hughes, Rex, "A Treaty for Cyberspace." **International Affairs,** 2010. Available free online at: < http://www.cyberdialogue.ca/wp-content/uploads/2011/03/Rex-Hughes-A-Treaty-for-Cyberspace.pdf>. This article considers the prospects for a cyber arms control treaty as governments and non-state actors develop methods and tools to wage war in cyberspace.

Information Warfare Monitor and Shadowserver Foundation, **Shadows in the Cloud: Investigating Cyber Espionage 2.0.** 2010. Available free online at: <http://shadows-in-the-cloud.net>. A major investigative report into a global cyber espionage network and a follow-on to Tracking Ghostnet.

Information Warfare Monitor, **Tracking GhostNet: Investigating a Cyber Espionage Network.** 2009. A landmark investigation into cyber espionage, beginning in the Offices of His Holiness the Dalai Lama and the Tibetan Government in Exile, led to the discovery of a network of compromised. highly sensitive computers in 103 countries.

Inkster, Nigel, "China in Cyberspace." **Survival**, 2010. Though Western policymakers have expressed growing concerns about Chinese intentions in cyberspace, this article takes a nuanced view that China itself has a lot at stake in a stable and secure Internet.

Walt, Stephen, 'Is the Cyber Threat Overblown?", **Foreign Policy**, 2010. Available free online at: <http://walt.foreignpolicy.com/posts/2010/03/30/is_the_cyber_threat_overblown>. A massive cybersecurity industry has arisen, but some of these businesses may have a stake in inflating security threats.

Visit **WWW.GREATDECISIONS.ORG** *for quizzes, seasonal topic updates and other resources to further your understanding*

Exit from Afghanistan & Iraq: right time, right pace?

by Michael O'Hanlon

Three Afghan soldiers in Khost, eastern Afghanistan, searching for Taliban camps and weapons near the Pakistani border. (PIETER-JAN DE PUE/LAIF/REDUX)

President Barack Obama inherited two major wars when he entered the White House on January 20, 2009. Both resulted at least in part from the September 11, 2001, terrorist attacks on the U.S. and their aftermath. The war in Afghanistan, now more than 10 years old, began just three weeks after those attacks by the al-Qaeda transnational terrorist organization. It led within a couple of months to the overthrow of the Taliban government that had tolerated al-Qaeda's presence on Afghan soil for years. But while the ouster of the previous government was a quick process, establishing a democracy and meaningful stability has proven far harder. Hamid Karzai was quickly chosen to lead the country, by popular acclaim within Afghanistan and throughout much of the international community, and was then formally elected president in 2004 and 2009. A constitution was also passed and parliamentary elections were held in 2005 and 2010. But in recent years the Taliban has mounted a comeback, at the same time that Karzai's

government has lost credibility among many Afghans and been challenged as well by less than cooperative policies across the border by the government of Pakistan. As a result, a North Atlantic Treaty Organization (NATO)-led coalition has responded with a major buildup of forces and has finally checked the growth of the insurgency, though it has not yet really reversed it.

The Iraq war was linked by the Bush Administration to 9/11 as well, even though Saddam Hussein's government had no meaningful operational ties to al-Qaeda. It did, however, have a track record of extreme brutality against its neigh-

---

MICHAEL O'HANLON *is a senior fellow and director of research at the Brookings Institution. He specializes in national security, defense and foreign policy, and is the senior author of the Iraq, Afghanistan and Pakistan Index projects. His most recent publications are* A Skeptic's Case for Nuclear Disarmament *(Brookings, 2010) and* The Science of War *(Princeton University Press, 2009).*

May 15, 2008, Baghdad, Iraq: An Iraqi woman escorts girls to school past a U.S. Army soldier during a morning patrol in the Baladiyat neighborhood. (CHRIS HONDROS/GETTY IMAGES)

bors and its domestic opponents, and unanswered questions about its possible programs to build weapons of mass destruction (WMDs) that had many worrying that it was holding chemical and biological arms while also again pursuing a nuclear weapons program as it had in the 1980s. These worries and suspicions then led to the March 2003 invasion of Iraq by a U.S.-led international coalition that, over the years, increasingly became U.S.-dominated. The Afghanistan operation had clear NATO approval; the Iraq invasion, by contrast, was endorsed by neither NATO nor the United Nations. Again, the goal was to leave behind a functioning democracy able to secure its own territory against violent extremists. The surge strategy of 2007–2008 dramatically reduced Iraq's violence, but it has not yet led to a firm establishment of a legitimate and law-abiding government. It appears that success in reaching that latter goal will soon be tested, as all main American military forces will have left Iraq by the end of 2011.

Obama is well on the way toward ending—or at least leaving—one of these wars, in Iraq, while he has dramatically escalated the U.S. role in Af-

Portions of this article were previously published in *Toughing it Out in Afghanistan* by Michael O'Hanlon and Hassina Sherjan (Brookings, 2010).

ghanistan. What are the prospects for successful conclusions to both in the coming months and years?

Iraq's finale

When former Prime Minister Ayad Allawi, whose Iraqiya party won the most seats in the March 2010 elections, could not find enough potential coalition partners to form a new government and Prime Minister Nouri al-Maliki was poised to do so, Washington counseled Maliki to form a government of national unity that included Allawi's party—and allowed the latter to play a major role in the selection of defense and interior ministers. Unfortunately, that approach has led to paralysis and a breakdown in the functioning of much of the Iraqi government, as Allawi and Maliki have not been on speaking terms and the key security positions have not been filled. This backdrop contributed to the difficulty Iraqis had in deciding whether to request an extension of the American military presence beyond 2011; ultimately they only offered terms that America found unacceptable, since they would have required American soldiers accused of crimes to be tried and potentially punished within the Iraqi legal system. Without immunity, the U.S. abandoned plans to leave troops in Iraq beyond the end of 2011. For this and other reasons, the grand-coalition strategy has been widely seen in retrospect

as a mistake.

Iraq has come a long way, but it is nowhere near being out of the woods. Bombings and killings continue, with the potential to result in high-level assassinations or other tragedies. There still are myriad political problems, too. They include unresolved constitutional debates about how much power the central government should wield and how much it should share with the provinces. They also include uncertainty over the future of the "Sons of Iraq" (as well as the so-called "Daughters of Iraq"), most of them Sunni, who did so much to check al-Qaeda in the role of community watch groups in 2007 and 2008—but who now worry that a Shi'a-based government will find it convenient to forget them rather than help them to find new jobs. Additional problems in Iraq include residual pockets of al-Qaeda as well as insidious influences from Iran and other neighbors. These create a real risk of resumed hostilities.

On the other hand, violence is down more than 95%, in terms of monthly war-related killings, since the carnage of 2004–2006, when at least 3,000 people a month were being killed due to acts of war, and when tens of thousands monthly were being driven from their homes. The progress that the surge, the Sunni awakening, the Basra and Sadr city offensives and related developments produced in the latter Bush years has been further solidified. The civil war as such is over, at least for now. Electricity production is up more than 50% and international energy firms are bidding enthusiastically to help develop new oil fields in Iraq. The central government is sharing revenues, and responsibilities, with Iraq's 18 provinces—even those dominated by Sunni and Kurdish communities. Politics are still rough and tumble, and the future is uncertain, but Iraq's progress has been extraordinary. And however unpleasant politics has been at times, debate and parliamentary maneuver and horse-trading, rather than violence and threats, have become the main means of trying to resolve differences in Iraq. As Vice President Joe Biden, who has worked hard on the issue in recent years, puts it, "politics has broken out."

Yet all is not well. Some say that the war is already over. But President Obama's Oval Office speech marking the end of the "combat mission" and the return of all combat troops from Iraq to the U.S. on August 31, 2010, was largely an exercise in semantics, since many well-armed American troops remained thereafter—and they continued to suffer casualties as well. And so the war may not truly be over. The U.S. role may in fact have ended prematurely, when it might be wiser to keep a modest presence in Iraq for a longer period of time to help Iraqis solidify their still very fragile peace. Countries emerging from recent civil war have a high likelihood of relapse—with one third to one half reverting to war. As Stanford University professor Steve Stedman and other scholars have shown, countries with neighbors bent on wreaking havoc, with "spoilers" within their own country who prefer to defeat a peace accord, and with abundant natural resources that provide tempting targets for exploitation are particularly vulnerable to renewed violence. Iraq has all three potential problems. In addition, though established democracies are prone to peace (with other democracies and also internally), young democracies are not—as the violence Iraq suffered after its election in 2005 suggests.

It is not that U.S. forces can or should be in a position to suppress any such violence if it occurs. The goal of the U.S. presence, rather, has been one of peacekeeping, confidence building and informal arbitration. The goal, in other words, has been to exercise American influence with relevant Iraqi parties in a preventive and confidence-building fashion. This task has been facilitated by the U.S. troops who could help man checkpoints, carry out joint patrols with Iraqi and Kurdish forces, and otherwise calm nerves and provide reassurance among still-jittery Iraqis as the wounds of civil war begin to heal. It will be a different situation with them gone.

The Obama Administration, while ambivalent about the continuing U.S. presence in Iraq, did appear willing to accept an ongoing presence under

the right terms. It was Prime Minister Maliki who insisted that the 2008 accord mandating this scheduled U.S. departure was reached, and it was the Bush Administration, not the current government in Washington, that signed the bilateral deal. Iraqi domestic politics still contain a healthy dose of anti-Americanism, and Iraqis remain a proud people who want to run their own country without help.

Yet there are reasons to worry. Maliki is driven not just by understandable national pride and coalition politics, but a personal tendency toward rash action—such as when he launched the campaign in Basra in the spring of 2008 with virtually no planning or coordination with American forces and when he wrongly tried to disqualify some opposition candidates for Parliament in early 2010. Maliki has also tried to consolidate many powers in his office, circumscribing the roles of Parliament and other actors on matters such as who

can propose legislation (sometimes Maliki has the help of the courts in this process). His unwillingness to work meaningfully with his main domestic rival, former Prime Minister Allawi, and his decision to retain the ministries of defense and interior under his own control cause further concern.

The most vivid way to understand the complexity of the situation is to focus on the contested city of Kirkuk and its environs in the north of the country, just below the autonomous region of Kurdistan proper. This is the oil-rich and historic city where Kurds, Turkomen, and Arabs interact—and compete for claims to the land and its resources. According to the Iraqi constitution, written with American help and passed in 2005, a referendum on Kirkuk's future must be held. In fact, it was supposed to have happened by 2007, but disputes over who should be allowed to vote and what options should be presented to voters have continued to delay the resolution

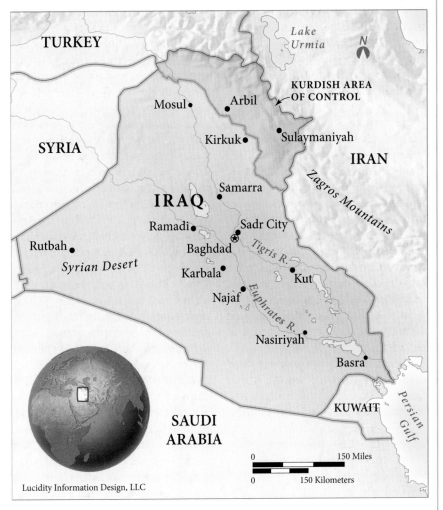

Lucidity Information Design, LLC

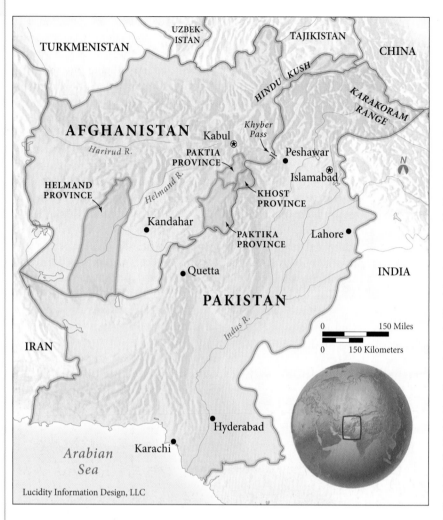

Lucidity Information Design, LLC

of the matter.

Kurds call Kirkuk their Jerusalem and believe Saddam tried to take it from them by diluting their demographic strength there through forced introduction of Arab populations in earlier decades. Arabs feel the Kurds have already gotten enough special deals and worry about the backsliding that might occur if yet another area were allowed to semi-secede from the center's control. Turkomen, numbering up to 1 million themselves, worry about being squeezed out of the area they have lived in for centuries by larger groups and larger forces around them. Some type of special status for Kirkuk and the environs—different from both Kurdistan's autonomy and the province's regular status within the rest of Iraq—might address the concerns of all parties. But that outcome will have to be worked out by Iraqis, who are nowhere near resolution.

"Peshmerga" (armed Kurdish fight-ers) forces and Iraqi army units have almost come to blows several times in recent years as they tried to influence the competition for these disputed lands in Iraq's north. Each time, cooler heads, shored up by the American military presence, have prevailed. The U.S. has been carrying out joint patrols and manning joint checkpoints with peshmerga and Army units. The U.S. has not threatened to fire on anyone, and its neutral status has been reassuring and stabilizing throughout.

There is a plan to create a mixed Arab-Kurd force that would continue this kind of effort after the Americans leave. But it will be made up of partisans to the very dispute that is not yet resolved. A couple of U.S. brigades could have continued to play the same stabilizing role that they have been for one to two more years at little risk to the troops and little additional strain to the U.S. Army—and very modest cost com-

pared with the nearly $1 trillion already spent. Perhaps some creative face-saving mechanism, like a NATO-led force under UN auspices, backstopped by American units with participation by other states as well, could still be used to help deal with the complex politics of the situation. Such a strategy might be possible if a crisis erupts after the U.S. departure. In other words, the U.S. may have withdrawn troops from Iraq, but rushing to leave may have increased the risk of serious problems down the road.

Afghanistan today

Afghanistan has become America's longest war. A decade after the U.S. set out to destroy the al-Qaeda terrorist network responsible for the September 11 attacks on New York and Washington, along with the Taliban regime that gave it sanctuary, American and NATO troops are still in Afghanistan fighting a resurgent Taliban in a war that has not achieved its original objectives and threatens to have negative effects on the stability of neighboring Pakistan. Obama promised during his presidential campaign that he would refocus on Afghanistan, that the previous Administration had made a mistake by turning away from it. But the Obama Administration's decisions in 2009 to increase America's commitment to the country, and the resulting intensification of fighting, have raised questions about how many American lives and how much of its wealth should be spent on the effort. Obama's June 2011 decision to hasten the drawdown of troops beyond what his commanders had counseled or preferred raises questions about the President's own commitment to the war now. Yet at the same time it does not constitute an exit strategy per se, since even after the first drawdown is complete at the end of September 2012, the U.S. will still have 68,000 troops in Afghanistan—twice the number Obama inherited when he assumed the presidency.

For many years the Afghanistan war was fought with minimal effort. U.S. troop commitments were typically one tenth as large as those for Iraq during President George W. Bush's first term (2001–2005). NATO allies contributed too, but their troop numbers were even more modest than America's during most of the effort. NATO sought to build an Afghan security force less than one fifth the size of Iraq's, even though Afghanistan is larger and about as populous as Iraq. And NATO did not provide the necessary trainers to help that smaller force; in early 2009, for example, only one fourth of all police units had embedded mentors from international partners like the U.S.

But this situation has changed. Combined foreign forces grew dramatically starting around 2008, and especially in 2009 and 2010. The intensity of combat has dramatically increased too. Since 2008, Afghanistan has, on average, been a more dangerous place for American soldiers to deploy than Iraq. Nearly 2,000 Americans had lost their lives there by the end of 2011. With annual costs exceeding $100 billion during the Obama years, it is hardly cheap in financial terms either.

The war is also Afghanistan's longest. It is essentially a conflict that goes back 30 years, to the Soviet invasion. Modern Afghanistan is about as old as the U.S., and over the last two and a half centuries, it has never seen such a protracted period of conflict. Britain and Russia played out their "great game" of geostrategic competition at Afghanistan's expense throughout much of the 19th century, but this was not a period of continued fighting such as the last 30 years have been.

The stakes

Just what does the U.S. want to accomplish in Afghanistan, anyway? This is a fair question as the nation doubles down its bets and commits more of its sons and daughters than ever before to a conflict in a remote part of the world.

The simplest answer is that the U.S. wants to prevent another 9/11 that might originate on Afghan soil, as the original September 11, 2001, attack did. All 19 hijackers trained there, as have many other anti-Western terrorists over the years. The leadership of al-Qaeda and associated movements have now pledged loyalty to Mullah Omar, head of the Afghanistan Taliban, and al-Qaeda has trained the Taliban in various

methods of attack. Intelligence reports also suggest growing ties between al-Qaeda and another major insurgent militia with an extremist ideology, the so-called Haqqani network operating in Afghanistan's east (especially in Khost, Paktia and Paktika provinces). So the triumph of insurgent groups in Afghanistan would likely lead to a renewed home and sanctuary for al-Qaeda within Afghanistan under the protection of a friendly government—greatly facilitating the terrorist group's training, coordination and command-and-control efforts globally. Such a sanctuary would be very troubling. Some say it would

Feb. 15, 2005, Kandahar, Afghanistan: An Afghan visits a massive Taliban memorial graveyard that holds the remains of Taliban soldiers killed in the northern city of Mazar-i-Sharif in 1997. Their remains were brought back to Kandahar by the Taliban after Mazar-i-Sharif was retaken. Pieces of the dead victims' clothing were placed on top of the graves. (ROBERT NICKELSBERG/GETTY IMAGES)

matter little, given al-Qaeda's various other options for organizing its followers, and also the weakening of the organization after the 2011 deaths at American hands of Osama bin Laden in Pakistan and Anwar al-Awlaki in Yemen (among other battlefield deaths of top leaders). However, the degree of brainwashing required of people being trained to be suicide bombers in the pursuit of a perverted version of jihad is extreme. The notion that it can happen on a large scale just anywhere or through the Internet is improbable; that is not the way extremist movements tend to develop devout followers.

As Gordon Smith, a Canadian official and scholar, plainly put it, in words that would apply equally well to most Western countries including the U.S.: "It is in Canada's interest that Afghanistan and the bordering regions of Pakistan not again be used as a base from which global terrorist attacks can be launched: think of London, Madrid, Bali and Mumbai, as well as 9/11." As bad as the first four examples on Smith's list were, 9/11 was far worse—and 9/11 was the plot that benefited in large measure from al-Qaeda's ability to organize on Afghan soil.

The stakes, however, go beyond simply denying al-Qaeda another sanctuary. Afghanistan has special importance in the minds of al-Qaeda members—and would-be recruits of al-Qaeda—as a symbol of a successful attack against the West. Were the U.S. to lose there, al-Qaeda would argue that its predictions about the West's weakness and lack of staying power were correct. It would claim momentum in its broader, global struggle against "infidels." That could help the terrorists find new followers who want to be on the winning side of history. It would also restore momentum to al-Qaeda, impetus that it has lost across the globe from Iraq to Saudi Arabia to Indonesia and elsewhere, and lost further with the May 2, 2011, killing of Osama bin Laden by a team of U.S. operatives. The head of the British armed forces, General Sir David Richards, stated that a NATO "failure [in Afghanistan] would have a catalytic effect on militant Islam around the world and in the region because the message would be that al-Qaeda and the Taliban have defeated the U.S. and the British and NATO, the most powerful alliance in the world. So why wouldn't that have an intoxicating effect on militants everywhere? The geostrategic implications would be immense."

Some say that the Taliban and other Afghan resistance movements are not the real enemies and that the U.S. should accommodate them. But those with firsthand experience of the Taliban in recent years would beg to differ. David Rohde of *The New York Times,* who was held captive in late 2008 and much of 2009 by the group, vividly described the extreme degrees of U.S. hatred, and support for al-Qaeda's global agenda, among its members. As counterterrorism expert Bruce Riedel says, terrorists "don't stay in their lanes." They tend to work together. That includes other groups in Afghanistan beside the Taliban, such as the Haqqani network. The goal of a large, growing fundamentalist movement that would attempt to create a caliphate throughout much of the Islamic world, and use extreme methods against American allies and interests as well as other dissenting groups and individuals in the process, is not confined to al-Qaeda. A victory for the Afghan resistance is effectively a victory, and a major one at that, for al-Qaeda and associated movements with a global and anti-Western agenda.

Another crucial reason to prevail in Afghanistan is to prevent Pakistani extremists from using Afghanistan as a sanctuary and training ground for launching attacks against their own country. A destabilized Pakistan, armed with about 100 nuclear weapons and thousands of extremist fighters, including al-Qaeda partisans, would be an even greater threat to the U.S. and other states than would a failed state in Afghanistan itself. Afghanistan is not very far from central Pakistan, and the border regions between the two countries are so hard to police that it would be highly undesirable to allow extremists such a safe haven so close to a strategically crucial state. At precisely the time that Pakistan is finally committing more of its resources to going after extrem-

ists in its own tribal regions, it would be an unfortunate moment to give them a sanctuary within Afghanistan. Moreover, there are growing reasons to fear that the Afghan Taliban, Pakistani Taliban and al-Qaeda have developed more links and more forms of cooperation in recent years. This is not a conclusive argument in favor of winning in Afghanistan at all costs, but it is an important reason why defeat would be worrisome. All that said, Pakistan needs to do more to help Afghanistan and the U.S. rein in the sanctuaries used by Afghan insurgents operating from Pakistani soil, and a central challenge of American foreign policy in the months and years ahead will be to use a combination of cajoling, pressuring, prodding and kindly requesting Pakistani help in the effort. Some willingness to reduce American aid in the absence of cooperation, and increase it in the aftermath of improved collaboration, may also be appropriate.

Some argue that the U.S.'s core goals in Afghanistan and Pakistan can be achieved through a more-narrow counterterrorism agenda, rather than a full-scale counterinsurgency approach in Afghanistan. That is, they favor "CT, not COIN," to use the acronyms commonly employed for each concept. They believe that another 9/11 could be prevented, and major destabilization of Pakistan averted, by a more limited approach. Under this strategy, special forces would periodically attack any cells that coalesced within Afghanistan, even in the absence of a stable central government. Drones, cruise missiles, and other forms of standoff attack would contribute as well, carrying out strikes in both Afghanistan and Pakistan. In this way, these critics say, the U.S. would accomplish its core objectives without engaging in huge risks to American personnel or unrealistic aspirations about constructing a functioning Afghan state.

But proponents of COIN argue that the CT plan is unrealistic—at least if pursued too soon. In essence, CT is the strategy that the Bush Administration tried in its early years; the plan clearly failed, leaving today's dilemma. To be effective, CT requires intelligence, but

Aug. 19, 2011, Kabul, Afghanistan: An Afghan security official runs past British armored vehicles at the site of a suicide attack and a clash at the British Council. At least three people were killed as a wave of suicide explosions rocked a British cultural centre in Kabul, on a public holiday marking Afghanistan's independence from Britain in 1919. (ROBERT NICKELSBERG/GETTY IMAGES)

obtaining solid intelligence on the locations of terrorists is very difficult without a strong presence on the ground and the cooperation of friendly local actors. Such friendly local Afghans are much harder to find, and protect, in a chaotic, destabilized country. At some point, if or when the Afghan insurgency prevails in combat—as would likely happen under a CT approach—the air bases and other facilities the U.S. currently uses to attack extremists in both Afghanistan and Pakistan could also be lost. CT might work as a U.S. strategy, once the Afghan army and police are strong enough to hold their own country together, but probably not yet.

Proponents of CT respond that the international community is trying a more minimal approach to countering al-Qaeda in places such as Somalia and some of the tribal areas of Yemen—two additional places largely unpoliced by any effective government. If such an approach works in these places, why not in Afghanistan too, one might ask? But Afghanistan is larger and more remote than Somalia or Yemen, and a place with more tribal networks and political actors favorable to al-Qaeda. As the Bush Administration learned, air strikes and commando raids against suspected terror targets are much harder to pull off quickly and effectively in Afghanistan. Afghanistan is therefore a safer, more convenient place for al-Qaeda to operate. And al-Qaeda has already proven its interest in operating from Afghanistan. Its leadership remains based nearby in the mountains of western Pakistan even today, and it would potentially be a mistake to assert that al-Qaeda after Osama bin Laden's death is permanently debilitated. There is currently considerable Pakistani action against extremists in these regions, so there is finally a chance to execute a hammer-and-tongs approach against the major redoubts for al-Qaeda and associated movements.

A third reason to try to succeed in Afghanistan is to make good on the U.S. commitment to an important Muslim people. The Afghans, who have suffered greatly as a pawn in great-power conflict over the last 30 years, deserve a

May 11, 2010, Washington, DC: President Barack Obama appears with President Hamid Karzai of Afghanistan during their joint news conference at the White House. Obama noted progress toward better governance in Afghanistan, but says he and Karzai agreed there is "much, much more that has to be done." (LUKE SHARRETT/THE NEW YORK TIMES/REDUX)

chance at a better future. Their decade-long stand against the Soviet invasion of Afghanistan weakened the U.S.S.R. and helped end the cold war. The debt is historical, therefore, as well as moral. It is also worth noting that the Afghans' drug production problem would not exist at today's current scale without a market for illegal narcotics in the Western world, a fact that further deepens the West's moral responsibility. Americans cannot build a new Afghanistan themselves, of course; only Afghans can do that. But the U.S., as well as the broader international community, has a certain moral obligation to give them a chance to do so. This is not an argument for staying forever, but it is an argument for trying to do the job right before going home. Such a strategy can help counter (at least somewhat) those cynics who claim that the U.S. does not care about the well-being of Muslim peoples and only uses them for its own Machiavellian purposes. Such arguments, reinforced by the stalemate in the Israeli-Palestinian peace process, hurt the U.S. because they help al-Qaeda and related groups recruit followers.

There is admittedly a flip side to this argument: if the Afghan people and, more to the point, the Afghan government, fail to do their part in this war, the American moral commitment at

some point will no longer be so binding. To put it differently, the U.S. and other countries could try their utmost and still fail because of mistakes made by President Karzai and other Afghan officials—and at that point, there would be little point in further investments in failure. Other means of stabilizing Pakistan, the most crucial country in the region for American strategic interests, would have to be explored. It is important that Karzai understand this, rather than view the international commitment to his country as open-ended, because his administration has a crucial role to play in improving U.S. strategy in Afghanistan. Success in Afghanistan—and depriving al-Qaeda of a new sanctuary and a major propaganda victory, and preventing Pakistani Taliban from gaining another redoubt of their own—is clearly desirable.

Is success possible?

The Afghan people, working with the international community, have a very good chance to succeed in this war. Success means defeating or at least containing the insurgency, gradually improving law and order, and creating infrastructure to allow for economic progress. The road will not be easy, and the outcome will not be a prosperous Western-style democracy. Former

Secretary of Defense Robert Gates was surely right when he said that there will be no Valhalla in Central Asia. But the U.S. can probably help the Afghans build a viable state that, over time, can assert control over its territory and improve the lives of its people. Perhaps it will resemble Colombia, which faced a brutal insurgency that controlled sizable chunks of its territory and terrorized its population, and which gradually made headway against that insurgency over the years with only modest outside help. But that goal, while less than ideal, is also consistent with core American security interests and with the prospects of an improved life for most Afghan citizens as well.

This may seem a modest set of goals. But attaining them would prevent Afghanistan from becoming a place where 9/11-type attacks are again planned and organized. It also would literally keep alive future generations of Afghan peoples—in contrast to the bloodshed of the last 30 years. Since the Soviets invaded in 1979, well over 1 million have died from violence, while nearly all the rest have lived in extreme poverty and deprivation.

Here are some reasons to hope for success. First, Afghans want a better future for themselves. This is true for Afghans in their own country, as well as for the diaspora of Afghans around the world—many of whom have moved back home to help build a new country, while others stand ready to invest and trade and assist in other ways. Most Afghans reject war. They also reject the Taliban, by 90% or more in most polls. Among the majority of the Afghan people who are not Pashtun, in fact, support for the Taliban is virtually zero. Even among the Durrani, one of the two main Pashtun tribal groupings, support for the Taliban has been limited (the Taliban's main support has come from the Pashtun Ghilzai tribe). In Kandahar City, the base for Taliban operations before they were ousted in 2001 and a central focus of the current insurgency, Taliban support reached an all-time high of 25% in 2009—but even there, three of every four Afghans had a favorable opinion of the government.

The Ulema Council of Afghanistan and other important religious groups also have supported the Afghan government and criticized the Taliban.

In fact, the Taliban is not a popular insurgency. It is in equal parts a narco-terrorist organization willing to use drug smuggling to finance its operations, an extremist Islamist movement with an intolerant view of nonbelievers, a backward view of the role of women and a ruthless organization willing to use brutal violence against innocent, law-abiding citizens to impose its version of Islam.

The way forward?

There is no clear consensus for Afghans on where to go from here. They are angry with the international community, and to a lesser extent with President Karzai, for doing a poor job in helping them build a viable state over the last eight years. And among some Afghans, that anger sometimes translates into support for insurgents—at least locally and temporarily. But it does not mean the Afghan people want a return to the Communist rule of the late 1970s and 1980s, or the anarchy and bloodletting of the late 1980s and early 1990s, or the tyranny of the Taliban thereafter.

Despite being devastated by decades of war, Afghans are resolute, resourceful and proud people. They have a real sense of national history and identity, even if some aspects of their nationalism have been weakened by decades of conflict and need to be rebuilt. They are a young, forward-looking people—70% of the population is under 30 and about one fourth of all citizens now live in cities. They are indeed good fighters, but they are not the caricature of backward, xenophobic warriors so often portrayed in the mass media. They are aware of the opportunity promised by a modern, democratic government supported by a strong economy and an educated population. There are many competent people in positions of power in government—cabinet ministers, governors and others—as well as in the private sector and civil society. The promising performance of the Afghan National Army also suggests that it is in fact possible to

build viable, national institutions—that the country is more than a collection of tribes with no regard for central authority and no sense of Afghan identity.

There are also many good and committed "average citizens." In Kandahar City citizens are telling authorities about the locations of up to 80% of all improvised explosive devices before they go off, allowing security forces to defuse them. This high percentage, higher than ever witnessed in Iraq, further suggests that efforts to quell the Taliban may have found unexpected support from the general population in one of the Taliban strongholds, support that a counterinsurgency can build upon. Progress is apparent in other places too. In Helmand province, for example, an infusion of U.S. forces in 2009 and 2010 had turned a previously lawless area held by the Taliban into a relatively secure area where ordinary people can begin to get back to their daily lives, using roads and attending schools and shopping markets. By various metrics, all such forms of normal activity have increased by 50% to 100% over the last couple of years as security has improved.

Second, elements of the Afghan security forces are improving fast. With NATO's International Security Assistance Force (ISAF) focused intently now on proper training and mentoring, the building of Afghan security forces that can protect their own people should accelerate.

Third, life in Afghanistan has actually improved somewhat compared with the recent past. As bad as many security trends have been in recent years, for most Afghans the country is far less violent today than it was in the 1980s and 1990s. Life in Afghanistan today is better in material terms too. Yes, the progress is uneven, and the poor remain very badly off. But overall the economy, education, health care, and similar indicators are moving more in the right direction than the wrong one. Material progress has contributed to a reservoir of good will among the Afghan people toward those in authority.

Fourth, NATO in general and the U.S. in particular know how to carry out counterinsurgency missions better than ever before. Troops are experienced in the art of counterinsurgency and knowledgeable about Afghanistan. Beyond top-level leadership, there are commanders at lower levels of authority—the ones who execute the strategy day in and day out—who are also seasoned and quite smart in the ways of this type of warfare. The importance of good leadership in counterinsurgency is very significant, and U.S. strengths in this area are a major asset.

Fifth, and hardly least, much of the basic strategy announced in March and December of 2009 is finally right. After seven years of treating Afghanistan as the forgotten war, the U.S. is seriously resourcing its effort there with combat troops, trainers for Afghan forces, development aid, top-notch leadership and other capabilities.

In mid-2008, the chairman of the Joint Chiefs of Staff, Admiral Michael Mullen, said, "Afghanistan has been and remains an economy-of-force campaign, which by definition means we need more forces there." He had been even more blunt in December 2007, when he said, "in Afghanistan, we do what we can. In Iraq, we do what we must." On the ground, at the tactical level, this reality prevented combined Afghan and NATO forces from securing many districts, towns and villages. Worse, it left troops stalemated in dangerous situations over extended periods of time because they did not have the capacity to seize land and sustain control. It left NATO forces relying too heavily on air strikes with all their potential to cause accidental deaths of innocents (a policy that General Stanley McChrystal changed in 2009; air strikes are generally allowed now only if NATO troops are in direct peril). And it left Afghan citizens who cooperated with NATO and their government vulnerable to reprisal. Only in 2009 and 2010 did these realities finally begin to change, and they continued to do so throughout 2011.

Historically, only 40% of modern counterinsurgencies have succeeded (and somewhat less in most recent times), according to research by Jason Lyall, Isaiah Wilson and Ivan Arreguin-Toft. However, 70% of the counterinsurgencies that focused on population security have been effective, according to research by Andrew Enterline and Joseph Magagnoli. Given the degree of commitment and excellence of U.S. and other NATO forces today, the odds would seem at least that great in U.S. favor today—provided everyone, including the Afghan government, can work together in support of the basic strategy. ■

Success or failure?

Sept. 14, 2011: A soldier, part of the coalition forces, holds his weapon during a gun battle with Taliban militants in a building in Kabul, Afghanistan. The 20-hour insurgent attack ended after Afghan police ferreted out and killed the last few assailants who had taken over a half-built downtown building to fire on the nearby U.S. embassy and NATO compounds. (MUSADEQ SADEQ/AP)

FOR ALL ITS PROMISE, Afghanistan could still fail—meaning a return to civil war, or a takeover by extremists and tyrants, some of whom could be allied with al-Qaeda. Any such outcome would provide the potential for al-Qaeda to reestablish a sanctuary in Afghanistan, meaning that the U.S. and its allies would fail as well and their security would be put at greater risk.

Despite its limitations, the Taliban-led insurgency has many strengths. It is well organized, cunningly led, and increasingly confident. Its use of roadside bombs and small-unit ambushes imperil NATO and Afghan troops. It has ample access to weapons and explosives, given the huge stocks of weaponry still scattered throughout the country from previous conflicts and the numerous smuggling routes across Central Asia. Afghans sense that the insurgency has momentum and are drawn to it for that reason. The Taliban have a shadow government structure, run out of Quetta, Pakistan, by what is famously known as the Quetta shura (leadership group), which maintains a system of governance throughout key parts of Pashtun-run Afghanistan (primarily the south and east of the country). While the Taliban may be corrupt in their reliance on drug money, they are by most accounts not corrupt in their interactions with normal Afghan citizens, who often comment that the Taliban operate with more discipline, and demand fewer bribes, than do government officials or police forces. The Taliban now operate in more than one third of Afghanistan's 368 districts. Their chilling use of threatening "night letters," assassinations and other forms of intimidation sows terror among local leaders as well as the general population, allowing the Taliban to maneuver relatively freely. By avoiding the mass atrocities used against civilian populations by other insurgencies, the Taliban may also have mitigated some of the

July 9, 2011: A Pakistani soldier stands guard on a road in Parachinar, capital of northwest Pakistan's Kurram Agency, which borders Afghanistan. (XINHUA NEWS AGENCY/EYEVINE/REDUX)

anger that would otherwise have been directed against them.

This leads directly to the second and related problem: the Taliban's ability to gain supporters among the growing number of Afghans disgusted by the government's incompetence and corruption (and by policy mistakes by the international community). If the government continues to flounder, there could come a day when, for many Afghans, the Taliban seem the lesser of two evils. Indeed, that is already the case for tribes that feel disenfranchised by the Karzai government. Tribes that feel badly served by the current government, and upset by the benefits that rival tribes may enjoy through patronage, are already inclined to support the resistance.

Corruption permeates many Afghan institutions, not least of which is the police force. In the eyes of most Afghans, the police force is a corrupt and distrusted organization. According to a 2009 survey by Carol Graham and Soumya Chattopadhyay, while 69% of Afghans said they trusted the army, only 21% trusted the police. That Afghanistan produces 90% of the world's opium, and that its farmers have relatively few alternatives to growing poppy, reinforces the problem of corruption and lawlessness—many police are drug us-

ers themselves and are susceptible to bribes. The drug trade is well organized in Afghanistan now. This culture is part of a broader problem of lawlessness; even if the Afghanistan war per se is not as violent as many other conflicts, the frequency of kidnappings, robberies and other crimes enormously weakens public morale and support for the government. The police must be reformed even as its size is further increased in the coming years from a population with relatively few potential recruits who are literate. This process has begun and is showing progress but has a ways to go.

The crime problem is exacerbated by the ever-present risk that key Afghan leaders, in government and out, will be assassinated or driven out of the country by fear. This consideration is especially worrisome given the country's shortage of experienced leaders and managers after 30 years of war. In the government, in particular, there is often a good minister at the top of a given organization but weak second- and third-tier leadership. The problem is compounded when the country's middle and upper classes give up hope and leave for destinations abroad.

Pakistan poses another major challenge. It has about 25 million Pashtuns, roughly double the number in Afghan-

istan—a significant population given that the Taliban in particular are a Pashtun-based movement. Pakistan represents a sanctuary for the Afghan Taliban (clustered largely in Quetta, near the border with Afghanistan's Kandahar province where the Afghan Taliban is headquartered, and in Peshawar near the Pakistani end of the Khyber Pass, where other militias have their headquarters as well). Particularly in the south of Afghanistan, most resistance fighters are indigenous Afghans. But some fighters do cross the border from Pakistan into Afghanistan to fight, especially in the east of the country. So do weapons. Elements of Pakistan's Inter-Services Intelligence Directorate (ISI) are believed to still support the Taliban and other militias—as for example in the July 7, 2008, suicide bombing of the Indian embassy in Kabul, which killed more than 50, and in summer 2011 attacks against the American embassy in Kabul as well as other prominent sites. In addition, Pakistan's Frontier Corps is believed to have provided supporting fire from border posts for certain insurgent operations within Afghanistan.

The exit strategy

So where does this leave the U.S. and NATO? NATO's two-part mission in Afghanistan—to protect the population while gradually training Afghan forces to assume that responsibility on their own—can be set to an approximate schedule.

Counterinsurgency doctrine suggests that a security force of 600,000 is needed to ensure robust security throughout a country of 30 million people, such as Afghanistan. But doctrine is only approximate. In the case of Afghanistan, the ratio of 20 security personnel for every 1,000 civilians probably needs to be applied only in that half of the country where the Pashtun ethnic group predominates. This is because it is only in these regions where the insurgency is intense. In the other half of the country, a ratio of fewer than 10 security personnel for every 1,000 citizens would likely suffice. This implies that security in Afghanistan could be maintained by a competent force of roughly 400,000 soldiers and police.

ISAF now has nearly 150,000 troops in Afghanistan. The Afghan security forces number about 300,000, with perhaps 150,000 of those in decent shape or in strong partnership arrangements with NATO troops. That means that there are roughly 300,000 competent security personnel in place, half foreign and half indigenous—about 100,000 forces shy of the overall target of 400,000. Given that shortfall, some parts of the country will have to be left relatively unguarded a bit longer. Ultimately, according to current plans as of late 2011, Afghanistan will have at least 350,000 uniformed security personnel (army, air force and police) plus another 30,000 to 50,000 in community watch groups known as the Afghan Local Police.

As the Afghan security forces build toward 400,000 competent soldiers and police, ISAF forces will be needed for two main reasons. First, to make up the difference between available, elite Afghan forces and the 400,000 goal. Second, to train and mentor and otherwise assist those Afghan forces.

How many forces are needed for the second mission? To get a rough idea, assume that partnering needs to be intense for one full year after a unit is formed. The current partnering concept requires ISAF units to team up with Afghan units of similar size, or perhaps one echelon larger. Thus, for example, a NATO battalion of 1,000 soldiers might pair with a relatively weak Afghan battalion of 1,000 or a relatively strong Afghan brigade of 3,000. This means that to add 75,000 Afghan personnel to the force, NATO needs to provide roughly 35,000 trainers, mentors and partners for them. It would also need to deploy additional forces to boost the aggregate (Afghan and foreign) security personnel toward 400,000.

Consider where the U.S. mission will be in mid-2012, when Obama will likely be running for reelection. According to U.S. projections, the Afghan security forces will by then have about 300,000 troops formed into units (plus a few tens of thousands more in training, not yet deployable). If ISAF deploys 35,000 troops to train, mentor and partner with Afghan units, that will make for a total security force of 335,000 in the

Jan. 13, 2011: A U.S. Marine with 1st Platoon, India Company, 3rd Battalion, 5th Marine Regiment goes over a map with Afghan National Army soldiers before a joint patrol in Helmand Province, Afghanistan. (MICHAEL KAMBER/THE NEW YORK TIMES/REDUX)

country. For the total to reach 400,000, another 65,000 ISAF troops would be needed. There would then be 100,000 ISAF soldiers in total and, factoring in contributions from NATO allies, roughly 70,000 of those likely would be American. This is roughly where President Obama's plan ends. His military commanders wanted the pace of the drawdown to be a bit slower so that they could take the fight to the eastern parts of the country in 2012, throughout the whole year, without depending on new Afghan forces to carry the major burden of that task. The basic arithmetic is similar for the two possible approaches, differing only by a few months' time.

After 2012, U.S. and other foreign forces would decline on a glide path from their initial levels of around 68,000 American and 100,000 total foreign troops to perhaps a total of 20,000 by the end of 2014, when the transition to nationwide Afghan primary security responsibility would be complete. Thereafter, remaining Western forces would operate primarily in support roles—training Afghans, helping them with intelligence gathering, cooperating on special operations raids, operating drones, and so on. This is the basic exit strategy implied by the current campaign plan for Afghanistan. Depending on what longer-term arrangements are reached, it might not amount to a com-

plete exit strategy as in Iraq; thousands of Americans might stay for a number of additional years in this strategically crucial part of the world. But personnel levels and thus costs would decline tenfold, and casualties would likely decline even more, relative to current numbers

This is, one should note, a happy ending—or at least a relatively tolerable one—to the Afghanistan saga. There are other possible endings too. One is that the U.S. leaves faster, for now, and takes its chances with what happens next. But depending on what happens next, such an approach could also increase the odds that the U.S. would have to return in force in future years.

Questions remain

Is the war in Afghanistan now a quagmire? Can the U.S. and its allies still "win"? Can Afghans really come together as a country to unify their land and build a modern state? Are the stakes really worth it for the U.S. as well as for other Western powers fighting in this part of the world? Finally, how will it be known if the strategy is succeeding as intended? These are questions increasingly being asked by the American public and Congress. ∎

Opinion Ballots after page 32

discussion questions

1. What are the challenges facing Iraq in the future? What is the U.S. role in Iraq's future? How does Iraq fit into the global terror strategy? To what extent is the U.S. responsible for the security of Iraq? What lessons can be learned?

2. Should the U.S. and NATO extend the size and duration of the commitment of troops to Afghanistan? At what point is Afghanistan responsible for its own security? How long should U.S. troops remain in the country, and in what capacity? What would a "successful" completed mission be?

3. What are the advantages and disadvantages of the counterinsurgency (COIN) and counterterrorism (CT) doctrines? Which strategy is best suited for Afghanistan? Why? What are the considerations that dictate military policy?

4. What are U.S. interests in Afghanistan? How have U.S. goals evolved since the beginning of the operation in Afghanistan? How does Afghanistan fit into the U.S.'s foreign policy for the Middle East?

5. What is the U.S. stake in Pakistani security? What are the concerns for the U.S. in engaging Pakistan as an ally? Is the author correct in asserting that a destabilized Afghanistan will contribute to a deteriorating security situation in Pakistan?

6. Why does the Taliban continue to enjoy the support of a segment of the Afghan population? Should the U.S. and the government of President Karzai engage with the Taliban as a potential partner in governing Afghanistan? How could U.S. policy undermine the Taliban's support base?

7. To what extent should international organizations, such as NATO or the UN, be involved with nation-building in Iraq and Afghanistan? Should other states—such as NATO partners or Iraq and Afghanistan's neighbors—step in? In what capacity?

8. Has the threat of al-Qaeda diminished or increased since September 11, 2001? Can al-Qaeda's change in stature be traced back to U.S. action in Afghanistan or Iraq? What is the significance of the death of bin Laden?

---

suggested readings

Barkey, Henri J., Lasensky, Scott B., Marr, Phebe, eds., **Iraq, Its Neighbors, and the United States: Competition, Crisis, and the Reordering of Power.** Washington, D.C., United States Institute of Peace Press, 2011. 300 pp. $19.95 (paper). This volume looks at the role of Iraq in its volatile region, analyzes Iraq's relations with its neighbors and discusses U.S. strategic interests and U.S.-Iraqi relations in the future. Includes case studies and policy recommendations.

Coll, Steve, **Ghost Wars: The Secret History of the CIA, Afghanistan, and Bin Laden, from the Soviet Invasion to September 10, 2001.** New York, Penguin, 2004. 738 pp. $18.00 (paper). This narrative, which won the 2005 Pulitzer Prize, was written by a former *Washington Post* journalist and examines U.S. engagement with the Taliban after the U.S.S.R.'s withdrawal and the CIA's hunt for bin Laden beginning in 1998.

Feifer, Gregory, **The Great Gamble: The Soviet War in Afghanistan.** New York, Harper Perennial, 2010. 336 pp. $15.99 (paper). This engaging account contextualizes the political and military conditions leading up to the U.S.S.R.'s invasion of Afghanistan, and traces the occupation from its beginning in 1979, from the point of view of a soldier on the ground.

Lyall, Jason, and Wilson, Isaiah, III, "Rage Against the Machines: Explaining Outcomes in Counterinsurgency Wars." **International Organization**, Winter 2009. 40 pp. Available free online at: <http://pantheon.yale.edu/~jml27/YaleWebsite/Publications_&_Data_files/Rage_Final.pdf>. This scholarly paper examines the factors for success and failure in COIN wars in the last century, focusing on mechanization.

Rashid, Ahmed, **Taliban: Militant Islam, Oil and Fundamentalism in Central Asia,** 2nd ed. New Haven, CT, Yale University Press, 2010. 344 pp. $17.95 (paper). This authoritative text from a *Far Eastern Economic Review* correspondent discusses the Taliban, fundamentalism and energy geopolitics in this volatile region.

Rohde, David, "Held By the Taliban," **The New York Times**, October 17, 2009. Available free online at: <http://www.nytimes.com/2009/10/18/world/asia/18hostage.html>. In this series, Pulitzer Prize-winner Rohde recounts his seven months of captivity in the hands of the Taliban in Afghanistan, and his daring escape.

U.S. Department of Defense, **Report on Progress Toward Security and Stability in Afghanistan.** October 2011. 147 pp. Available free online at: <http://www.defense.gov/pubs/pdfs/October_2011_Section_1230_Report.pdf>. The eighth and most recent installment of this semiannual report to Congress evaluates the status of U.S. objectives in Afghanistan.

Visit **WWW.GREATDECISIONS.ORG** *for quizzes, seasonal topic updates and other resources to further your understanding*

State of the oceans: waves of change
by Sara Tjossem

Endangered goliath grouper congregate on deep shipwrecks along Florida's east coast during the spawning season in August and September. The giant fish, often found in the Gulf of Mexico and the Caribbean Sea, can weigh as much as 800 pounds and are often accompanied by cigar minnows. (MICHAEL PATRICK O'NEILL/PHOTO RESEARCHERS)

FOR MANY AIR TRAVELERS, crossing the ocean is measured in interminable hours of unremitting blue flatness. Perhaps a flash of light or twist of wave might punctuate this boredom with thoughts of whales or other deep-sea creatures. Over a century ago the American writer Henry David Thoreau observed, "The ocean is a wilderness reaching round the globe, wilder than a Bengal jungle, and fuller of monsters...." Indeed, the ocean's aerial monotony masks a remarkable diversity of form, function and use. Although one can speak of a single ocean of salt water, its regional variation is hinted at by names such as the Atlantic, Pacific, Indian, Arctic and Southern Ocean, along with a multitude of smaller seas. The global ocean plays an integral role in climate and weather, supports at least half of all species, and provides about a quarter of the animal protein in the human diet. A billion people count on seafood for their primary source of protein, while countless towns and cities rely on the economic engine of fisheries to provide direct employment to some 200 million people. The global economy is predicated on cargo ships that move almost all internationally traded goods.

Despite the ocean covering over two thirds of the world's surface, humans have explored less than 5% of it. Generations of people thought and acted as though it was so vast as to be beyond human influence, an inexhaustible source of fish and adventure. The most recent scientific consensus, however, suggests that the ocean is highly vulnerable to cumulative human action, including fishing, resource extraction and pollution—effects that are exacerbated by climate change. An increasing number of citizens and policymakers fear that the rapidly deteriorating conditions of the oceans will profoundly reduce human welfare. Advocates for a

SARA TJOSSEM *is a Senior Lecturer at Columbia University in the School of International and Public Affairs. She wrote* The Journey to PICES: Scientific Cooperation in the North Pacific *(Alaska Sea Grant, 2005). Her research interests are the intersection of science and society, history of marine science and the development of environmental policy.*

71

holistic, unified marine policy warn of imminent global marine collapse, especially as climate change magnifies other long-standing threats. The global reach of oceans has made international maritime governance both critical and difficult to achieve. In order to understand what options exist for future ocean governance, it is necessary to assess the shift in mankind's relationship with the oceans and in turn, the implications for current resource management and governance initiatives underway around the world. Only renewed public attention to the vital role of the oceans will lead to their lasting future.

Growing scientific and popular understanding

Although the oceans have provided fish and access to new lands since prehistoric times, scientific exploration began only in the mid-19th century. Matthew Fontaine Maury—dubbed "Pathfinder of the Seas" for having developed a uniform method for recording currents and winds—published the first extensive book on oceanography in the 1850s. The 1870s voyage of the HMS *Challenger* produced the first systematic scientific explorations of the biological, physical and chemical marine environment. Its scientific results required 50 volumes that took almost a quarter

century to compile, and only touched upon the vast complexity of the oceans.

Scientific accounts were matched by an outpouring of popular stories to excite the layperson through a mix of adventure, science and natural history storytelling that built upon Americans' fascination with the myth of the Wild West. Some of these stories were pure scientific adventure, while others began to question what they saw as the arrogance of man's exploitation of the seas. By the 1950s, the biologist and writer Rachel Carson introduced a new generation of readers to the unfolding mysteries of the seas with her trilogy portraying ocean life from its shores to its surface and finally to its profound depths. Her love of the sea led her to question the wisdom of the exploitation of its riches before understanding the full consequences for the future of both ocean and mankind. The adventures of French marine biologist Jacques Cousteau and his crew brought the wonders of the deep into even more homes and inspired a new generation of marine adventurers and scientists. Popular and scientific research interest throughout the 1960s and 1970s helped a broad audience see the ocean as a wonderous frontier rather than a watery "desert."

In fact, at the 1964–65 New York World's Fair, the General Motors (GM)

Futurama exhibit envisioned that "mankind can make great future strides in every area of the globe if it exercises its full potential." The wild frontier of ocean exploration and exploitation promised such a future. In prose conjured up by GM's styling staff, the publicity brochure explained: "Three quarters of our earth lies beneath the cold still deeps of the sea. A water world in which we now can find abundance far beyond our dreams. Now we can farm and harvest a drifting, swimming, never ending nourishment; food enough to feed seven times the population of the earth. In aquacopters search the ocean floor to find, miles deep, vast fields of precious minerals and ores. And in the deepest trenches of the seas, study at first hand long hidden secrets of survival. Work easily the rich oil deposits of the continental shelves while trains of submarines transport materials and goods along the waterways of the under sea."

How have these aspirations been realized in the modern world, with a global population that has just exceeded seven billion people? An increase and intensification of ocean use, compounded by the development of new types of coastal and ocean activities, has led to increased user conflicts and loss of functional habitats. It is now known that the ocean plays a vital role in the global climate system, absorbing carbon dioxide (CO_2) from the atmosphere and producing oxygen. Increasing levels of greenhouse gases are bringing about changes in the ocean as rising sea levels and acidification are putting both marine ecosystems and coastal communities at risk. Effective ocean policy and management plans must take into account past and current uses and mitigate their impacts.

At the international level, the United Nations has been the forum where nations and intergovernmental organizations develop and monitor plans for the usage and conservation of the global ocean commons beyond the limits of national jurisdiction. Its efforts to bring order and stability to "the common heritage of mankind" produced a constitution for the seas, the UN Convention on the Law of the Sea (UNCLOS). Along

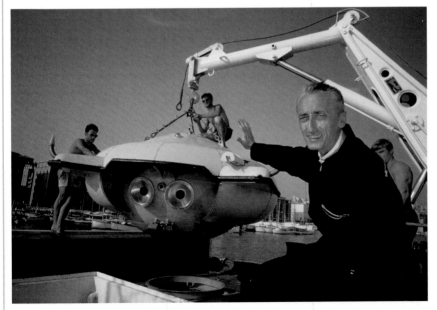

Jan. 1, 1960: Jacques Cousteau gestures at his latest underwater research vessel, the bathyscaph Calypso, *in Puerto Rico.* (THOMAS J. ABERCROMBIE/NATIONAL GEOGRAPHIC/GETTY IMAGES)

with protection of navigation rights and coastal state authority over offshore resources, one of the driving motivations for a treaty was the prospect of commercial seabed mining. Meanwhile, governments and nongovernmental organizations (NGOs) had developed a variety of regional and local initiatives for management inside their national jurisdictions.

Early resource management

Because the ocean is vital to national security and economic vitality, it has spawned both conflict and cooperation. International and local policy initiatives must grapple with an apparent "tragedy of the commons" condition, further complicated by the interaction between international governance—or collective action—and the protection of state sovereignty.

Perhaps the most instructive example of conflict and attempted cooperation on the seas is the management of living marine resources. Marine fish populations are notoriously difficult to assess because they can move from near shore to open ocean without regard for artificial political boundaries. Coastal and open ocean management influence each other in complex ways. Informal fisheries management has existed for hundreds of years, while formal, government-based attempts only started in the last century. Concern about fish stocks grew in Victorian times, as some near-shore fisheries were overfished, but it seemed inconceivable that open-sea fish stocks were vulnerable. The British scientist Thomas Henry Huxley famously held that the great sea fishes must be inexhaustible so it was unreasonable and unfair to try to regulate poor fishermen.

At first when a fishery failed, it was natural enough to suggest that the fish had moved elsewhere, or that ocean conditions had turned unfavorable, but the collapse of more and more fisheries prompted increased efforts at regulation. The number of bilateral and multilateral fisheries treaties proliferated over time as managing different species required different approaches. By the 1900s in Europe, growing concern over the condition of fish stocks in the North

August 1955: A fisherman knee-deep in water casts his net just off the shore at the fishing colony of Arnala, about 40 miles from Bombay. (FOX PHOTOS/GETTY IMAGES)

Sea combined with developing marine research produced the first international marine scientific organization in the world: the International Council for the Exploration of the Sea (ICES), which still produces and supports cutting-edge marine research and provides advice on fisheries management to its member nations and the 27 members of the European Union (EU). An analogous

regional organization, the North Pacific Marine Science Organization (PICES), now promotes and coordinates research for the far North Pacific, though without a fisheries management component.

Early management efforts tried to achieve "rational fishing," where both fish and fishermen would be managed together. The adoption of the strategy called maximum sustainable yield

Nova Scotia fishermen at sea off the Grand Banks of Newfoundland throw cod onto the ship. (PETER STACKPOLE//TIME LIFE PICTURES/GETTY IMAGES)

Collapse of Atlantic Cod

Atlantic cod stocks off the east coast of Newfoundland have been severely depleted since their collapse in 1992.

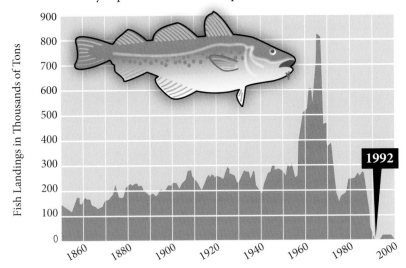

Fish Landings in Thousands of Tons

1992

SOURCE: Millennium Ecosystems Assessment

to estimate critical harvest points where the catch would be maximized and yet sustained—considering the benefits, but not the costs—of fishing. The theoretical construct of MSY gained popularity as an apparently simple, logical and scientific management tool for fish where no fish would be "wasted." One of its key assumptions was that fish and the ocean system are completely resilient and that stocks have surplus production. If a stock was overharvested, one just had to relax fishing pressure and the stock would recover, or as with salmon, help them along by building fish hatcheries. The MSY calculations did not require knowing the size and age of the fish, its reproductive status or its function in the ecosystem—factors that are now proving critical in trying to rebuild collapsed fisheries.

Current fisheries management depends on more nuanced stock assessments based on scientific survey and past catch information. While fisheries scientists formulate sustainable catch levels, fisheries managers are under constant sociopolitical pressure to allow greater harvests in order to generate short-term benefits of jobs and profits. The burden of proving harm falls on them, not the fishing industry. ∎

(MSY), developed in the early 1930s, however, quickly distracted scientists from this more comprehensive goal. The U.S. High Seas Fisheries Policy of 1949 established the goal of maximum production of food from the sea using MSY, and since then, the concept has become embedded in law and policy. It

reflects a utilitarian philosophy familiar to the Progressive Era (the 1890s through the 1920s), in which resources are to be used and that not to harvest them is wasteful. The logic was that thinning out a fish population through fishing would make more prey available to the remaining fish. It attempted

Creating a law of the sea

AFTER WORLD WAR II, efforts got underway to reach an international agreement on the use of ocean resources. The 17th-century principle of "freedom of the seas" limited national rights and jurisdiction to a narrow coastal strip, while the remainder of the seas was free to all. The oceans proved to be an early canvas for international policies on access to fisheries, ocean dumping and pollution, and oil and gas rights.

By the 20th century, rapid technological advancements had opened new ways to exploit offshore resources, with offshore oil production moving to increasingly deeper waters and long-distance fishing fleets harvesting unprecedented tons of fish, while transport ships and oil tankers increased the hazards of pollution. In an effort to de-

crease conflict over competing claims, the UN General Assembly (UNGA) resolved to create a common law of the sea that would determine the limits of coastal state authority and promote greater use and better management of ocean resources in both territorial and high seas. (See Box on p. 75.)

The first attempt to codify international law for the seas failed to determine a new breadth for territorial waters, but ensured the principle of freedom of fishing, which encouraged the development of long-distance industrialized fishing fleets. In 1954 the British stern freezer trawler *Fairtry* introduced to the Grand Banks off Newfoundland a new era of large vessels equipped with the latest technology for unprecedented hauls of fish. Seven years later

the first Soviet vessels appeared there, quickly growing to a fleet of over 100 ships. The post-World War II (WWII) development of such factory ships that could stay for months at sea with new, more powerful equipment to find and harvest fish signaled an intensified level of efficiency and destruction as both targeted and "incidental" fish were caught. When fisheries collapsed, people saw a classic example of a tragedy of the commons; too many boats chasing too few fish.

After an inconclusive second conference in 1960, the third UN Conference on the Law of the Sea (UNCLOS III, 1973–82) labored for nine years to write a comprehensive treaty for the oceans that would address the contentious issues of resources, sovereignty and su-

Evolution of the 'law of the sea'

FOLLOWING WORLD WAR II, advances in technology for offshore oil development and ocean fishing led to national claims over marine resources and territory beyond the traditional three-mile territorial sea. With the Truman Declaration in 1945, the U.S. led the way by announcing a unilateral right to resources on its continental shelf. Other states soon followed, claiming fisheries zones of 4 to 200 miles. These competing claims posed a serious threat to military and civilian freedom of navigation, open seas fishing and other maritime activities.

In the early 1950s, the International Law Commission, established by the UNGA in 1948, attempted to promote the codification of these new claims into international law. In 1958, four conventions were produced, addressing the territorial sea, fisheries, the continental shelf and the high seas. The conventions defined rights and duties, but failed to reach agreement on the outer boundaries of national authority over territorial waters, fisheries or the ocean floor. A second conference in 1960 was unable to resolve these same issues.

In the 1960s a new approach was taken: instead of negotiating separate treaties, the goal was a comprehensive convention on the ocean that could address the essential security interests of all nations and accommodate their most important economic, environmental and scientific concerns. Championed by the U.S. and the then-U.S.S.R., the goal was also to obtain universal ratification of the convention in order to manage future ocean issues through a peaceful process involving all nations.

After years of painstaking negotiations, UNCLOS was completed in 1982. It achieved almost all of the ambitious objectives set for it. It provided protection for navigational freedoms while establishing a 200-mile EEZ in which coastal states managed all economic development; developed a new set of provisions governing the marine environment and scientific research; and created a regime to manage the exploitation of minerals of the seafloor beyond the limits of national jurisdiction.

It was this last issue—deep seabed minerals—however, that derailed the final agreement. The Reagan Administration (1981–89) conducted a thorough review of the draft convention as it stood in early 1981. The U.S. review found the regime for deep seabed minerals—which had been negotiated during the turmoil of decolonization and ideological disputes between developing countries and the industrialized world—to be unacceptable. Before the final negotiations began, Reagan laid out six criteria, all related to the seabed minerals regime, that were necessary in order to make the convention acceptable to the U.S. In the final version, these criteria were not met, so the U.S. opposed the adoption of the convention and pressured its allies not to sign it. President Reagan did declare in 1983 that the U.S. would abide by all parts of UNCLOS except for the deep seabed mining provisions.

In 1990, as the number of ratifications slowly rose toward the 60 needed to bring the convention into force, developing states and industrialized allies prevailed on the U.S. to seek a modification of UNCLOS that would meet all six of Reagan's criteria. This effort proved successful, and in 1994 the Agreement Relating to the Implementation of Part XI of the UN Convention on the Law of the Sea that modified the implementation of the seabed provisions along with the rest of the convention was signed by President Bill Clinton. The Agreement and the Convention were then sent to the U.S. Senate for its advice and consent, where both have languished ever since, despite strong support from every President and Cabinet, all of the Navy and Coast Guard leadership, heads of shipping, energy, fishing and telecommunications industries, and the environment and conservation community. However, partisan politics and other business deemed more pressing than the oceans have prevented the convention from being debated by the full Senate. ■

perpower rivalry. In the meantime, the U.S. enacted the Magnuson-Stevens Act in 1976, which established eight regional councils made up of commercial and sport fishers along with agency staff to manage stocks. Their overarching goal was to achieve optimal yields from fisheries while restoring depleted stocks, with the right to determine how many fish could be caught, by whom and with what gear. They had good success at rebuilding stocks where regulations were faithfully enforced, but that was difficult and expensive to do. The political pressure to maintain the livelihoods of fishing communities and the fishing industry could overwhelm conservation ideals. In 2011 the National Marine Fisheries Service reported to Congress that of the 197 stocks monitored for overfishing, 39% of them were subject to overfishing or clearly overfished.

UNCLOS III finally came into force in 1994. A veritable "constitution for the ocean," it provides a legal framework within which all legal ocean activities must operate, defining maritime zones, such as the 200-mile exclusive economic zone (EEZ) that gives coastal states exclusive rights to manage and share living and nonliving ocean resources in this space while ensuring freedom of scientific research. That management provision required that nations protect stocks from overexploitation and that they either harvest their entire allowable catch or give access to the "surplus" to other countries, an arrangement that some scientists have argued fosters mandated overfishing.

By 1992, international cooperation had also led to a successful ban on large-scale drift-net fishing in international waters. This fishing method

high seas in some areas so completely that coastal stocks declined. Smaller drift nets are still used in EEZs around the world, however, and illegal fishing persists. To date, 161 countries and the EU have signed and ratified UNCLOS while only 35 nations, including the U.S., Libya and North Korea, and many landlocked states in Asia and Africa, have yet to do so. The U.S. is the only major maritime country that has failed to ratify the convention. It is a signal achievement for international law to govern the oceans, however, it ultimately relies on national legislatures and regional treaty organizations to implement and oversee its provisions. While this allows for national autonomy, it means that individual nations must be willing to view action on the oceans as a priority. ∎

Competing uses for ocean resources

HUMANS HAVE LONG used the ocean to provide food, energy, transportation and waste disposal while weaving it into social and cultural life. The most recent excitement has been over the potential for energy and food generation, including possible offshore wind farms up and down the north- and mid-Atlantic coast, and fish farms off the coast of Chile. As technology allows new and greater exploitation of the ocean's resources, ongoing challenges surrounding jurisdictions, governance and sustainability—in addition to the will to implement and execute any policy decisions—will continue to confront policymakers around the world

Mining and drilling

In the 1970s, the eccentric billionaire Howard Hughes was credited with fostering excitement over the potential riches of manganese nodules plucked from the ocean floor, though his ship, the *Hughes Glomar Explorer,* was never meant for that use (it was used for the secret retrieval of a sunken Soviet submarine). Other attempts in the 1970s and early 1980s to mine the sea floor for manganese nodules did not result in commercial operations since growth in demand slowed as new land-based sources came on line, but they nevertheless produced both interest and the techniques for later exploration of other geologic formations like hydrothermal vents. The first underwater geyser was discovered in 1977 by oceanographers, and was seen as a geological curiosity. It is now known that vents influence ocean chemistry, temperature and circulation, and play host to unique species of tubeworms, clams, shrimp and bacteria. Since these first observations, commercial firms have intensified their search for vents with the realization that vents accrete dense and pure mineral deposits on their flanks in potentially commercial amounts. The particularly harsh conditions of low light and oxygen combined with extreme temperatures may also provide building blocks for new industrial processes and products derived from this bacterial action, similar to what has occurred in better-known terrestrial hot springs.

Advances in marine geology and deep ocean technology have opened up depths previously unattainable. In the past few years, deep-sea mining firms from Canada, Australia, Russia and China have intensified their interest in exploiting copper, gold, silver, lead and zinc in deepwater areas around the world, often off small island nations like Papua New Guinea. In some cases, the deep-sea robotics now used by the offshore oil and gas industry has prompted mining interests to see water as an easier barrier to overcome than an equivalent amount of rock. That access comes with drawbacks, however. Hydraulic pumping increases nutrients in deepwater areas and potentially produces harmful algal blooms, while the sediments stirred up will certainly interfere with or kill filter-feeding organisms that are a critical component of marine ecosystems. More than land-based mining, these pollutants are likely to spread via currents through large areas of water.

In further mining developments, the International Seabed Authority (ISA), established under UNCLOS, regulates mining in international waters beyond a coastal country's EEZ. In its 17-year existence, the ISA has issued 12 contracts for exploration, recently deciding in favor of allowing China to explore for

Aug. 29, 1975: The Glomar Explorer *is seen off the coast of Catalina Island, CA. In August 1974 the ship fished a sunken Soviet nuclear-armed submarine out of the Pacific Ocean.* (AP PHOTO/FILE)

deep-sea minerals in the Indian Ocean. All this economic interest in mining the sea floor has raised concern among small island nations, legal experts, scientists and environmentalists about the ecosystem effects because there are few international standards and safeguards. The island nations with jurisdiction over rich deposits have neither guidelines nor sufficient information to balance environmental interests against the potential income from selling mineral concessions.

Destructive fisheries practices

There is growing concern about how the ecosystem effects of mineral extraction add to the long-standing degradation of fish stocks and habitat. Recent research suggests that the indirect effects of fishing can have more important consequences for ecosystem structure and dynamics than the direct loss of target fish. Fragile deep-sea habitats can take centuries to grow and yet can be quickly destroyed by dredging or bottom trawling. Bottom trawling drags large nets weighted with chains across the seabed to catch long-lived ground fish species such as cod, sole and rockfish. Using bottom trawls has been likened to clear-cutting a forest because the gear scrapes clear habitats such as rocky ledges and coral gardens that are vital habitats for biodiversity. Repeated trawling and dredging is not sustainable because it seriously decreases sea floor productivity.

The management of deep-sea fishery methods used beyond national jurisdictions has been under debate for a decade at the UN. A resolution adopted in 2004 called for states either individually or through regional fisheries management organizations to act to end destructive practices like bottom trawling. A report just published in September 2011 found, however, that five years after the UNGA passed the first resolution outlining how countries should protect vulnerable habitats and biodiversity, many nations have yet to act on their commitments to end the practice. One critical issue is that researchers do not know the most fundamental biological characteristics and status of most target and by-catch spe-

Feb. 27, 2007: A view of fish seized at the port of Abidjan, Côte d'Ivoire, from two Chinese ships (seen in the background), which were intercepted using bottom trawling in disregard of national fishing laws. (KAMBOU SIA/AFP/GETTY IMAGES)

cies. It is becoming increasingly clear that at least some species are extremely long-lived with low reproductive rates, making them highly vulnerable to unsustainable harvesting practices.

Jurisdiction over polar use

The South and North Poles have long intrigued explorers and played a part in strategic interests. The Polar regions are now known to be quite fragile ecosystems, particularly affected by adverse effects of climate change. During the cold war (1945–91), the race to explore and lay claim to the continent and its potential riches prompted the successful negotiation of the Antarctic Treaty of 1961, which banned mineral mining indefinitely and reserved the region for peaceful uses such as scientific research, and more recently, tourism. Its harsh conditions are speculated to have helped treaty negotiations as the costs of exploration were so high that it was a relief to avoid such expenditures. No such treaty was sought for the Arctic, however, and now as the distribution and formation of sea ice changes, mining and energy companies eagerly anticipate the mineral riches unlocked from the ocean floor and the newly accessible Arctic coast.

The Arctic may hold as much as a quarter of the world's remaining oil and gas reserves, and neighboring countries are eagerly eyeing its potential riches while fearing competing territorial claims. In 2007 Russia sent a submarine to the Arctic to plant its flag on the sea floor before taking samples that it hoped would show that the underwater Lomonosov Ridge is an extension of the Siberian continental shelf, thus putting its resources under Russian jurisdiction. The sea off Russia is also becoming less

Dec. 13, 2006: An Adelie penguin leaps above a crack in the sea ice off the penguin colony at Cape Royds on Ross Island, Antarctica. Researchers say rising temperatures are melting and thinning the seasonal Antarctic pack ice. (CHRIS WALKER/CHICAGO TRIBUNE/MCT/GETTY IMAGES)

Fishing on land?

OFTEN WHEN PEOPLE THINK about overfishing they think about the dramatic collapse of once-abundant fisheries like the cod off of Georges Bank, or sardines off the California coast. A more unusual story of systems linkage comes from Ghana, where the EU's taste for West African seafood may be unintentionally causing the decimation of "charismatic" wildlife such as hippos, antelopes, monkeys, lions and leopards. What mechanism can possibly connect eating fish in Europe with the dramatic loss of local wildlife? A few years back, environmental scientist Justin Brashares and colleagues used data from six Ghanaian nature reserves to document how the amount of bushmeat—illegally hunted wild game—for sale in local markets rose in concert with the decline in regional fish supplies. It turns out that the local people rely primarily on fish for their protein, and when they cannot get their protein from fish, they turn to bushmeat for survival. Ghana's formerly thriving local fishing industry has declined simultaneously with a 10-fold increase in regional fish harvests by large foreign and domestic fleets. Financial subsidies to the EU fleet had risen from around $6 million in 1981 to more than $350 million 20 years later, and had allowed them to buy rights to access African waters with unintended knock-on effects. The problem is further exacerbated by illegal fishing operations. The displacement pattern from fish to wildlife is likely true not just for Ghana, but many other developing countries around the world. The phenomenon is in some ways analogous to the recent "land grab" occurring as wealthier countries like Saudi Arabia, China and India lease prime agricultural land from underdeveloped countries such as Ethiopia and Tanzania, decreasing access to that resource by local people. ∎

Mar. 26, 2007: Fishermen work at the fishing port of Elmina on the Cape Coast, Ghana. (LUC GNAGO/REUTERS/CORBIS)

ice-bound, and in August 2011, *The Wall Street Journal* reported that ExxonMobil had beaten out BP for a deal with the Russian-state owned oil company Rosneft to explore for oil north of Siberia in the Kara Sea.

The Arctic differs from the Antarctic in that it is a maritime domain for which a comprehensive treaty, UNCLOS, is already in place. The Arctic coastal states have agreed to resolve all disputes in accordance with the law of the sea and they respect the right of coastal states to establish environmental regulations over their EEZs in the Arctic.

While there is no top-down regulatory regime for the Arctic, in 1996, the Arctic states (Canada, Denmark, Finland, Iceland, Norway, Russia, Sweden and the U.S.) and the region's native peoples created a high-level forum, the

Arctic Council, for discussion of Arctic issues. Mindful of the lessons after the 2010 Deepwater Horizon explosion and blowout in the Gulf of Mexico, the council began discussions for a code of practice and operational guidelines for oil development in the Arctic Ocean.

In an assessment of the lessons to be learned from the accident, the National Commission on the BP Oil Spill noted that there must be an "unbending commitment to safety by government and industry" before moving forward in the Gulf of Mexico or new U.S. frontiers. In particular, the commission noted the need for better scientific information on the Arctic ecosystem for more informed decisionmaking with respect to oil and gas exploration and development.

In March 2008, almost two years before the BP oil spill, the executive body

of the European Commission acknowledged "environmental changes are altering the geostrategic dynamics of the Arctic with potential consequences for international stability and European security interests." It issued a paper that constituted "a first step towards an EU Arctic policy" by detailing Europe's interests in the region's natural resources, potential shipping routes, security concerns and environmental perils. Its three main policy objectives are to protect and preserve the area while promoting sustainable use of resources and improving multilateral governance under the umbrella of an Integrated Maritime Policy for the EU.

In 2009, the Bush Administration (2001–2009) issued a presidential directive, laying out the initial goals for U.S. policy toward the Arctic. Of all

On left: Fish swimming around pink gorgonian coral on a reef off Papua New Guinea. (GEORGETTE DOUWMA/PHOTO RESEARCHERS) *On right, Jan. 23, 2006: On right: Dr. Paul Marshall from the Great Barrier Reef marine park photographs bleached coral heads off the Keppel Islands, Brisbane, Australia.* (OVE HOEGH-GUIDBERG/AFP/GETTY IMAGES)

the Arctic states, Russia has taken the most significant actions, including establishment of Arctic land and marine conservation areas, cleaning up oil and gas dumps, and making initial efforts to clean up nuclear waste sites left over from the cold war as part of a larger national plan for development of its Arctic zone.

Growing threats to reef systems

Although humans have found increasing uses for the ocean's resources, a growing list of threats to marine systems is pushing the world's oceans toward what some fear is a paroxysm of extinctions unrivaled for millions of years. Healthy coral reefs are some of the most economically valuable ecosystems on earth, providing food for some 500 million people, protecting coastlines from storm damage, and creating income from fishing, recreation and tourism. They are also of particular cultural importance to small island nations whose very land is composed of coral skeletons. One estimate of the value of coral ecosystem services came to nearly $30 billion per year. Nevertheless, one fifth of the world's coral reefs—nurseries for tropical reef fish— are effectively lost from damage such as coral bleaching and show little prospect for recovery, while another 15% are seriously threatened with loss within the next 10–20 years. The rates of fish depletion, loss of corals, open-water "dead zones" and toxic algal blooms have exceeded even the worst-case scenarios of just four

years earlier, and their combined effects are even more alarming. A number of researchers conclude that scientists and the public have underestimated the overall risks to a functioning oceanic system.

Climate change

Climate change has been called a "threats multiplier" for any existing environmental and social condition, whether it is changes in weather patterns, shifts in ocean temperatures or even the stability of regional political relations. A recent international workshop convened by the International Program on the State of the Oceans found

Mar. 17, 2007: In this aerial image, Tuvalu's capital Funafuti is seen, surrounded by the rising Pacific Ocean. (ASAHI SHIMBUN PREMIUM/GETTY IMAGES)

global climate change to be the greatest threat to the continued functioning of the ocean. The effects of climate change can appear as acidification from increased CO_2 emissions, rising sea levels, changing patterns of currents, and increasing intensity and frequency of extreme events like hurricanes. Although scientists are wary of saying rising sea levels are permanent given their long-term variability, a recent paper finds that sea-level rise has accelerated since the early 1990s, although it has been increasing since the 19th century. These recently recognized effects join earlier threats to marine wildlife such as overfishing, seabed damage and loss of biodiversity, polluted runoff of toxic substances, heavy metals, excess nutrients and pathogens, noise pollution and ubiquitous plastics—adding up to what some have called "the Perfect Storm."

Climate change also is predicted to have profound effects on ocean currents. Ocean currents are driven not only by wind and tides, but also by differences in water density. Air temperatures in the Arctic have been increasing at twice the global average, and its sea ice has been rapidly fragmenting and shrinking. American climate scientist Wally Broecker is best known for his work in assessing the role of oceans in both gradual and abrupt climate change. He developed and popularized the idea of a global "conveyor belt" linking the circulation of the global ocean. Widespread melting of ice and changing rain patterns could create a large layer of freshwater that could slow or alter the path of this ocean conveyor belt, something that has happened in the deep past. If that were to happen again, it would likely have dramatic "knock-on effects" contributing to changes in regional weather patterns, particularly precipitation, thus driving agricultural productivity and vegetation shifts that would affect the current viability of agricultural crops around the world—similar to what oceanic regime shifts like the warmth of El Niño and the cooling of La Niña do.

Although developed countries have historically produced the most greenhouse gases, the effects of climate change will be unevenly distributed, being first felt in low-lying areas prone to inundation. Least developed and small island developing states (SIDS) are particularly vulnerable. For example, climate projections suggest that Tuvalu, a tiny archipelago of nine South Pacific islands, could be unlivable within 50 years. Extreme weather has become

more frequent, and so its low-lying land has suffered from repeated saltwater flooding while its fisheries have also declined due in part to increasing average water temperatures. The UN has called for helping SIDS mitigate and adapt by planting mangrove barriers and more salt-tolerant crops, but these efforts cannot hold back any significant rises in water levels. Small island nations are at risk from collective inaction on climate change mitigation. ■

Policy options

THE FEARED COLLAPSE of ocean ecosystems from synergistic threats is raising calls for coordinated and concerted efforts by governments in their national waters and on the high seas to manage resource rights, enforce sustainable fisheries, reduce pollution and decrease climate change. While UNCLOS serves as a foundational milestone for international maritime governance, addressing the multitude of existing and new challenges that confront the oceans will require the persistent attention of stakeholders and policymakers, from consumers and communities to national and international bodies.

UNCLOS: Yes or No?

Although the U.S. provided crucial leadership in the negotiation of UNCLOS,

the U.S. has yet to formally accede to the convention, which requires a two-thirds majority vote in the U.S. Senate. In 2012, the Obama Administration and the Senate leadership will need to decide whether to make a concerted effort to bring the convention to a vote in the full Senate, a vote that will only happen if leaders are certain they have the 67 votes required for "advice and consent."

A diverse array of stakeholders are in favor of accession for various reasons. For instance, the U.S. Navy is concerned that as a nonparty, the U.S. has lost its leadership role in protecting the security and naval mobility rights detailed in the convention. If the U.S. joined the convention, there would be additional channels for diplomatic co-

operation rather than resorting to sending ships to demonstrate U.S. objections to excessive maritime claims.

U.S. industry worries that it cannot get internationally recognized rights to exploit mineral resources beyond the EEZ and will lose development opportunities and high-tech jobs to foreign competitors if the U.S. fails to accede to the convention. The U.S. ocean mining industry has been stalled for more than a decade, while currently, 12 foreign operations involving 14 nations have mine sites recognized under the convention. Conservation and environmental groups seek reestablishment of U.S. leadership on conservation issues, which has eroded as the U.S. remains outside of the international ocean regime.

Globally, the U.S. pursuit of maritime partnerships to combat piracy and the transport of weapons of mass destruction and efforts toward cooperation in humanitarian and disaster response has been deterred by its outsider status. For example, the attempt by the U.S. to rely on UNCLOS to limit China's expansive goals in the South China Sea is seriously undercut by its own failure to join the convention.

Domestic opponents no longer raise President Reagan's concerns about access to deep seabed minerals, although contemporary objections to the convention fall broadly into four groups. One group advocates autonomy of U.S. military activities unrestrained by international law. A second opposes restraints on U.S. actions that result from membership in international organizations, including the UN. A third segment generally opposes regulation of industry and views the international regime es-

Sept. 10, 2007: UN Secretary General Ban Ki-Moon chats with scientists in Torres del Paine, Patagonia, Chile, one of the stops in his Latin America tour aimed at investigating global warming. (RODRIGO ARANGUA/AFP/GETTY IMAGES)

tablished by the LOS Convention as a mechanism for rule-making on the international level, particularly in areas such as marine environmental protection. Finally, there are those who are advocates for private property rights on land, and see the convention as a threat to private rights in both offshore and inland waters.

In the past, arguments for accession have emphasized the national security benefits in joining the convention, with only limited attempts to appeal to business or conservation groups and no attention to the general public. Since 1994, the opposition has relied on three main methods: using procedural mechanisms to slow progress, mobilizing conservative groups not normally associated with security issues (such as "family values" groups) to pressure uncommitted senators, and emotional outreach to grassroots networks that mobilize extensive e-mail and letter campaigns to senators. For the only major sea power remaining outside the convention, 2012 will be a crucial year in determining whether the U.S. will pursue its maritime interests through international engagement based on a collaborative legal framework, or whether it will adopt a unilateral approach that rejects external limits placed upon U.S. national sovereignty.

A new domestic oceans policy for the U.S.?

In the early 2000s, the U.S. began to formally reexamine its ocean policy, a review of which had not officially taken place since 1969. Congress passed the Oceans Act of 2000 to create the U.S. Commission on Ocean Policy (the Watkins Commission), which released a series of recommendations. At the same time, the privately funded Pew Oceans Commission also published its report, "America's Living Oceans: Charting a Course for Sea Change." Both commissions strongly advocated early U.S. accession to the Law of the Sea Convention. After the two commissions disbanded, the members of each joined forces to form the Joint Ocean Commission Initiative, a bipartisan group with the objective of fostering improved ocean policy, management, science and

Circa 1990: Loading halibut in Alaska . (JEAN-ERICK PASQUIER/GAMMA-RAPHO/GETTY IMAGES)

funding in the face of climate change, energy security and a struggling economy.

Last year, President Obama signed Executive Order 13547, establishing a national policy for the Stewardship of the Ocean, Our Coasts and the Great Lakes. This new policy is the realization of one of the key recommendations urged by the Joint Ocean Commission Initiative. It is designed to address the lack of coordination within the federal government and among federal, state and local management bodies by moving to a regionally based planning process. Implementation of the new policy is to be based on a scientific, comprehensive ecosystem approach to ocean conservation and management. More significantly, decisionmaking is to be guided by a "precautionary approach" as reflected in the Rio Declaration of 1992, which states that "[w]here there are threats of serious or irreversible damage, lack of full scientific certainty shall not be used as a reason for postponing cost-effective measures to prevent environmental degradation."

As a result of these features, and others, the new initiative has its proponents and its opponents. Those in support generally note the need for far greater coordination of ocean policy at all levels of governments in the U.S. federal system and better and more science-based decisionmaking with respect to current and future uses of ocean space. Those

strongly opposed fear it is simply more costly bureaucracy that will restrict long-standing ocean use, increase regulations and reduce jobs. Questions have also been raised about the President's authority to issue an executive order that is as encompassing as the one establishing the new national ocean policy. Regardless, the new policy includes a clear and unambiguous statement about the Obama Administration's intent to support accession to UNCLOS.

Mar. 9, 2011: A tractor dumps dead fish into a trash bin as workers and volunteers continue to clean up millions of dead sardines for a second day in King Harbor, Redondo Beach, CA (DAVID MCNEW/GETTY IMAGES)

New tools for ocean marine management

In addition to the UNCLOS framework, the complexity of the oceans calls for a multipronged approach to threats, and some of the more innovative ideas for both top-down and bottom-up governance are coming from fisheries because they directly impact so many people. The increasing number of overfished populations suggests that fisheries management has failed to achieve a principal goal of sustainability, in part due to constant sociopolitical pressure for greater harvests. Providing incentives for fishers to change their behavior has proven helpful, but may not be enough in the face of climate change.

Abolish government subsidies for fishing

Government subsidies for fishing fleets artificially increase their profitability despite declining fish stocks. Given the asymmetry in economies, industrialized nations can usually negotiate very favorable fishing license agreements with poor countries. The agreements typically give a set number of boats access to fishing grounds for a specified time with no limits on the catch. Reductions or cutting of subsidies tends to decrease both the number of trawlers and the distance they can afford to travel, thus reducing the capacity of global fishing fleets and their impact on local fisheries.

Individual fishing quotas or catch shares

In many fisheries, like the Alaskan halibut fishery, regulators closed the fishing season when the catch reached the harvest target for the year. Because the fastest fishermen caught the most fish, it encouraged them to invest in faster and faster boats that forced shorter and shorter seasons. Those races, or "derbies," produced seasons only a few days or hours long. The practice threatened both human safety and livelihoods as fishers went out regardless of the weather and flooded the markets with their catch. Under individual fishing quotas (IFQs) or individual transferable quotas (ITQs), individual fishers are al-

located a share of the total catch for the whole year, so they can choose when to fish, spread their catch over more time and thus get better prices. ITQs can be bought and sold, and the criticism has been that it has raised the cost of entering the fishery. Although not a panacea, as a conservation tool it has worked well in New Zealand and Australia.

Ecosystem approach to sustainable fisheries

The state of global fisheries is difficult to assess because the best available information is about what is harvested rather than whole-system conditions. Under UNCLOS, control over ocean resources has been divided by geographic boundaries that simply cannot reflect the complexity of organisms in nature. Recent analysis of catch statistics from around the world suggest that fishing may be changing the very structure of food webs from large piscivorous fishes to smaller invertebrates and planktivorous fishes. Small, lower-value schooling fish like anchovies make up more and more of catches, and increased jellyfish swarms may be associated with global change.

Canadian marine scientist Boris Worm and his colleagues analyzed fish harvest results from around the world and found 63% of fish stocks need rebuilding. Looking more closely at 10 well-studied ecosystems, they found that exploitation rates for half of them have dropped to a point of MSY. They suggest modifying MSY so that it can achieve high yields while maintaining multiple rather than single species.

A flexible combination of fisheries management tools such as catch restrictions, modified fishing gear and closed areas will provide the best chance to rebuild fisheries. This multifaceted approach is what some are calling an ecosystem approach, where whole communities are managed.

Figuring out what constitutes ecosystem management is being hotly debated, however. The Gulf of Maine Census of Marine Life is a pilot project for this type of management. Ecosystems management proposals often call

for abolishing distorting government subsidies, establishing new incentives for sustainable practices and creating more zones for protecting resources.

Marine protected areas and reserves

The 1992 Convention on Biological Diversity (CBD) is the flagship international convention for promoting international cooperation to protect the broad diversity of life on the planet. The convention states that biological diversity is "a common concern of humankind" and argues for using the precautionary principle in the face of biodiversity loss. The U.S. has signed but not ratified the treaty due to its concern over intellectual property rights since the CBD calls for the fair and equitable sharing of benefits arising from genetic resources. The CBD has a goal of putting 10% of the world's marine areas under Marine Protected Areas (MPA) designation by 2020. Currently, however, less than 0.5% of the ocean's waters have some level of natural resource protection, and most of these areas are tiny. Few have the more restrictive marine reserves designation of "no-take" zones, a designation somewhat equivalent to U.S. wilderness areas. These zones serve as safe havens for spawning fish, but are susceptible to illegal fishing and the effects of climate change. Slightly more than 3% of U.S. territorial waters are protected as marine reserves, most in one area off the northwestern Hawaiian Islands.

Shaping consumer demand

Most fish management has focused on regulating the supply of fish, but demand-side efforts are beginning to grow under the logic that increased consumer demand for more sustainable fisheries products will lead to better practices as fishers vie for the premium price that gives them incentive to keep stocks at healthy levels. One approach is through community-supported sustainable fishery programs that work like similar institutions in agriculture. Once a person signs up for a subscription, he receives

On left, Mar. 26, 2008: A fish farm near Puerto Montt, Chile, owned by Marine Harvest, a Norwegian company that is the largest producer of farm-raised salmon. (JOAO PINA/THE NEW YORK TIMES/REDUX). On right, Sept. 10, 2011: Shaw's Supermarkets, a grocery chain in New England, launches an aggressive sustainable seafood program, highlighted by the new availability of products certified by the Marine Stewardship Council (MSC). (SUZANNE KREITER/THE BOSTON GLOBE/GETTY IMAGES)

harvest from boats that are part of the conservation program. The only drawback is that participants have to live in the area to be able to pick up the "produce." A second, complementary approach is certification of fisheries. The Marine Stewardship Council (MSC), a product of collaboration between the World Wildlife Fund and businesses, was created in 1997 to certify and label wild fisheries as sustainable, and thus reward sustainable practices with premium prices. The "blue label" should indicate that the fishery operates in an environmentally responsible way. As of 2010, more than 1,600 retailers, restaurants and processors were trading MSC-labeled fish around the world. Aquaculture operations are served by the Aquaculture Certification Council (ACC), which is oriented toward buyers rather than end consumers. The giant chain Walmart reported that as of 2011, 73% of its fish products in North America came from either MSC- or ACC-certified operations.

Improved governance at the local level

For many decades, the "tragedy of the commons" was approached through top-down state control or privatization. Work in the last two decades, like that of Nobel laureate economist Elinor Ostrom and others, has suggested a third way—how groups can avoid the "tragedy of the commons" by managing resources themselves. These self-organized enterprises share

in short-term sacrifices of profit for the long-term rewards of sustainable stewardship. For example, over 200 co-managed fisheries exist worldwide, ranging from tiny artisanal cooperatives to the billion-dollar pollock fishery in the Bering Sea. A strong, trusted community leader is one of the most critical components of successful management, particularly where government control is not trusted or possible. These co-management arrangements can work in concert with other tools such as marine protected reserves.

A global approach

Marine policymakers are increasingly turning their attention to the edge of the sea for answers on how to sustain the oceans. The majority of the ocean's pollution comes from land-based human activity, and half of the world's population lives within 60 miles of a coast. The increased vulnerability of those people to climate change may be the policy window necessary to produce a unified oceans policy. UNCLOS may purport to establish a strong and robust international oceans policy, but that aspiration must be matched by vigorous commitments of its member nations. Advocates for a unified oceans policy hope that the developing ocean crisis will make that cooperation in both name and deed a reality.

How oceans should be governed to balance protection of resources necessary for human livelihoods—from food to fuels—will continue to be an ongoing challenge for policymakers, resource

industries, conservationists and artisanal fishers. The establishment of two ocean commissions in recent years in the U.S. and their similar findings of serious governance issues speaks volumes about the growing recognition of the need for governments to find that proper balance between ocean resource development and protection.

Policies can be divided into two categories: top-down approaches, whether at the international or national level, and bottom-up initiatives that begin with local communities concerned about their livelihoods and a sustainable future. The top-down approaches have often been focused on the production of resources, but recently the growth of consumer awareness and buying power suggests that ordinary people may have more influence than previously envisioned on the growth of sustainable resource use. An increase in co-management arrangements and organizations like the MSC suggest that bottom-up policy may integrate well within an international oceans framework provided by UNCLOS, though it is unclear whether these mostly small-scale efforts will be sufficient to stem unsustainable harvests. In light of technological advances, perhaps it is time to not only consider conforming to existing UN maritime resolutions, but also to explore new ways that may help us govern the use of ocean resources. ■

Opinion Ballots after page 32

discussion questions

1. What are the strategic considerations that should be incorporated into U.S. ocean policy? What is the role of the ocean in the global economy? How should conservation be approached? Where does the ocean fit into the national security and counterterror agenda? How does the ocean affect U.S. relations with its neighbors? How does the ocean figure into food security?

2. The U.S. has signed but not acceded to the Law of the Sea Treaty (UNCLOS) and recognizes it as codification of existing international law. Should the U.S. ratify UNCLOS? Would doing so be detrimental to economic or foreign policy interests?

3. What are the U.S. interests in the Arctic? How should the U.S. respond to Russian exploration? Is a treaty similar to the Antarctic Treaty feasible? How might competing claims to resources affect U.S. relations with Russia, Canada and other nations with sovereignty in the Arctic?

4. How is climate change affecting the oceans? How should the U.S. respond to the effects of global climate change? Is multilateral action by regional groups (such as the Arctic Council) more appropriate than wider international action (such as the UN)? Who should enforce climate change policy?

5. What are the goals of successful fisheries management? Consider the different methods proposed and attempted. Is local governance, as with the pollock fishery in the Bering Sea, most appropriate? What about quota systems? What about demand-side policy that would influence behavior of consumers of fish?

6. Rising sea levels and temperatures acutely affect island nations and nations with fish-heavy diets. How should the international community manage the seas? Should all countries bear responsibility equally? Should ocean management be led by countries that are more dependent on the ocean?

7. What is the best approach to conservation? Are agreements that protect single species appropriate? What about regulations governing methods such as bottom trawling? Is the solution the creation of marine protected areas (MPAs)?

suggested readings

Borgerson, Scott, **The National Interest and the Law of the Sea.** Council Special Report No. 46. New York, Council on Foreign Relations Press, 2009. 80 pp. Available free online at: <http://i.cfr.org/content/publications/attachments/LawoftheSea_CSR46.pdf>. This report examines the seaborne commerce and discusses the economic importance of the sea.

Emmerson, Charles, **The Future History of the Arctic.** New York, PublicAffairs, 2010. 448 pp. $28.95 (hardcover). Emmerson presents a comprehensive history of the Arctic and examines its legacy—and future—as an economic corridor and a source of political conflict and natural resources.

Finley, Carmel, **All the Fish in the Sea: Maximum Sustainable Yield and the Failure of Fisheries Management.** Chicago, University of Chicago Press, 2011. 224 pp. $35.00 (hardcover). This book traces U.S. policy on fisheries management in the 20th century and discusses the larger economic interests behind these policies.

Freestone, David, Barnes, Richard, and Ong, David, eds., **The Law of the Sea: Progress and Prospects**, 4th ed. 504 pp. $185.00 (hardcover). New York, Oxford University Press, 2006. This collection of essays provides a comprehensive, scholarly view of the Law of the Sea.

Howard, Roger, **Arctic Gold Rush: The New Race for Tomorrow's Natural Resources.** New York, Continuum, 2009. 272 pp. $27.95 (hardcover). This book discusses the implications of climate change on the Arctic and analyzes the international competition over exploiting the natural resources unlocked by the melting ice.

Kurlansky, Mark, **Cod: A Biography of the Fish that Changed the World**. New York, Penguin, 1998. 294 pages. $15.00 (paper). In this accessible volume, Kurlansky traces cod's prominent role in history from the Viking exploration of North America to the depleted fisheries of the present day.

Pauly, Daniel, and Maclean, Jay, **In a Perfect Ocean: The State of Fisheries and Ecosystems in the North Atlantic Ocean**. Washington, DC, Island Press, 2003. 208 pp. $32.50 (paper). Pauly and Maclean provide an original, scientific assessment—the first of its kind—of the status of fisheries in the North Atlantic.

Visit **WWW.GREATDECISIONS.ORG** *for quizzes, seasonal topic updates and other resources to further your understanding*

Indonesia:
prospects for prosperity
by James Castle

Mar. 17, 2011: Workers install steel reinforcement columns at the construction site of a high-rise office and residential towers in Jakarta. Indonesia has been one of the best-performing emerging economies. (ROMEO GACAD/AFP/GETTY IMAGES)

THE 1997 ASIAN FINANCIAL CRISIS devastated Indonesia, leading to economic collapse, rioting and ultimately the resignation of Suharto, Indonesia's president for 32 years. In the wake of the dramatic collapse of Suharto's authoritarian "New Order" government in May 1998, many Indonesians and members of the international community feared that the country would fragment into a failed state of epic proportions, not only destroying itself but also threatening the security and prosperity of its neighbors.

Instead, the country held together. The interim Habibie government that succeeded the Suharto administration initiated a critical reform process that helped stabilize the country and make recovery possible. Shortly after being sworn in, President B.J. Habibie unshackled the press, released political prisoners, removed restrictions on formation of political parties and announced that new elections would be held.

Although the puppet legislature had been reelected to a new five-year term just two months before Suharto fell, it quickly produced legislation in support of these dramatic

democratic reforms and declared elections would be held in 1999, four years earlier than required. Although many feared the worst, the June 1999 elections—with a full complement of international and local observers in attendance—proved to be free, fair and peaceful, unmarred by significant violence, coercion or voter fraud. During this same period, the powerful military peacefully accepted a major reduction of the dominant political, administrative and social roles it had assumed during the Suharto era.

These remarkable achievements set the stage for a flurry of economic and social reforms that enabled Indonesia

JAMES CASTLE *is the Chairman of CastleAsia and an adjunct professor at Johns Hopkins School of Advanced International Studies. Resident in Indonesia for over 30 years, he has advised in the establishment of many foreign investment projects and serves on the boards of several companies. He has consulted on numerous projects for governments and international agencies and is on the Advisory Board of the East-West Center.*

to return to a pattern of progress and growth that led to its inclusion in the Washington, D.C., summit of the Group of Twenty (G-20, leading world economies) in 2008, when it was the third-fastest-growing member.

Indeed, many are seeking clues to Indonesia's transition to a stable, prosperous democracy from rigid authoritarianism that might serve as guidelines for other predominantly Muslim countries

that are now trying to make a similar transition as the Arab Spring sweeps across the Middle East. Two of the most important keys to Indonesia's relatively peaceful transition were an aging dictator's willingness to leave the stage rather than fight to the death and a military willing to take a backseat to civilian forces.

Another important key was the fact that the Suharto era had delivered substantial economic progress during its

three decades in power. The educated, increasingly prosperous middle class and the prosperous business and technocratic elite that emerged from this economic success were key drivers in making democracy possible and the military willing to step back. Absent these conditions, Indonesia still offers a practical example of secular and sectarian organizations working together in a democratic framework. ∎

Transition to democracy

Feb. 27, 1967: Indonesian President Sukarno, left, surrenders his executive powers to General Suharto in Jakarta. (AP)

IF INDONESIA had not achieved political stability rapidly after the fall of Suharto, strong economic growth would have been impossible. The successful implementation of democratic elections was a key element in this process.

In the 1999 elections, although voting was not mandatory, 110 million out of 118 million registered voters went to the polls, a turnout of 93%. This turnout stands as a dramatic testament to the awareness of and commitment to the democratic process among all strata of Indonesian society and produced a national government that was recognized by all significant elements of society and the world community as the legitimate government of Indonesia.

The impressive success of Indonesia's rapid switch from authoritarian to

democratic government is even more noteworthy given the tremendous size and diversity of the country, which has the world's largest Muslim population, and encompasses up to 300 ethnic groups with distinct languages and traditions, dispersed over 6,000 inhabited islands that span the equator for over 3,200 miles, with widely diverse levels of educational and economic development.

National elections are currently held on a five-year cycle. Since the 1999 elections, Indonesia has held two more successful national elections that have also been noteworthy for the high voter turnout, the virtual lack of violence and the low number of cases involving electoral fraud or other antidemocratic behavior. In 2004, the country switched from indirect to direct presidential elec-

tion, with a limit of two five-year terms.

Popular retired general Susilo Bambang Yudhoyono won Indonesia's first direct presidential election in a run-off against the incumbent, Megawati Sukarnoputri, the daughter of Indonesia's legendary, charismatic "founding father" and first president, Sukarno. SBY, as Yudhoyono is popularly known, was reelected to a second and final term in 2009, winning over 60% of the vote in a first-round victory over Megawati again and the candidate from Golkar (the government party of the New Order), Jusuf Kalla, who was SBY's first term vice president.

Military yields power

Given how integral the military was to the success of Suharto's New Order and how much power and wealth individual officers derived from its structure, it is remarkable how readily the army yielded power to the civilian leadership when Suharto fell.

While the New Order was much more complex than the stereotypical military dictatorship that is often portrayed, the military was critical to the success of the regime at every step, suppressing left-wing opposition (1965–67), establishing law, order and stability (1967–78), being deeply involved in government administration throughout the entire period and, finally, abandoning Suharto in support of the transition to democratic rule as the New Order collapsed in 1998.

The Indonesian military has always seen itself as the single unifying force capable of holding the country together in the face of squabbling politicians and incompetent civilian leadership. This sentiment evolved into the doctrine of *dwi fungsi,* or "Dual Function," before Suharto came to power, but quickly became the organizational philosophy of his New Order regime. Simply put, because the officer corps was better trained, educated and disciplined than society at large, military officers should, for the good of society, share these abilities by holding both military and civilian positions.

While there is more than a little self-serving rationalization in this formulation, there have indeed been numerous occasions in Indonesian history when the competition among civilian political forces seemed to weaken the country and make sensible governance virtually impossible.

Along with its territorial command structure that places army divisions throughout the country, dwi fungsi formed the key element of central control over the sprawling archipelago because it justified filling traditionally civilian posts at all levels of government. Throughout the entire New Order era, most of the provincial governors and many lower level "civilian" provincial and local officials were military officers. It paralleled the division command structure and embedded the military deeply into every aspect of Indonesian life.

As with the civil service, the police have historically been and remain a national organization in the employ and under the control of the central government. There are no local or provincial police forces. All security and law enforcement personnel remain under the ultimate control of the national leadership.

This strong central structure is the result of a concentrated effort to deal with the greatest fear of the Indonesian state: the divisive forces, real and imagined, that have troubled this sprawling, ethnically diverse archipelagic nation throughout its history.

After the fall

In 1998, during the final days of the New Order, there was a power struggle between the commander in chief at the time, Wiranto, and his main rival, Kopassus (special forces) commander and

May 21, 1998: Indonesian President Suharto, left, announces his resignation. After Suharto ended his 32-year autocratic rule of Indonesia, Vice President Baharuddin Jusuf Habibie, at right, was immediately sworn in as the new president. (CHARLES DHARAPAK/AP)

Suharto son-in-law, Prabowo Subianto. Wiranto (along with his chief of staff for sociopolitical affairs, SBY) supported a transfer of power to civilian rule, while Prabowo sought the imposition of martial law. The struggle was won by Wiranto. Prabowo was charged with human rights abuses and discharged from the service, but he was not imprisoned.

Because Wiranto and his supporters had concluded in early 1998 that the aging Suharto's position was ultimately untenable, they actively sought cooperation with civilian forces. Prabowo led the hard-liners, who sought to mobilize militant Islamic networks in support of martial law. He and his colleagues had little support in civil society, however, and they were outmaneuvered by Wiranto, who made common cause with much more prominent Islamic leaders, such as Amien Rais, head of the large Islamic organization Muhammadiyah, and Abdurrahman Wahid (Gus Dur), along with the secular leader Megawati Sukarnoputri, all of whom supported the return to democratic civilian rule.

At this critical juncture, Suharto trusted Wiranto more than he trusted his son-in-law and purportedly offered to put Wiranto in charge. This would have paved the way for the army to stay in power and for Wiranto to try to follow in Suharto's footsteps. Wiranto and

his camp, however, had already decided that such a solution would be rejected in the streets, putting the army in the position of having to kill thousands of Indonesians to maintain order and stay in power, a prospect the Wiranto faction found untenable.*

In the event, it was agreed that Suharto would step aside and his vice president, Habibie, would take over, as provided for in the constitution.

Under democracy since 1999, the military has generally accepted civilian rule, but it remains a formidable power and has successfully resisted a number of important reforms, including the abolition of the territorial command structure and the withdrawal from hundreds of businesses that it uses to obtain nonbudgetary funding for both institutional and personal uses.

But there was one more tragic event to occur during the transition to democracy that threatens to overshadow all of the responsible behavior of the military during the transition period

*This would be the first of two occasions when the Army had a chance to take over in the post-Suharto era. The second was to come in July 2001, when embattled president Wahid was on the verge of being voted out of office by Parliament. He declared a national emergency that was, in effect, an open invitation for the military to take control. His declaration was ignored by the military and Wahid was legally ousted by Parliament a few days after the declaration.

The Shame of East Timor

DESPITE GAINING INDEPENDENCE from Portugal in 1975, Timor-Leste—commonly known as East Timor—was not free until May 20, 2002. Indonesia invaded East Timor—an area roughly the size of Connecticut, located on half the island of Timor—in 1975 and annexed it as the province of Timor Timur the next year. The Indonesian occupation lasted until 1999, with a large loss of life due to killings as well as to hunger and illness.

The UN supervised a referendum on independence in August 1999 where the Timorese voted overwhelmingly for independence. The referendum, however, was surrounded by violence. Pro-integration Timorese militias, with the support of the Indonesian military, unleashed a brutal campaign of intimidation before and retribution after the referendum. The violence did not cease until the UN-mandated peacekeeping force, the International Force for East Timor (INTERFET) arrived in late September 1999. Several hundred Timorese were killed and more than 200,000 were made refugees in post-referendum violence that required the intervention of a UN peacekeeping force led by Australia to restore order. Indonesia gave permission for the force to enter the area, but it could hardly have done otherwise under the circumstances. Many cases of human rights abuses perpetrated during this period remain unresolved to date. The entire East Timor debacle remains one of the blackest marks in the history of the military and the nation.

Sept. 24, 1999: Australian soldiers arrest a suspected militant, as tensions rise in Dili, the capital. (PAULA BRONSTEIN/GETTY IMAGES)

Since Timor-Leste achieved independence, internal violence has erupted several times. A military strike in April 2006 fractured the country and resulted in 150,000 internally displaced persons. Amid questions of whether Timor-Leste had become a failed state, an International Stabilization Force, led by Australia, was dispatched at the request of the government to restore order. In the same year, the UN established an Integrated Mission in Timor-Leste (UNMIT). Two years later, however, President José Ramos-Horta was gravely injured in an assassination attempt launched by ex-military rebels. The country suffers from corruption, an infrastructure decimated by the years of violence and the continued existence of armed rebels. ∎

and will blacken its legacy until it is acknowledged and accounted for. This was the awful brutality that occurred when Timor-Leste (East Timor) voted to leave Indonesia in a UN-supervised referendum on autonomy in August 1999, the outcome of a process initiated by President Habibie (see box above).

The military has successfully resisted calls for a more transparent accounting of military abuses in East Timor. Activists also continue to point out that the role of intelligence forces in the murder of Indonesian human rights and anticorruption activist Munir Said Thalib in 2004 has not been fully investigated. At the request of human rights activists, the U.S. has on several occasions raised the issue with the Indonesian government, to little effect.

Nevertheless, the most important reforms include the withdrawal of active-duty military personnel from civilian posts, the separation of the police from the armed forces, a declaration of political neutrality, withdrawal from Golkar, the appointment of a civilian as minister of defense and the elimination of reserved seats for the military in Parliament.

The next steps in reform are to get the military out of business, continue judicial reforms that will ultimately make military personnel fully subject to civil law, get all military funding on budget and to provide enough funding, especially to the navy and the air force, to create a modern, well-trained military capable of keeping the country's important sea lanes open and defending Indonesia's territorial waters against military, economic and environmental intrusion. The U.S. is playing a small but important role in facilitating this transition.

For all its shortcomings, Indonesia has made great strides in reforming its military and subjecting it to civilian rule with the military's active cooperation and no reform-related violence, something only the most rosy-eyed optimist would have dared to consider possible in 1998. Perhaps as a consequence of these changes, the military remains one of the most important and respected institutions in Indonesia.

Regional autonomy and decentralization

After the institution of democracy and a free press and the elimination of the military's direct role in government and politics, the next most important reform undertaken in the post-Suharto era has been radical decentralization. During late colonial rule and under the Japanese occupation of World War II, the colonizers (the state) essentially owned natural resources rather than the people who occupied the land where the resources were found or grown. When the colonizers were gone, the successor state became the new owner.

The granting of exclusive stewardship of resources to the central government and the lack of recognition of local property rights and traditions, created grievances that contributed significantly to the tension between the central and local governments in Indonesia.

In this context, it is useful to think of Indonesia's central government as a huge vacuum cleaner that historically has sucked the vast majority of the country's wealth into the national treasury and redistributed it through the national budget and increasingly corrupt bureaucratic favoritism. Suharto did not create the system of corruption and crony capitalism that characterized his rule. He merely perfected it.

The most destructive effect of this high degree of centralization has been the concentration of wealth and human resources in Jakarta to the detriment of the rest of the nation. Until decentralization legislation came into effect in 1999–2000, for example, two thirds of both the deposits and the credits in the banking system were held in Jakarta and in the 1990s almost 70% of the cash in circulation in the country was within 100 kilometers of Jakarta. Thus,

an area that encapsulates less than 15% of the population with none of the material resources enjoyed two thirds of the country's wealth.

Equally disruptive, the high concentration of wealth and power in Jakarta created a devastating domestic brain drain. Since the early days of the republic, bright, ambitious young Indonesians had to go to Jakarta if they wanted to get ahead. One of the political strengths in the country's early history was that each of Indonesia's numerous ethnic groups quickly established strong Jakarta communities to make sure their group was able to share in the national booty.

But as time passed and the economy grew, these Jakarta elites became less connected to their original homelands. The Jakarta elites made sure they shared in the national pie, but little trickled back to their ethnic homelands, and those who did not migrate to the capital evolved into distinctly second-class citizens with no control over local resources and no say in how tax and resource revenues were spent.

With the passage of comprehensive decentralization legislation in 1999, the new Parliament took an important step to correct this historic injustice. This legislation transferred numerous administrative functions—health and education, to name just two—to local administration. Most important, it mandated that a specific amount of tax revenues be automatically transferred to the regions each year. The formula for calculating the amount of the transfers essentially draws from two pots of money, one based on general revenue and one based on resource revenue. The first is shared by each district (*kabupaten*) through a formula based on population and land area, heavily weighted to population. The second is based on revenues from natural resources, where all counties get something, but those that contribute more, get more. This latter is designed to make each area feel they do, in fact, benefit from the exploitation of resources in their home regions. While there are some problems with the formula, it is transparent and has resulted

Lucidity Information Design, LLC

7

in over 30% of the national budget being returned, essentially unearmarked, to the control of county administrations.

As a result, a historic redistribution of wealth from the center to the regions has been under way for just over a decade. The economies of most Outer Island communities are now growing much faster than those on Java and regional tensions are much diminished. This trend has been strongly supported by the direct election of most key local government officials, which began in 2005.

While decentralization has contributed to a greater sense of fairness and social justice across the land, supported by a real shift in wealth, it has flaws. Critics charge that few regions have adequate human resources to properly handle the new authority and the relatively large sums of money they have been given, and that government decentralization has resulted in the decentralization of corruption.

There are strong elements of truth in both these concerns. The lack of human resources can be simply explained by the brain drain noted above and the fact that until 2000 local governments were expected to merely be implementing agencies for diktats delivered from Jakarta. But the answer is surely not to return authority to Jakarta. It is to provide technical support and increase training. The central government is doing both.

And, while it is early in the process, it is also important to note that there now seems to be a "reverse" brain drain under way. There are numerous examples of prominent individual bureaucrats and businesspeople who, having made their mark in Jakarta, have returned to their home areas, taking the skills, knowledge and connections of a successful career in Jakarta back to the regions. The one-way street of talent and money from the regions to Jakarta is now a highway that runs in both directions.

The second charge—that corruption has also been decentralized—is of more consequence. There is no doubt that weak controls and inexperienced administrations have created fertile ground for dishonest officials. The media are full of stories of regional offi-

cials being booked or convicted on corruption charges. One can either be discouraged by the large number of cases reported or encouraged by the fact that so many are coming to light and perpetrators are being convicted.

Despite the obvious corruption problems, local government is generally much more transparent than national government institutions and this transparency can result in quicker improvements at the local level than the national. Meanwhile, the central government bureaucracy is hardly a model of fiscal rectitude so it cannot seriously claim the high moral ground on corruption issues and use this as a basis for reducing regional autonomy.

This is not to say that Jakarta does not have substantial technical and management resources lacking in the regions. But these resources should be applied to strengthen the competence of the regions, not to reassert central authority or claw back central control.

The bottom line is that Indonesia's great decentralization program has strengthened, rather than weakened, national unity by creating a greater sense of fairness and opening the channels for one of the most radical revenue redistribution programs ever conducted, one that has been voluntary and nonviolent. It has been a great success to date and should continue to contribute substantially to Indonesia's growth and increasing sense of social equity.

The journey

Indonesia has come a long way since the Asian financial crisis, during which its economy collapsed and its gross domestic product (GDP) contracted by nearly 14%. The establishment of a legitimate, democratic government, fully recognized and welcomed by the international community, has provided the foundation for Indonesia's formidable economic recovery, which in turn has played a large part in the country's stability. It has weathered the current global economic crisis comparatively well. While much of the world slid into recession in 2009, Indonesia's GDP growth only slowed to 4.5% in 2009, compared to a growth rate of over 6%

in the two preceding years. It averaged 5.7% GDP growth from 2005 to 2010.

With GDP growth still strong and foreign exchange reserves, exports and the domestic stock market reaching record highs this year, direct investment levels steadily increasing and commodity prices stable to strengthening, the Indonesian economy is very strong and prospects for steady real growth in the future are excellent.

This positive prognosis is strengthened by the fact that badly needed infrastructure investment, stalled for years by government indecision and infighting, is now moving ahead, albeit slowly. And while there is legitimate concern about the pace of reforms today compared to the burst of badly needed legislation and regulation designed to promote transparency and curb corruption in the first half of the decade, progress continues to be made.

Although the continued weakness of the economies of Europe and the U.S. has generated much concern about the potential impact on the high-growth economies of Asia, Indonesia is among the least vulnerable. Indonesia's weak manufacturing links to the global supply chain have become a virtue, making the country less susceptible to the current global downturn than its more globally integrated neighbors. In 2010, Indonesia's exports were equal to about 27% of its GDP compared with, for example, over 200% for Singapore and Hong Kong, 97% for Malaysia, 71% for Thailand and 35% for the Philippines.

And, while much remains to be done on the poverty-reduction and job-creation front, the country is making progress there, too. In terms of GDP per capita, the country reached $1,000 in 1997, then dropped to $500 in 1998 and did not recover to 1997 levels until 2004. Since then, however, GDP per capita has tripled and now stands at just over $3,000, with purchasing power parity (PPP) at $4,200 per capita.

The number of open unemployed (those not working or looking for work) in the country's 116-million-strong labor force has dropped to 7% today, compared with 12% in 2005, and the percentage of people living below the poverty line has dropped from almost 25% during the Asian financial crisis to around 13% today. However, that leaves about 30 million people living below the poverty line.

In spite of the country's solid economic performance and excellent prospects for the future, there are many serious problems. The regulatory climate in most sectors is far from optimal. The U.S. has identified increased protectionism and slowly growing economic nationalism as two of its main concerns about Indonesia's prospects moving forward, along with a weak rule of law and a judicial system that is riddled with incompetence and corruption. There is also little doubt that the space for foreign investment has slowly but steadily narrowed over the past decade, although Indonesia remains one of the more open economies in the region and foreign investment is high.

In areas like education and health care, much-needed private-sector investment is blocked by outdated regulations and the strong protectionist sentiments of the coddled professional classes, which have long resisted the application of global standards. The growing middle class is becoming increasingly aware of the deficiencies of these two vital sectors and frustrated at either going abroad for quality education for their children and health care or going without. The government is belatedly starting to realize that Indonesians who can afford it are spending billions of dollars annually in neighboring Singapore, Australia and Malaysia, effectively funding the growth of health and education services in these more-advanced economies while Indonesia's sectors drop further and further behind.

The point is not that the economy is doing poorly, just that it could be doing so much better with stronger leadership and greater encouragement of private-sector investment, including foreign investment.

Challenges remain

For all its progress, Indonesia remains a developing country. A number of its health, education and other social indicators lag behind many of its neighbors, even those with lower per capita

June 28, 2011: Miners use bamboo rafts to dredge for tin ore on a lake in the Sungai Liat area, Bangka, Indonesia. Surveys suggested that tin would fetch $30,000 per metric ton at the end of 2011. (DIMAS ARDIAN/BLOOMBERG/GETTY IMAGES)

incomes. Most of its institutions were hollowed out by decades of authoritarian rule when independent thought was dangerous. Institutions that seemed robust in the Suharto era have been exposed under the floodlights of democratic transparency as ill-equipped for the demands of modern government, which call for independent, professional analyses and the ability to articulate and negotiate positions with competing institutions of equal authority and legitimacy. Rebuilding these institutions remains a major challenge.

There is also no doubt that the election of the popular, consensus-building SBY for two five-year terms has brought badly needed stability and continuity after the chaotic period that followed Suharto's exit. After over 30 years of strongman rule that ended in 1998 and having experienced only two presidents in its first half-century of independence, Indonesia suddenly had three different presidents from 1998 to 2001. These transitions were conducted without serious violence, but the rapid turnover and the more numerous cabinet changes that accompanied them badly weakened administrative control of the bureaucracy.

It is troubling, however, that neither SBY nor his party has groomed a successor generation and no broadly popular figures have emerged from the other political parties that tend to be dominated by aging party functionaries with little broad appeal. The lack of new political leaders with even modest national credentials gives little clue to who might succeed the popular Yudhoyono when his term expires in October 2014.

Adding to these concerns is a growing perception that administrative reforms and anticorruption activities, particularly legal and judicial reforms, have stalled due to resistance from powerful vested interest groups that survived the downfall of Suharto and have seen their political power eroded by democracy and their cash flows reduced by anticorruption agencies. Many continue to occupy powerful positions in government, the Parliament and business, and regularly mount counterattacks against anticorruption activities from their privileged positions.

Outlook for Indonesia

In spite of its problems, Indonesia is in a very good place right now. Economic growth is sound and politics are stable, although dangers from global economic uncertainty cannot be ignored.

Among Indonesia's economic advantages are strong macroeconomic fundamentals, prudent fiscal management and youthful demographics.

Strong, stable economic growth in Indonesia is essential to regional stability and will enable Indonesia to play a constructive regional role commensurate with its size. The median age of the Indonesian population is 28 and there are over 50 million middle-class Indonesians creating a rapidly growing market today, nearly double the entire populations of Malaysia or Australia.

Among Indonesia's greatest drawbacks are the lack of political will to tackle intolerance, inefficient government bureaucracy, widespread corruption in the legislature and judicial establishment, the security apparatus and the bureaucracy, poor rule of law and governance, a great human capital/skills shortage, a huge

subsidy burden that consumes 18% of the national budget and unaddressed infrastructure bottlenecks.

There is legitimate concern that Indonesia may not be able to deal with its many self-inflicted problems like high subsidies, poor infrastructure, education and health care in a timely fashion, missing its current window of opportunity, but pessimism is not yet in order.

If the 2014 election goes smoothly and infrastructure investment continues to increase, Indonesia is likely to maintain its position as one of the top G-20 countries by GDP growth over the next 25 years. This growth should be enough to ensure political stability and buy time while the country's political system ma-

tures and its bureaucracy becomes more seasoned.

Indonesia's greatest danger today seems to be an overconfidence bred of the political and economic success it has achieved over the past decade. But by resting on its laurels, the country is missing the chance for more rapid growth and greater institutional improvement. This will make it more vulnerable than it needs to be in the future as new challenges emerge. Nevertheless, the current trajectory is strong and if continued, Indonesia could well become the fourth largest economy in the world by mid-century. It is within the county's reach, a prospect that would have seemed a cruel fantasy just a decade ago. ∎

Trouble spots, terror and tolerance

I N THE CONTEXT of America's concern with global terror, it is not surprising that radical Islamist terrorism in Indonesia has attracted the most official and media attention. It is only part, however, of Indonesia's complex security picture that can usefully be divided into three broad areas of concern: first, religious terrorism, which is being driven by

A Muslim leader exhorts militants to shout "jihad" (holy war) and "Allahu Akbar" (God is great) during a show of force on the grounds of the parliamentary complex in Jakarta. (WEDA/AFP/GETTY IMAGES)

loosely connected webs of atomistic cells that range across the country under the broad patronage of elements within groups like Jemaah Islamiyah (JI), Hizb ut-Tahrir and others; second, localized trouble spots like Aceh, Papua, Maluku and Central Sulawesi, which are driven by local issues and have generally not welcomed the support or involvement of outsiders; and finally, organized vigilante groups that promote intolerance and bigotry by attacking minority religious groups, the most prominent being the Islamic Defenders Front (FPI, Front Pembela Islam) and the Betawi Brotherhood (FBR, Forum Betawi Rempug). These groups have been active in support of local groups attacking minorities, most recently the Ahmadiyah, a small Islamic sect considered heretical by many mainstream Muslims, and in blocking construction of Christian churches. Religious terrorism as practiced by elements of JI and fellow travelers is the most notorious because of the involvement of some of its members in a series of high profile suicide bombings of foreign targets, including two incidents in the tourist mecca of Bali (2002 and 2005), and three in Jakarta (JW Marriott Hotel in 2003 and 2009 and the Australian Embassy in 2004).

The Indonesian police have created a special antiterrorist unit, Densus 88, which has had a great deal of success in catching the perpetrators of these atrocities and disrupting their networks. In all, Indonesian antiterror forces have killed or captured about 500 terrorists in the past decade. It is generally felt that this effort has decimated their networks and, while it takes only a few dedicated people to perpetrate such outrages, the number of active participants seems to be in decline, along with their funding sources. Perhaps most important, unlike terrorist hot spots to the west—Afghanistan, Pakistan, Yemen—these groups have no sympathizers in the security apparatus. They are considered by police and military alike as criminals.

For all the headline-grabbing violence of terrorist bombings, however, Indonesia's localized trouble spots have accounted for much more death and destruction. Between 1999 and 2002, several thousand people were killed in sectarian violence in Maluku alone, and perhaps 500,000 people were displaced, compared with about 260 who have been killed by suicide bombers in Indonesia in the past decade, including 202 in the first Bali bombing in 2002. And over 700 persons were killed in a two-month period of sectarian violence in Poso, Central Sulawesi, in 2002. These areas are unique in Indonesia because the number of Muslims and Christians are roughly in balance, unlike most other areas of the country where one or the other tends to be a substantial majority. There is little doubt that the virtually equal competition for local jobs and resources has contributed to local tensions. While both of these areas have calmed down considerably over the past decade, small-scale violence still flares up.

Aceh and Papua offer a different set of challenges. In both areas, perceived injustices inflicted on the local population by the central government are at the core of the discontent and separatist sentiments exist. While Acehnese tend to be conservative Muslims, the main issues are ethnic and territorial; the Acehnese resent the predominantly Javanese central government intrusion in local affairs, and tensions exist between competing local elites. The ethnic nature of the dispute—Acehnese against others—is also well-reflected in the fact that outside sympathizers from the radical Islamic underground like JI were not welcomed by Acehnese rebels. In any event, in 2005 the central government reached a peace accord with the Free Aceh Movement (GAM, Gerakan Aceh Merdeka), which had been waging sporadic guerilla warfare for nearly 30 years. This settlement continues to hold today.

In Papua, local autonomy grievances are exacerbated by the distinct ethnicity of ethnic Papuans and the fact that they are predominantly Christian. Papua is also the only area of today's Indonesia that was incorporated after the UN recognized Indonesian independence in 1949. It was incorporated into Indonesia after a UN-sanctioned Act of Free Choice in 1969 in which the U.S. played a key brokerage role. Not all Papuans accepted this result, particularly the Free Papua Movement (Organisasi Papua Merdeka, OPM) that was founded in 1963 when Papua was still under UN supervision. While small and scattered, the OPM remains the most prominent anti-integration force in the territory.

Papua now has a special autonomy agreement with the central government, but the Indonesian military still plays a dominant role and access for outsiders, particularly the media, is strictly controlled. Sporadic violence and allegations of human rights violations by security forces are endemic and certain international groups, particularly Christian groups in Australia and the U.S., monitor the situation closely. ■

Indonesia and the U.S.

INDONESIA has been playing a much more assertive role in international and regional affairs under the Yudhoyono Administration. Indonesia was the 2011 Chair of ASEAN (Association of Southeast Asian Nations), the most important multilateral organization in the region, and has taken the lead in establishing and nurturing the Bali Democracy Forum, which promotes democracy in the Asia-Pacific region. These efforts, along with Indonesia's well-deserved international recognition as the world's third-largest democracy, have earned it a place at the G-20 table that it prizes highly.

All of this activity is highly constructive and makes Indonesia an increasingly attractive friend if not partner not only for the U.S., but also for the many countries with substantial interests in Southeast Asia, including China, India, Japan and Korea. As the competition between the U.S. and the growing Asian powers increases, the importance and influence of Indonesia as linchpin of Southeast Asia will continue to grow.

The U.S. clearly has come to recognize the increasing importance of the ASEAN region and the leadership role Indonesia is poised to play. Following

A Malaysian marine policeman stands guard on the deck of his patrol boat while patrolling past a tanker in the Malacca Strait, one of the world's busiest shipping lanes, amid threats of a terrorist attack on oil tankers. The strait runs between the Indonesian island of Sumatra, western Malaysia and southern Thailand. (JIMIN LAI/AFP/GETTY IMAGES)

President Barack Obama's state visit to Jakarta in late 2010, there has been a flurry of U.S. diplomatic activity in Indonesia. Recently, Defense Secretary Leon Panetta attended a meeting of ASEAN defense ministers where an agreement was announced for Indonesia to obtain 24 F-16 fighter planes. Parliament subsequently approved the deal. This reflects both the growing importance of Indonesia and U.S. concerns about China's long-term intentions in the region.

Indeed, the U.S.-Indonesia relationship is long and deep. The Indonesian archipelago has always been of great strategic importance for global trade and the great navies of the world. Today over half of the energy supplies that feed the industries of Japan and China pass through the archipelago's waters. The two-way flow of manufactured products is nearly as great.

U.S. involvement in Indonesia began with Indonesia's declaration of independence immediately after the fall of Japan in 1945 and was initially driven by America's desire to stabilize the region after World War II. This phase culminated with UN recognition of Indonesia's independence in 1949, when the U.S. played a major role in persuading the Netherlands to cease its attempt to reoccupy its former colony. Over the next two decades the relationship deteriorated from this high point, a victim of cold-war tensions, as the young republic turned leftward and the U.S. gave ill-advised support to the easily quashed Permesta separatist movement in Sumatra and Sulawesi in the late 1950s.

By the mid-1960s the U.S. was deepening its entanglement in Vietnam as the Communist party of Vietnam was making significant gains. Combined with the consolidation of Communist rule in China and the success of the Soviet Union in space exploration, global communism seemed ascendant. In this context, the increasing influence of the Indonesia's Communist Party (PKI) was viewed with alarm.

In late 1965, six right-wing generals were murdered in an abortive left-wing coup attempt. The origins of the coup remain murky, but its outcome changed the course of Indonesian history. It resulted in the fall of Sukarno, a takeover by right-wing military officers led by General Suharto, one of the highest ranking survivors, and unleashed more than a year of violence that left several hundred thousand dead and the PKI destroyed.

Although the U.S. certainly welcomed the fall of Sukarno and demolition of the PKI, it was caught by surprise both by the coup attempt and the rise of Suharto, who was virtually unknown to U.S. intelligence and, indeed, to the Indonesian population at large at that time.

At the height of the cold war in the 1960s, the U.S. body politic was by no means as sensitive to human rights concerns as it would become from the 1980s onward. The choice for the U.S. then seemed stark and simple. An anti-communist general had replaced a left-leaning dictator and the largest Communist party outside of the U.S.S.R. and the People's Republic of China had been smashed. Suharto's takeover was welcome and U.S. support was forthcoming, initially in financial support and food for Indonesia's starving population, at that time one of the poorest in the world. The U.S. was even more encouraged when Suharto quickly turned to a group of

American-educated technocrats, subsequently dubbed "the Berkeley Mafia," to take over the nation's economic management, including opening the country to foreign investment.

The U.S. has remained heavily engaged in development activities in Indonesia, primarily through the U.S. Agency for International Development (USAID), the Ford Foundation, the Fulbright Scholarship Program, The Asia Foundation and numerous other NGOs and government programs ever since. In the 1970s and 1980s, the U.S. also played key roles helping the country achieve rice self-sufficiency and develop its highly successful, noncoercive family planning program, which brought live births per female down from 5.6 in the 1950s to 3.1 in 1990 and 2.1 today. Thousands of Indonesian university students and government officials were sent to the U.S. during this period, reaching a peak of over 13,000 a year in the 1990s.

While educational and economic development efforts generally went well during this period, Suharto's authoritarian style and his obvious intention to maintain power as long as possible began to grate on both significant elements of the Indonesian population and some of his major international supporters, including the U.S. Suppression of political opposition and strong press censorship led to numerous human rights abuses.

Indonesia's attempt to annex East Timor compounded the problem. Although the U.S. initially welcomed the occupation in 1975 because it seemed to crush another leftist independence movement, continued local resistance was met with brutal suppression. This brutality eroded international support for Indonesia's occupation, which was never accepted by the UN and resulted in numerous highly publicized cases of human rights abuse, culminating in the infamous Santa Cruz massacre in 1991, when Indonesian security forces opened fire on several thousand mourners who had peacefully assembled to attend a memorial service for an East Timorese resistance member who had been killed two weeks earlier. Over 200 mourners were killed in the attack, which was se-

Members of the Youth Wing of the Indonesian Communist Party are guarded by soldiers as they are taken to prison in Jakarta in 1965, following an abortive coup d'etat that prompted Sukarno's government to crack down on Communists. (AP)

cretly filmed by a foreign journalist and broadcast around the world.

This attack led to restrictions on U.S. military sales to the Indonesian Armed Forces. Limited IMET (International Military Education and Training) continued until 1999, but was halted in the wake of the brutal response of Indonesian-supported paramilitary forces to the Timorese landslide vote for independence, in a UN-sponsored Act of Self Determination agreed to by Indonesia.

As the cold war faded into history, however, the U.S. increasingly recognized Indonesia's importance as a linchpin of regional stability, and as one of the most successful developing countries in the struggle to reduce poverty. However, Indonesia's lack of progress in promoting basic human rights and its suppression of political and social dissent presented an obstacle to closer relations with the U.S.

Indonesia's transition to democracy has made things easier for the relationship, and both Presidents Bush and Obama have given special attention to the country. Initially the Bush Administration focused on Indonesia because of the importance of the Indonesian role in combating global terror, particularly after the 9/11 attacks on the World Trade Center and the Pentagon. This in turn led to a much greater appreciation of Indonesia's size, strategic location and economic and leadership potential in Southeast Asia. In terms of the Asian strategy of the U.S., the relationship with Indonesia has historically been relegated to the second tier, with priority given to treaty allies Japan and South Korea, along with support for Taiwan. Obama's decision to attend the East Asia summit in Bali, Indonesia, in November 2011, marked the first time a U.S. President had attended the meeting. The decision shows a more assertive U.S. policy, no doubt partly in response to the growing Chinese economic presence in the Asia-Pacific region and China's confrontational strategy in the South China Sea.

There is much more to the U.S.-Indonesian relationship than security issues. In November 2010, Presidents Obama and Yudhoyono signed the

U.S. President Barack Obama speaks with Indonesian President Susilo Bambang Yudhoyono at the 2010 G-20 Summit in Seoul, South Korea. (YONHAP/GETTY IMAGES)

Comprehensive Partnership agreement in Jakarta. This agreement specifically covers: Socio-Cultural Affairs, Security and Regional Cooperation, Science and Technology, Education, Environment and Climate Change, Health, and Trade and Investment.

The partnership agreement reflects a high point of mutual engagement that has been building since the collapse of the New Order and Indonesia's return to democratic rule. While government-to-government relations improved dramatically under President George W. Bush, who had a good personal relationship with SBY, public attitudes toward America deteriorated sharply during his Administration because of the U.S. military intervention in Iraq. According to the Pew Research Center's Global Attitudes Project surveys, 61% of Indonesians had a favorable attitude prior to the 2003 Iraq war. This figure dropped to only 15% the year after the war started. It recovered to 38% in 2005, undoubtedly due to the massive level of U.S. support provided after the December 2004 tsunami that left over 170,000 dead and over 500,000 homeless in northern Sumatra. (It is also worth noting that the U.S. Peace Corps returned to Indonesia in 2010, 45 years after being thrown out of the country by Sukarno in 1965.) The percentage of Indonesians with a favorable view of

the U.S. stayed around this level for the next several years, until the election of President Obama, the son of an African father and American mother, who has an Indonesian half-sister and had spent several years of his childhood in Jakarta. Although American policy toward Indonesia did not change, the number of Indonesians with a favorable view of the U.S. leapt back up over 60% after his 2008 election.

While the remarkable coincidence of having a U.S. President with a strong personal connection to Indonesia offers a unique opportunity to enhance the relationship, this rapid reversal of public opinion may also be taken to indicate that the view of the U.S. among the general public in Indonesia is "a mile wide and an inch deep" and perhaps argues that the U.S. perception in Indonesia has suffered badly because of a steadily reduced public diplomacy program over the past 20 years.

The next chapter of the U.S.-Indonesia relationship must consider a wide range of issues, such China's intentions in Southeast Asia, the global war on terror, military cooperation, concern for human rights and the rapid development of Indonesia's economy. ∎

Opinion Ballots after page 32

discussion questions

1. What are the challenges facing Indonesia's democracy in the future? To what extent can these challenges be traced back to Indonesia's history? Are there drawbacks to speedy democratization and economic growth? Is there an optimal pace for transitioning to democracy?

2. To what extent is the democratization of Indonesia a "special case"? What circumstances contributed to the success of Indonesia's rapid modernization and democratization? Could this success be replicated in other countries transitioning from authoritarian or military regimes?

3. How important is Indonesia to U.S. policy in Southeast Asia? Should Indonesia be prioritized over Japan, South Korea, Taiwan or other U.S. allies? Where does Indonesia fit into U.S. strategic economic and political interests regarding China? What is Indonesia's place in regional security?

4. Consider the U.S. response to Indonesian atrocities in East Timor in the 1990s. Was the U.S. reaction appropriate, and if not, what action should U.S. policymakers have taken? How does Indonesia's problematic history with human rights abuses inform its future? What lessons can be learned from the actions or inaction of the international community in the 1990s? Has sufficient action been taken on the atrocities that Indonesia perpetrated during its occupation? How should the legacy of East Timor inform U.S.-Indonesian relations?

5. Indonesia has not been hit as hard as some other countries by the global economic crisis that began in 2008. What are the prospects for Indonesia's economic future? Consider that some scholars have observed correlations between economic development and democratization; when it comes to economic health, is there more at stake for Indonesia? Could—or should—the U.S. and its allies act to support the economies of new democracies?

6. Compared to other Muslim-majority nations, Indonesia has seen relatively few Islamic fundamentalist and militant groups. What factors have contributed to the unique profile of Islamic terrorism in Indonesia? What lessons for the global war on terror can be learned from Indonesia's experiences?

suggested readings

Abuza, Zachary, **Political Islam and Violence in Indonesia.** New York, Routledge, 2007. 176 pp. $39.95 (paper). Abuza, a Southeast Asia security expert, analyzes Islam in Indonesian society and politics and discusses radical Muslim groups in the post-Bali bombing era.

Bresnan, John, ed., **Indonesia: The Great Transition.** Lanham, MD, Rowman & Littlefield, 2005. 336 pp. $37.95 (paper). This study from Columbia University's Weatherhead East Asian Institute provides an introduction to the upheaval and crises in Indonesia's recent history and examines Indonesian politics.

Haseman, John, **The Military and Democracy in Indonesia.** Santa Monica, CA, RAND Corporation, 2002. 170 pp. $20.00 (paper). This book examines the role of the military in Indonesia in the post-Suharto era and discusses the implications for U.S.-Indonesian relations.

Mietzner, Marcus, **Military Politics, Islam, and the State in Indonesia: From Turbulent Transition to Democratic Consolidation,** Singapore, Institute of Southeast Asian Studies, 2008. 444 pp. $71.90 (hardcover). The best description and analysis of the important social and political changes that took place after the fall of Suharto and creation of today's democratic Indonesia. To be read with *A Nation in Waiting* below.

National Commission on U.S.-Indonesian Relations, **Strengthening U.S. Relations with Indonesia: Toward a Partnership for Human Resource Development.** 2003. 58 pp. Available free online at: <www.nbr.org/publications/specialreport/pdf/USICR.pdf>. This report, prepared by specialists on Indonesia, provides an introduction to U.S.-Indonesian relations and identifies critical challenges facing Indonesia.

Nevins, Joseph, **A Not-So-Distant Horror: Mass Violence In East Timor.** Ithaca, NY, Cornell University Press, 2005. 296 pp. $21.95 (paper). Nevins documents the atrocities that Indonesia perpetrated in East Timor over the last 25 years and discusses the role of the international community in the bloodshed.

Schwarz, Adam, **A Nation in Waiting: Indonesia's Search for Stability,** New York, Westview, 1999. 552 pp. $53.00 (paper). The best description and analysis of the tensions facing Indonesia as the Suharto era was drawing to a close. Originally published well before Suharto fell in 1998, it was republished at the end of 1999 with two additional chapters on Suharto's fall and the transition to democracy. To be read with *Military Politics, Islam and the State in Indonesia.*

World Bank 2011, **Indonesia Economic Quarterly: Turbulent Times.** October 4, 2011. Available free online: <http://web.worldbank.org/WBSITE/EXTERNAL/COUNTRIES/EASTASIAPACIFICEXT/INDONESIAEXTN/0,,contentMDK:23016714~pagePK:1497618~piPK:217854~theSitePK:226309,00.html>

Visit **WWW.GREATDECISIONS.ORG** *for quizzes, seasonal topic updates and other resources to further your understanding*

96

Energy geopolitics: quandaries intensify
by William Sweet

Sept. 4, 2010: An employee of the company PPS Pipeline Systems prepares to lay an 800-meter-long section of pipe and connect it to the southern OPAL pipeline. OPAL is part of the Nord Stream Pipeline project, which runs from Lubmin on the north German coast to Olbernhau near the German-Czech border, where it connects with other transmission pipelines. (CHRISTOPH GOEDAN/LAIF/REDUX)

TRADITIONALLY GEOPOLITICS evokes classic *Realpolitik* or what goes by the name of *raison d'état* or Machiavellianism—the notion that in a world of sovereign states, each has no choice but to maximize its own interests and security, construed in a rather narrow geographic and military sense. But what is thought of as energy geopolitics today has come to encompass much more than physical control over resources to advance state interests. It also refers to the ability to influence or even set world prices for fuels and technologies, and to leverage energy power to achieve a larger political end or ward off interference from other states and nongovernmental bodies. Energy geopolitics can still mean expanding one state's power and security at the expense of another's in a zero-sum game, but it also can involve human rights or humanitarian intervention.

Since energy geopolitics can encompass so much, discussion of energy policy often suffers from what the Austrian philosopher Ludwig Wittgenstein might have called a confusion of discourse. When the discussion is about energy independence, which has been a major recurrent theme in U.S. politics since 1973, is it about the danger of an organization like the 12-member Organization of the Petroleum Exporting Countries (OPEC) using its oil power to tempt the U.S. into betraying a friend like Israel—or, conversely, into overextending its military reach in an attempt to better control world oil reserves? Or is it really the influence that world oil prices

WILLIAM SWEET *blogs about energy and climate for IEEE Spectrum magazine and about nuclear arms control and weapons of mass destruction for the Foreign Policy Association.*

have on U.S. energy prices and the general economy that is the chief concern?

The same kinds of ambiguities arise in anxious discussions of Europe's dependence on natural gas imports from Russia and former Soviet Union (FSU) states that are in effect Russian protectorates. Are Germans seriously concerned that Russia might exploit its market power and start to push them around the way it has bullied former constituent parts of the U.S.S.R., like Ukraine, Belarus and Georgia? (See "Europe's 'Far East': The Uncertain Frontier," *Great Decisions* 2010.) Or is the real issue that Russia might take actions in its own sphere of influence that seem morally or politically unacceptable, but which must be accepted because of Russia's energy power?

Such situations could involve the sort of very sticky issues of gross human rights violations and humanitarian intervention that arose during the dissolution of Communist Yugoslavia. But they also can involve entirely different questions, e.g., environmental issues that some people consider urgent matters critical to earth's and humankind's fate.

A tale of two pipelines

Consider two immensely controversial pipeline projects that received wide attention in 2011: the Nord Stream natural gas pipeline, connecting Western European consumers with suppliers in Russia and Central Asia; and Keystone XL, which would take petroleum from Canadian oil sands in Alberta and transport it to refineries in Louisiana and Texas. Both projects raise basic geopolitical issues—but issues representing different types of geopolitics.

Nord Stream is controversial because it carries gas from Russia under the Baltic Sea directly to Germany, bypassing Poland and Ukraine. This means Russia could curtail gas shipments to Ukraine, which it has done several times to exact financial and political concessions, or to former Soviet satellite countries, without affecting supplies to Western Europe.

Former German chancellor Gerhard Schröder has served as chairman of Nord Stream, fronting for the project and acting in effect as an employee of Russian Prime Minister (and soon to be president again) Vladimir Putin. In some countries such an intrinsically conflicted arrangement would not be tolerated.

Keystone XL is controversial for a very different set of reasons. It would bring 1.3 million barrels per day (mbpd) of heavy crude oil to the U.S. from Canada. As Canada is a completely reliable supplier, unlike some OPEC countries or Russia, the new pipeline would contribute materially to U.S. energy security.

The objections to Keystone XL are not politico-military, as with Nord Stream, but environmental. The pipeline would lead to more oil sands extraction, an energy- and carbon-intensive process that critics charge devastates the local environment. Meanwhile, delivery of the heavy oil to U.S. refiners will enable continued reliance on fossil fuels, a dependence that environmentalists say is incompatible with President Barack Obama's pledge to cut greenhouse gas emissions 80% by 2050.

For those reasons, environmentalists' opposition to Keystone XL has been fierce, unanimous and pointed. Hundreds of demonstrators were arrested at the White House during the late summer and early fall of 2011, among them some eminent environmental and scientific leaders. Twenty scientists, including several top U.S. climate experts, wrote to Obama saying Keystone XL would be flatly incompatible with the nation's professed climate goals. All the top U.S. environmental organizations joined in a letter asking the President to kill the project—and warning him of domestic political repercussions if he did not. The groups described the pipeline as "perhaps the biggest climate test you face between now and the election," and said that "if you block it, you will trigger a surge of enthusiasm from the green base that supported you so strongly in the last election," clearly implying that if he did not block it, that enthusiasm would be absent.

It presented a major quandary for the President, pitting the security of oil supplies against the long-term risks of catastrophic climate change. Obama opted for delay. The State Department, which was responsible in this case for preparing an environmental impact statement (because a cross-boundary project is involved), announced in November that exploring alternate routes would push the controversial decision beyond the 2012 election.   ■

Sept. 1, 2011, Washington, DC: Protestors were arrested in front of the White House during two weeks of daily demonstrations to highlight opposition to the Keystone XL pipeline. The protestors want the Obama Administration to reject a permit for the pipeline, which would carry tar sands oil from Canada to Texas. (PETE MAROVICH/ZUMA PRESS/CORBIS)

Tight global oil market

OBAMA'S DILEMMA is all the more acute in that the relationship between affordable energy, economic growth and jobs creation appears to be close. In particular, oil prices and the balance of oil supply and demand show a high sensitivity to global economic trends, and, reciprocally, business cycles show a high sensitivity to oil market trends.

Oil prices spiked at the end of 2008 at over $140/barrel, when the world economy was crashing. In the next year prices dropped precipitously to about $30/barrel, despite OPEC's decision in December 2008 to cut production targets by 4.2 mbpd. Prices climbed back more gradually in 2010–2011 to as much as $115/barrel or more.

Though OPEC's ability to closely control prices has its limits, the organization's continued centrality is noteworthy. During and after the oil crises of 1973–74, free-market theorists predicted that as the organization tried to limit world production and drive up prices, competing suppliers would enter the market, causing the organization eventually to wither away. In the short term, something like that happened. From 1975 to 1985, OPEC's share of world production fell from almost 50% to below 30%. But then it climbed back in the next decades to over 40%, where it has held steady.

Evidently there was a limit to how much oil was readily available in non-OPEC countries. Today, a Worldwatch figure indicates that OPEC countries have almost as large a share of total estimated world reserves as they did in 1973.

In terms of production, OPEC and non-OPEC countries (not counting the FSU) each account for about 42% of total supplies, with the FSU states accounting for a sharply rising share of 16.8%. In 2011, for the second year running, Russia was the world's largest oil producer, displacing Saudi Arabia in the top spot. It is an increasingly important supplier of oil to Europe as North Sea reserves dwindle.

June 1, 1973: Leon Mill spray paints a sign outside his Phillips 66 station in Perkasie, PA, to let his customers know he is out of gas. An oil crisis was the culprit, squeezing U.S. businesses and consumers who were forced to line up at gas stations for hours (AP PHOTO)

The insurgency and civil war in Libya led to a loss of that country's production and exports equivalent to about 1.5% of the world market. That relatively small and transitory decrease sent world prices soaring, showing just how closely balanced global supply and demand are.

U.S. and European dependencies

During the last decade, the U.S. has become significantly less reliant on OPEC exports, while Europe has become somewhat more dependent on OPEC and the Russian sphere. The U.S. accounted for 25% of OPEC exports in 2009, versus 31% a decade earlier; Europe's share grew to 30% from 28% in the same period. As a percentage of total oil consumption, Europe's imports grew dramatically to 72% in 2009, from 54% in 1999.

Even when the U.S. was more dependent on OPEC, its imports from the Middle East were smaller than one might suppose. It obtains large quanti-

ties of petroleum from countries like Venezuela, Mexico, Nigeria and Angola; less than a fifth of its oil imports comes from the Persian Gulf. A major disruption in a Persian Gulf country— whether the result of "Arab Spring" rebellions or war—can have very adverse short-term effects on supplies and prices, as seen during the 2003 Persian Gulf war, but such disruptions will not bring the U.S. economy to a standstill.

Europe's dependence on Mideast oil is significantly greater. Starting in the mid-1990s, there was an enormous amount of squabbling between the Europeans, the Russians and their client states, the major oil companies, and the U.S. over development projects and pipelines in the Caspian region. Two major reserves were developed in Azerbaijan and Turkmenistan, at the cost of tens of billions of dollars. The U.S. played an aggressive role in the pipeline politics connected with those projects and had some real success in securing routes that largely bypassed Russia. The

April 4, 2010: A natural gas wellhead stands on an Alta Resources LLC drill site near Montrose, PA. Companies are spending billions to dislodge natural gas from a band of shale-sedimentary rock called the Marcellus shale formation, which underlies Pennsylvania, West Virginia and New York. (DANIEL ACKER/BLOOMBERG/GETTY IMAGES)

total addition to world oil exports from these efforts, however, came to about 2.8 mbpd, amounting to barely more than 3% of world consumption.

A 25-year energy perspective

The 2011 International Energy Outlook released by the U.S. Department of Energy (DOE) expects the main trends seen in recent years to accelerate, with big long-term consequences. The report anticipates that world oil consumption will grow from 85.7 mbpd in 2008 to 112.2 mbpd in 2035. Driven by strong economic growth in large, fast-developing countries, total energy use in the non-OECD (Organization for Economic Cooperation and Development) countries will increase 85% in the next 25 years, while OECD energy use will climb just 18%.

Because of fundamental trends such as conservation, enhanced fuel efficiency and electrification of transportation, the overall share of liquid fuels in total energy consumption will shrink, from 34% (in reference year 2008) to 29%. But liquid fuels will remain critical, and increasingly they will be made from unconventional sources: oil sands, extra-heavy oil, biofuels (from biological raw materials), coal-to-liquids, natural-gas-to-liquids and shale oil.

Greater dependence on unconventional liquid fuels will mean, in some measure, still greater reliance on some countries not deemed wholly dependable. To be sure, the U.S. is beginning to produce significantly more oil from unconventional sources, notably North Dakota shale. As a result, the U.S. has been importing a smaller share of the oil it consumes in recent years. To the extent biofuels replace petroleum and electric motors displace the internal combustion engine, U.S. import dependence may continue to contract.

But there are good reasons to be skeptical about the medium- and even long-term prospects for biofuels and vehicular electrification, and there is every reason to assume that U.S. gasoline prices will continue to be determined by overall trends in a world market where oil can be obtained only by increasingly expensive methods.

The end of easy oil

In 2005, a former chairman of Chevron memorably said that the age of easy oil was over. What that means, basically, is that if world oil prices start to drop significantly, production in difficult environments will slow down and available supplies will contract; that in turn will push prices back up, prompting producers to resume production in the tough places. As that kind of cycle continues and gathers momentum, oil companies will find themselves working in some of the toughest environments of all.

One such environment is Alberta in western Canada, the location of the oil sands that Keystone XL hopes to pipe to the Gulf of Mexico. Another is off Venezuela's coast in the Orinoco Belt, the site of giant oil-sand reserves that are considered higher-grade and easier to extract than Canada's. The combined quantity of oil contained in these two huge deposits could be nearly 2 trillion barrels of oil, roughly equivalent to total world reserves of conventional oil.

Canada can be safely considered an appealing business partner, but not many Americans would say the same of Hugo

Sept. 13, 2007, 200 miles east of Caracas, Venezuela: A billboard featuring a happy Hugo Chávez, Venezuela's president, overlooks the complex that refines crude from the heavy oil of the Orinoco Belt. The refinery is a joint venture between Venezuela's state-owned oil company PDVSA and foreign companies Chevron, BP, Total and Statoil (a Norwegian company). (DIEGO GIUDICE/REDUX)

Chávez's Venezuela, which already is a significant oil exporter to the U.S.

The stakes may be highest in what is probably the toughest environment of all, the Arctic. Shell Oil is expected to get permission from the U.S. government to begin exploratory drilling in the Beaufort Sea, north of Alaska, in the summer of 2012. According to the U.S. Geological Survey, the Arctic may hold about one fifth of the world's remaining oil and gas reserves.

Russia, which has coasts going about halfway around the Arctic Ocean, is of course the big gorilla in the room. On August 2, 2007, Russia got the world's attention when one of its submarines planted a Russian flag on the seabed at the North Pole. No doubt the main purpose of the expedition was to assert a point, but it also had a quasiscientific purpose—to gather geological evidence to bolster Russia's claim to a continental shelf reaching to the North Pole.

Some Russian planners take the Arctic to be crucial to the country's economic strategy and prospects, starting as early as 2020. Already, Russia's state-owned natural gas company Gazprom is involved with France's Total and Norway's Statoil in developing the Shtokman gas field, on Russia's northern coast.

Until recently, areas along that coast were considered barely accessible, but with the summer ice thinning radically, ships are now able to go through the fabled Northeast Passage, linking the North Atlantic to the northern Pacific. As one recent report noted, "A Norwegian cargo ship has already traversed the Northeast Passage faster than expected and without encountering any major challenges." As the earth continues to warm, the cost of extracting Arctic oil and gas will fall. No wonder there is some overheated rhetoric comparing the Arctic race that is shaping up to the "scramble for Africa" and the California gold rush. There has been loose talk of developing a 1946 George F. Kennan-style containment doctrine for the Arctic, to push Russia back and give the North Atlantic Treaty Organization (NATO) a new mission.

However inflated that kind of language may be, the stakes are not trivial. Norway and Russia are maneuvering

August 25, 2010: The Canadian Coast Guard's medium icebreaker Henry Larsen *is seen in Allen Bay during Operation Nanook, as Canadian Prime Minister Stephen Harper visits Resolute, Nunavut, as part of his five-day northern tour of Canada's Arctic.* (SEAN KILPATRICK/CANADIAN PRESS/AP)

for position in the Barents Sea, where Statoil recently made its biggest oil find in decades, advancing their claims at the United Nations Commission on the Limits of the Continental Shelf. Denmark is engaged in the same kind of struggle with Russia over seabed jurisdiction north of Greenland.

Canada, which is increasingly concerned about control of newly opening sea routes as well as resource claims, is purchasing eight new armed ice-breaking patrol ships, has been conducting Arctic military exercises and is constructing a base on Ellesmere Island. The European Union (EU) is bidding for a seat on the Arctic Council, which currently consists of Canada, Denmark, Finland, Iceland, Norway, Russia, Sweden and the U.S.

Biofuels and electrics

To judge from statements frequently heard in politics and seen in the press, there is a widely held perception that a fast transition to hybrid and then fully electrified vehicles might sharply cut U.S. dependence on the world oil market and make the country less subject to the vagaries of energy geopolitics. That expectation is probably misplaced. Right now hybrids yield only modest fuel savings and often not as much as what could be obtained from cheaper standard cars with improved fuel efficiency. All-electric cars like the newly introduced Chevy Volt and Nissan Leaf sell at very high premiums.

Bringing to maturity all the technologies and infrastructure to support ubiquitous plug-in hybrid or all-electric cars will be the work of decades, not years. China, which gives domestic manufacturers of electric vehicles very generous subsidies, has retreated somewhat from its ambitious goal of having 10% of the cars produced in 2015 to be electrics.

Recognizing that automotive electrification is running into some strong headwinds, onetime enthusiasts like former Central Intelligence Agency (CIA) Director R. James Woolsey are backing off a bit, too. Having once conjured up visions of plug-in hybrids that would get 500 miles to a gallon and run on electricity generated almost entirely from domestic resources (coal, natural gas, nuclear and wind), Woolsey now is talking up the idea of first adopting biofuels before negotiating the electric transition.

Aug. 2, 2007: A Russian TV image shows a robotic arm of the Mir-1 mini-submarine as it places a Russian state flag in the seabed of the Arctic Ocean, 2.5 miles beneath the North Pole. (AFP/GETTY IMAGES)

May 1, 2006, Marshall, MO: Corn is the main ingredient used to produce ethanol, which can be used to power automobiles. Most corn is grown in America's heartland. (STEVE HE-BERT/POLARIS)

Last year, for the first time more of the U.S. corn crop went to the manufacture of ethanol fuel than for livestock feed. It is in part a sign of the fuel's growing maturity that ending direct U.S. support for ethanol production is under serious consideration. The Senate voted in mid-2011 to terminate both the 45-cent federal subsidy for every gallon of ethanol blended into U.S. gasoline and the 54-cent-per-gallon import tariff protecting the U.S. industry. Though the measure was not expected to pass the House immediately, its success in the Senate was taken as a sign that the end of ethanol subsidization was looming.

Aug. 27, 2007: A sugarcane cutter works in Batatais, Brazil. (ANDRE PENNER/AP)

Growing misgivings about corn ethanol are also playing an important role in domestic politics. Critics have been pointing out and substantiating for years that switching from gasoline to ethanol has almost no net impact on greenhouse gas emissions and little impact on net energy consumption because of the big energy inputs required in growing corn and fermenting it to make ethanol. Meanwhile, adverse impacts on the domestic and global food markets are visible and disturbing.

The U.S. is overwhelmingly the world's largest producer and exporter of corn. It grows about two fifths of the globe's total, more than twice as much as the next largest grower (China) and almost six times as much as all the EU countries combined. It accounts for more than half of corn exports, with Argentina running a distant second. Naturally, because of world demand for maize as feedstock and food, and with a fast-growing share of the U.S. crop going to ethanol production, world prices for maize have climbed sharply.

As ethanol comes to be a standard ingredient of U.S. gasoline and subsidies on its production are lifted, along with import tariffs, it seems obvious that U.S. corn ethanol will be displaced by much cheaper sugarcane ethanol now made on a large scale in Brazil. The net geopolitical effect of federal biofuels' promotion

will be to make the U.S. more dependent on tropical and subtropical sugarcane producers, including perhaps Communist Cuba, and somewhat less dependent on oil exporters.

Conservation and fuel efficiency

The really big changes in U.S. gasoline demand in the next decades will occur spontaneously in reaction to sustained higher prices, and not because of vehicle electrification or biofuels inroads. During the summer of 2011, both the number of miles driven and the amount of gasoline consumed were significantly lower than the year before, which is surely the beginning of a major trend.

Five years ago, a blue-ribbon panel assembled by Princeton University's Woodrow Wilson School proposed in effect that the U.S. government should deliberately drive the price of gasoline to about $5 a gallon over 10 years, from roughly $2.50 in 2006. Assuming that in the long run (perhaps 10–25 years), Americans cut gasoline use about 50% in response to a 100% price hike, a gasoline price of $5 a gallon ought to eventually result in total consumption that is half of what was consumed in 2006.

With actual prices headed toward $5 a gallon, it is to be expected that Americans will continue to trade in their SUVs and vans for smaller, more fuel-efficient vehicles. That will translate into significantly lower oil imports and lower greenhouse gas emissions. That happy result will be not the consequence of policy but rather the failure of policy. Because the U.S. has been unable to reduce its oil imports enough to cause a drop in world oil prices, Americans are buying smaller cars and driving them less.

The inconvenient truth is, even if the U.S. were to reduce its oil imports to zero, unless it also completely insulated itself from the world oil market, gasoline prices still would be determined by world petroleum prices, and they still would be sky high. As Yale economist William Nordhaus said in a recent article, "Our vulnerability depends on the global market. It does not depend upon the fraction of our [oil] consumption that is imported." ■

Natural gas revolution

OVERWHELMINGLY, the major development in world energy during the last years has been the revolution in "unconventional gas," specifically shale gas extracted by means of hydraulic fracturing, or "fracking." The upheaval started in the Southwest about a decade ago, is now sweeping the U.S. Northeast, and soon will transform parts of Western Europe, China and Central Asia.

Experts describe what is going on in natural gas as a "game changer," one that "is already changing the national energy dialogue and overall energy outlook in the U.S.—and could change the global natural gas balance," as Robert Ineson and Daniel Yergin wrote in late 2009 in *The Wall Street Journal*. Yergin, chairman of IHS Cambridge Energy Research Associates and for decades one of the top names in energy analysis, has meanwhile amplified that assessment in a major new book about energy, *The Quest*.

Two and a half years ago, reacting to the development of gas fracking methods, the Potential Gas Committee, a consortium of academic and industrial experts coordinated by the Colorado School of Mines, boosted its estimate of U.S. gas reserves by 45%. Taking DOE assessments into account as well, the total available future supply in the U.S. is now nearly 2,074 trillion cubic feet—enough to meet the country's gas needs for about 90 years at current rates of consumption, or perhaps half that long if consumption is doubled.

And double it likely will. That is because—as advertisers constantly remind us—gas is now very cheap relative to oil, available right here in the U.S. in vast quantities, and much cleaner than coal in terms of both standard pollutants and greenhouse gas emissions. On a per-unit-energy basis gas generates about half as much greenhouse gas as coal. Therefore, as coal-generated electricity accounts for about a third of U.S. greenhouse gas emissions, if the country were to close half its coal plants

and replace them with gas, the net effect would be about the same as doubling gasoline prices.

Fukushima's impact

The revolution in unconventional gas has been a lucky break for the U.S. and will continue to do its work for decades to come. It is unlikely, however, to have a similar impact in Europe, at least in the near term. Though a big find was recently announced in northwest Britain—possibly as much as 200 trillion cubic feet—it remains to be seen whether comparable reserves will be identified elsewhere. Exploratory drilling so far is largely confined to Poland, Germany and Britain.

What is more, because Europe is so much more densely populated than the U.S., concerns about the impact of gas fracturing on water reserves are bound to be even more acute. In 2010, France's Parliament voted to ban fracking outright, pending more research into its effects.

Europe's dependence on gas imports, accordingly, will remain great and is almost sure to grow. Currently, Europe gets about a quarter of its natural gas

from Russia, and some major countries like Germany and Italy obtain 40% or more from the Russian sphere. The reason that dependence will grow in the next decade is, in a word, Fukushima.

The nuclear crisis at Fukishima has been quite different from the two major previous accidents, Three Mile Island in 1979 and Chernobyl in 1986. But all three had this in common: What happened was quite a bit worse than anybody would have expected. Not only was there a fuel meltdown in at least one reactor, but two containment buildings exploded and a spent fuel cooling pond caught fire. The spectacle of a large reactor complex almost completely out of control had an immense international impact and fundamentally changed the terms of the nuclear debate in Germany, Italy and Japan itself.

Germany, which had been dithering for decades about whether to phase out nuclear power, and which is led by a government that had sought to negotiate "an exit from the nuclear exit," threw in the towel and decided to shut down its nuclear reactors by 2022. Italy soon followed suit, and Japan may as well.

Mar. 16, 2011: People look on as they wait to be scanned for radiation at a temporary scanning center for residents living close to the quake-damaged Fukushima Dai-ichi nuclear power plant in Koriyama, Fukushima Prefecture, Japan. (GREGORY BULL/AP)

That means those countries will have to rely more on coal and natural gas in the coming decades to generate electricity, which in turn implies increased greenhouse gas emissions. Because the carbon intensity of coal is so high, the preference will always be when possible for gas, and so gas imports will increase.

Eurasian geopolitics

Putin's frankly stated and unswerving ambition has long been to make Russia's prodigious fossil fuel assets—above all its gigantic natural gas reserves—the foundation of the country's economic and military recovery.

This is why during his first term as president Putin reconsolidated state control over the oil and gas industries (much improving management of Gazprom and nationalizing Mikhail Khodorkovsky's much improved Yukos). By provoking a series of gas supply crises with neighbors (mainly Ukraine and Belarus), Russia was able to get a firm lock on pipelines to Western Europe and to dictate export terms.

Ukraine is the major hub of the European pipeline network, and so Putin has seen it as essential to keep Ukraine firmly in line.

Ultimately, as demand for natural gas rises sharply in northeast Asia as well, Russia stands to be in a pivotal position to play one continent off against the other, exercising significan market power to keep prices as high as consumers can bear.

Putin, a shrewd, skillful, determined and ruthless operator, is not to be underestimated. The disconcerting thing about his exercise of energy power, indeed, is that it has tended to work. In the wake of the last gas confrontation with Ukraine, that country's voters appear to have decided that Russia had too much influence on their fortunes for them to risk provoking it again. They voted out Prime Minister Yulia V. Tymoshenko's government, which had been seeking membership in the EU, and voted in the pro-Russian party headed by Viktor Yanukovich. Promptly after taking power, the new government agreed to an exten-

sion until 2042 for Russia's naval base at Sevastopol on the Black Sea (within Ukrainian territory), one of Putin's major diplomatic objectives.

Then, in what might be ranked as a record-setting act of political cynicism, the pro-Russian government brought criminal charges against Tymoshenko, accusing her of having caved into Russian demands in the gas dispute. In fact, it was Tymoshenko, a harsh critic of Putin, who had tried hardest to stand up to Russia. As of this writing, she languishes in a Ukrainian jail.

While Europe continues to maneuver to open a new gas pipeline into Central Asia that would make it less dependent on Russia-controlled routes, Russia seeks to build South Stream, which would connect its fields with Italian customers the way Nord Stream connects with major German utilities.

When it comes to the geopolitics of building pipelines in the Caucasus and thereabouts, Russia has historical experience, political relationships and economic clout that would be hard to match. ∎

Climate geopolitics

ARGUABLY, European dependence on Russian natural gas (and all that it implies) is basically a European problem, not a U.S. one. This indeed is why German Chancellor Angela Merkel has been much more cautious about extending NATO membership to former Soviet constituent states that the Atlantic Alliance might not be willing to defend militarily, if push came to shove.

But Europe's backsliding into greater dependence on fossil fuels has implications that directly concern the U.S., notably the ramifications having to do with greenhouse gas emissions and climate change. During the first decade following the adoption in Rio de Janiero, Brazil, of the United Nations Framework Convention on Climate Change (UNFCCC) in 1992, Europe carried the burden of cutting emissions so as to prevent what the convention calls "dangerous" climate change.

Between 1990 (the base year specified in the 1998 Kyoto Protocol to the UNFCCC) and 2009, the EU-15—those countries party to the UNFCCC at the time it was adopted—cut their emissions about 15%. U.S. emissions increased during that same period by 5.6%. Britain and Germany, the world leaders in climate policy, cut their emissions by 28% and 23%—three or four times as much as Kyoto prescribed.

European leaders have been remarkably restrained in complaining publicly about the performance of the U.S. compared with theirs. But among Europe's educated publics there has been a simmering anger, which may account for the sharpness of differences between Europe and the U.S. that erupted last year over emissions from commercial aircraft.

The EU has taken the position that U.S. carriers will be required, beginning in 2012, along with European carriers

and any other airlines landing planes in Europe, to buy emissions credits as part of the 2010 EU Emissions Trading System (ETS). Connie Hedegaard, EU Commissioner for Climate Action, has been quite insistent on that point. That by itself might not mean much: As former Danish environment minister and chairperson of the 2009 global climate conference in Copenhagen, Denmark, her efforts to obtain a strong binding agreement were torpedoed and she personally was sidelined. But with European carriers insisting that all airlines must be subject to the same carbon taxation, it seems improbable that Europe will back down—and not just because of resentments associated with Rio and Kyoto.

Kyoto ironies

The history of the Kyoto Protocol has been riddled with paradox. As Yergin recounts in *The Quest*, aggressive inter-

On left, May 5, 2010: Black, dense smoke is emitted from chimneys at a Sinopec petrochemical plant in Lanzhou city, northwest China's Gansu province. (IMAGINECHINA/AP) *On right, July 6, 2011: A worker checks solar panels in Xigaze Prefecture, southwest China's Tibet Autonomous Region. The largest solar power station in Tibet, its annual electricity generation of 20 million kilowatt hours can displace some 9,000 tons of coal, and is enough to meet the annual power demands of 100,000 local households.* (XINHUA NEWS AGENCY/EYEVINE/REDUX)

vention by the U.S. in the 11th hour of negotiations resulted in the Europeans agreeing—kicking and screaming—to the principle of carbon trading; the U.S. delegation led at the end by Vice President Al Gore, persuaded them that cap-and-trade would be the price of a meaningful agreement, with binding emissions reductions targets for the industrial and near-industrial countries.

But then, before the ink was dry, the U.S. made clear that the treaty could not and would not be ratified by the U.S. Senate. Though, in the following years, the idea of setting up a U.S. cap-and-trade system won bipartisan backing—at one time or another Senator John McCain (R-AZ), Joseph Lieberman (I-CT) and Lindsay Graham (R-SC) co-sponsored legislation—in the end the Obama Administration declined to push such legislation.

At the Copenhagen meeting in December 2009, the U.S. made clear it would not "do" Kyoto in any sense. In effect, the U.S. and China conspired to kill a strong follow-on agreement—the U.S., because it did not want binding reduction targets unless countries like China were subject to them too, and China, because it considered such targets incompatible with rapid economic growth.

What Americans have tended to lose sight of is that their country stands isolated on Kyoto: The protocol has won virtually universal adherence,

and the U.S. is now the lone holdout. So, Kyoto joins other international agreements—such as those banning land mines, protecting children and migrant workers, and establishing the International Criminal Court, among others—that the U.S. has chosen not to affirm despite a general presumption that they have come to have binding force, morally and legally. (In international law, if a treaty or body of law is seen as expressing the general opinion of humankind it can be considered binding on a country, whether or not the country has agreed to it.)

What the Europeans have tended to lose sight of, on the other hand, is that in practice, there is by no means a one-to-one relationship between Kyoto status and actual performance. Under George W. Bush's presidency (2001–2009), which explicitly repudiated the case for climate action, the U.S. actually did as good a job as Europe of cutting its greenhouse gas emissions: Indeed, in the period from 2000 to 2009, in which U.S. policy consistently fell short of what Kyoto parties have sought, the U.S. cut its emissions by about 12%, whereas Europe cut its a little more than 11%. Canada, which was supposed to cut its emissions by about the same amount as Europe and the U.S. between 1990 and now—roughly 7% to 8%—has seen its emissions climb 30%.

So, seen in the perspective of the UNFCCC, if the U.S. approves the Key-

stone XL pipeline, it will not merely be out of keeping with its Copenhagen greenhouse gas reduction pledge—the U.S. will be enabling a country that is in violation of its supposedly binding Kyoto commitment.

The China price

While the U.S. and to a lesser degree the Europeans have been complaining about China's refusal to even promise when growth in its emissions will stop, let alone when it will be in a position to reduce them, the People's Republic has been busily gobbling up subsidies that rich countries offer to those developing and deploying renewable energy.

A major source of capital for wind and solar projects in countries like China has been the ETS, working in combination with the Kyoto Clean Development Mechanism, which enables parties unable to meet reduction targets in the rich countries to purchase emissions credits from parties installing clean energy in poor countries. In practice the ETS has been the main source for such funds. According to the *Financial Times* (London), somewhere between $25 and $100 billion appears to have been transferred from emitters in Europe to green energy developers in countries like China.

Meanwhile, Chinese wind and solar manufacturers have been collecting the generous subsidies that countries like Germany and Spain—not to mention the U.S.—offer to those who develop and deploy renewables. That has had drastic effects on the fortunes of green energy companies in the rich countries, above all in photovoltaics, where the Chinese have radically driven down the price of the workhorse material poly-silicon, making life very difficult for all solar manufacturers.

Inexplicably, leaders of the rich countries have been painfully slow to react to that dilemma. The Chinese, on the other hand, seem to have gotten it right away. They do not extend the generous subsidies they give Chinese consumers buying China-made hybrid and electric cars to foreign manufacturers of such vehicles. The foreign manufacturers and their state patrons have humbly gone along with those requirements.

No regrets

The outlook for renewables and issues of subsidization and commercial viability are crucial because, for all practical purposes, when energy resources that can enhance energy independence or reduce climate risk are discussed, the topic is predominantly renewables.

The idea of strongly promoting low-carbon and zero-carbon sources of energy emerged in the 1990s and often went under the name of "no regrets." If, as scientists were saying at the time,

global warming might turn out to be a problem, then it made sense to do things addressing climate risks that would have made sense to do anyway. Since the OECD countries—Europe, North America and Japan—were all worried about their chronic dependence on imported fossil fuels, why not do things that would help reduce that dependence and also would help, in the long run, cut greenhouse gas emissions?

That philosophy is, in a sense, now obsolete. The scientific community, since the last assessment by the Intergovernmental Panel on Climate Change in 2007, has been saying that the human-induced global warming is definitely a serious problem. As such, it calls for a more robust approach than mere "no regrets."

But, in practice, no regrets is what there is. Public concern about climate change, though widespread throughout the OECD countries, so far has turned out to be rather shallow. U.S. voters are not demanding their leaders deliver on climate commitments, and European voters are not calling for sanctions to be imposed on the delinquent Americans.

Green outlook

So how much can be expected of wind and solar? In its mid-year 2011

report, the World Wind Energy Association found a total of 18,405 megawatts (MW) of wind power had been installed in the first half of the year around the world, up from 16,000 MW in 2010. Unsurprisingly, China accounted for a huge chunk of the 2011 installations, with 8,000 MW of new wind power. The U.S. lagged far behind, at 2,252 MW, followed by India (1,480 MW), Germany (766 MW) and Canada (603 MW).

The world's total wind energy capacity reached 215,000 MW at the end of June 2011. In terms of the ability to generate electricity, 215,000 MW is equivalent to the construction of 215 nuclear power plants. However, when comparing wind or solar capacity to nuclear, it is important to bear in mind that a reactor generates electricity 90% of the time or more while intermittent sources of energy like wind and solar generate power only a third, fourth or even a fifth of the time.

Prospects for continued strong growth in wind energy are good in the U.S. but somewhat dimmer in Europe. Germany and Denmark appear to have already exhausted most suitable on-land sites, forcing them to more expensive offshore sites. In Britain, unusually strong hostility to on-land installations has had the same effect.

Energy Daily has reported another arresting number, based on figures from the Energy Information Administration (EIA): In 2009, for the first time, renewables matched nuclear energy in U.S. primary energy production—not just capacity, but actual energy generated. However, primary energy includes all energy, not just electric power, and renewables, as defined by the EIA, comprise hydropower and biomass, among other things. Specifically, biomass and biofuels accounted for 52% of the renewables share in primary energy production, and hydropower for 31.5%. Wind made up 10.5% of the energy generated from renewables, and solar less than 1.5%.

Although widely seen as a panacea, solar energy is far from demonstrating its commercial viability. Photo-

July 19, 2011: Energy company EnBW has constructed this offshore wind park, Baltic One, which generates electricity for 45,000 households, 16 kilometers north of the Darss Peninsula, Zingst, Germany. (PAUL LANGROCK/ZENIT/LAIF/REDUX)

voltaic power plants are rarely, if ever, installed without generous subsidies. That means there are severe limits to how quickly solar energy can be scaled up; it may in fact never be scalable.

Critical elements

Continued advances in storage technologies are seen as crucial both to electric power, where wide use of intermittent green energy will require electricity to somehow be saved, and in the automotive sector, where much wider use of plug-in hybrids and all-electric vehicles will depend on the invention of much cheaper batteries. Those technologies will depend on scarce resources from places that may also be problematic.

The list of elements that are critically needed in energy is extensive and includes some truly obscure items like the transition metal vanadium, a standard steel strengthener that also could be key to the development of grid-scale "flow batteries." The rare earth neodymium is needed in the magnetic alloys used in hybrid vehicle motors; each Toyota Prius requires an estimated 2.2 pounds. Altogether, according to a report on "energy critical materials" prepared by a committee of the American Physical Society (APS) and the Materials Research Society (MRS) last year, there are more than a dozen of them in addition to the 17 rare earths, some of which are crucial to wind turbines, solar collectors and electric cars.

Perceived manipulation of rare earth markets by China, overwhelmingly the dominant supplier of most of these minerals, has given rise to concern in the last year. The U.S. imports about 90% of the energy-critical materials it needs, the APS-MRS report found, which is not a problem when suppliers are widely diversified. But when they are highly concentrated, there is the danger of the supplying country being exploited by outsiders, and the danger of the supplying country exploiting outsiders. "The present 'rare earth crisis'—involving dramatic price escalations and possible shortages— appears to be an example of government policy," said the report.

Feb. 25, 2010, Salar de Uyuni, Bolivia: Lithium, a soft silver-white metal, is the lightest metal and the least dense solid element. It is highly reactive and erodes quickly. Bolivia's reserves exceed 5.4 million tons, much of which will be sold to produce batteries for cars. These lithium salt mounds are a major source of income for Bolivia. (MEHDI CHEBIL/POLARIS)

Right now most hybrids and electric vehicles have employed lithium-ion batteries, drastically scaled-up versions of the batteries found in laptops. The main source of lithium is the Altiplano desert straddling Chile, Bolivia and Argentina. Globally, Chile is the No. 1 exporter, and Argentina is second.

Policy options

Though efforts are being made to find green technologies that avoid reliance on rare earths, the fact remains that trying to reduce dependence on oil can breed other dependencies, some of which could turn out to be just as awkward geopolitically. Given that the U.S. is only somewhat dependent on Mideast oil, and considering that Americans almost certainly will be stuck with higher gasoline prices no matter how much oil the country imports, is "energy independence" really a suitable goal?

An alternative policy approach would make reduction of climate risks the priority, with reduced reliance on imported fuels a fringe benefit, however dubious. In this approach, for example, the U.S. would not necessarily promote electric and hybrid-electric cars if their introduction meant even greater reliance on electricity generated from fossil fuels. Nor would it encourage use of biofuels, whose production yields little climate benefit while incurring huge costs in terms of ecology and food.

Wherever the emphasis is put, there is the question of what policy instruments are most suitable. A higher tax on fossil fuels would discourage oil imports but also domestic production of natural gas. A carbon tax reflecting the widely varying carbon intensities of different fuels would enhance prospects for renewables and nuclear energy, but do little to discourage oil imports. A cap-and-trade system would have similar effects.

Finally, there is the matter of energy dependence among major economies that are intimately intertwined with the U.S. economy. This country's fortunes are highly dependent on the prosperity of Europe and Northeast Asia, but does that mean it is necessarily America's responsibility to guarantee the continued supply of fuels to those economies? It is an increasingly onerous responsibility at a time of severe budgetary challenges.

Outgoing Defense Secretary Robert Gates, bidding a farewell to NATO allies, called on them to pay for a larger share of the common defense. That too is a kind of energy policy. ∎

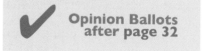

Opinion Ballots after page 32

discussion questions

1. Increasingly, global warming is seen as the mirror image of energy use. To what extent do energy goals coincide with and complement climate goals, and to what extent do they conflict? When they collide, should energy security or greenhouse gas reduction take priority? How can policymakers balance these interests?

2. What should be the priority of the U.S. government: security of energy supplies or the cost of oil and gasoline? Can these interests be reconciled with each other? Should policy emphasize guaranteeing supplies, diversifying them, or reducing dependence on existing supplies by developing alternative fuels and technologies?

3. Where does energy security rank among U.S. foreign policy interests? What are the appropriate methods for securing energy supply? Should the energy wealth of other nations be a consideration in foreign policy? Consider, for instance, U.S. military involvement on the side of the National Transitional Council of oil-rich Libya in 2011.

4. How should the U.S. balance the interest of environmental conversation with the energy potential of regions like the Arctic and the Beaufort Sea? Should U.S. policy be driven by the consideration that countries such as Russia and Canada are already grappling over claims for oceanic and Arctic energy hotspots and countries late to the Arctic game may be left behind?

5. Lower energy prices translate into higher economic growth but also greater energy use—and higher greenhouse gas emissions. During economic crises, should economic growth take precedence over the reduction of greenhouse gases? Should the U.S. discourage consumption by imposing taxes to increase energy prices? Can reduction of oil imports make the economy less vulnerable to price increases?

6. To what extent is the security of Europe's natural gas and oil supplies from Russia and FSU states a legitimate U.S. concern? Should the U.S. involve itself in negotiation of Eurasian pipelines routes?

suggested readings

Crane, Hewitt D., Kinderman, Edwin M., and Malhotra, Ripudaman, **A Cubic Mile of Oil: Realities and Options for Averting the Looming Global Energy Crisis**. New York, Oxford University Press, 2010. 328 pp. $29.95 (hardcover). For those unable to negotiate quads, kilowatts, barrels and bushels, and for those visually inclined, this is the book to have. Everything is stated in terms of a cubic mile of oil, as the title implies.

Hallett, Steve, and Wright, John, **Life Without Oil: Why We Must Shift to a New Energy Future**. Amherst, NY, Prometheus Books, 2011. 375 pp. $26.00 (hardcover). Puts the age of oil in a broad historical perspective and conjures the specter of ecological collapse when energy consumption exceeds resources. Coauthored by an academic and a journalist.

Huber, Peter W., "Broadband Electricity and the Free-Market Path to Electric Cars," **Energy Policy & the Environmental Report**, The Manhattan Institute, New York, March 2011. Available free online at: <http://www.manhattan-institute.org/pdf/eper_07.pdf>. The author's core observation is that about half of electricity generating capacity, an even higher fraction of grid capacity, and 90% of automotive power lie idle. He argues that certain free-market policies could link the power system and car battery storage, to achieve great efficiencies and savings.

Klare, Michael T., **Rising Powers, Shrinking Planet: The New Geopolitics of Energy**. New York, Henry Holt and Company, 2008. 352 pp. $17.00 (paper). The third and perhaps the best so far of the author's books to sound alarms about the geopolitical implications of scarce resources. A fourth book by Klare on the same subject is forthcoming.

Jacobson, Mark Z., and Delucchi, Mark A., "Providing All Global Energy with Wind, Water and Solar Power Technologies," **Energy Policy**, 2010. Available free online at: <http://www.stanford.edu/group/efmh/jacobson/Articles/I/JDEnPolicyPt1.pdf>. The authors argue that a world powered exclusively by electricity and hydrogen separated electrolytically from water would require only 40%–60% more land to be dedicated to energy production, resulting in 30% less energy consumption.

Viktor, David, and Yanosek, Kassia, "The Coming Crash in Clean Energy," **Foreign Affairs**, July–August 2011. The value of clean-energy companies has been dropping and is destined to fall still more, bringing tough foreign policy challenges.

Yergin, Daniel, **The Quest: Energy, Security, and the Remaking of the Modern World**. New York, The Penguin Press, 2011. 816 pp. $27.95 (hardcover). Hot off the press, the latest grand survey of the scene by the person who is probably the most quoted and most highly regarded energy analyst. Authoritative and comprehensive, though Yergin this time has no particular message to convey.

Visit **WWW.GREATDECISIONS.ORG** *for quizzes, seasonal topic updates and other resources to further your understanding*

Global Discussion Questions

No decision in foreign policy is made in a vacuum, and the repercussions of any single decision have far-reaching effects across the range of strategic interests on the U.S. policy agenda. This new GREAT DECISIONS feature is intended to facilitate the discussion of this year's topics in a global context, to discuss the linkages between the topics and to encourage consideration of the broader impact of decisionmaking.

---

1. Consider the U.S. interests in "Promoting Democracy" in the context of the new landscape of concerns that have arisen in "Cybersecurity." What is the role of cybersecurity in the democracy agenda? How does the interest of promoting democracy compare to the other interests—military, intellectual, economic—that the U.S. has in cyberspace?

2. "Energy Geopolitics" raises concerns about the effects of climate change and the ways in which policy decisions may cause the existing problems to worsen. How do these concerns resonate in "Oceans"? Could the ocean, with its hidden treasures of biodiversity and mineral and resource wealth, be compared to the land atop rare earth minerals or fossil fuels? What should be the conversation about the relationship between energy independence and marine conservation?

3. "Exit from Afghanistan & Iraq" details two missions that brought democracy to the Middle East. How were methods suggested in "Promoting Democracy" applied? What methods might have been more effective? Why?

4. How might the experiences leading up to the "Exit from Afghanistan & Iraq" informed the U.S. reaction to the mass protests in the Middle East and North Africa? How have Afghanistan and Iraq influenced the U.S. response to the "Middle East Realignment"?

5. In the context of the "Middle East Realignment," what can be learned from the example of "Indonesia"? What conditions seen in Egypt, Tunisia, Libya, etc. were or were not present in Indonesia prior to democratization? How can the example of Indonesia be applied to other nations emerging from authoritarian rule?

6. "Mexico" discusses a variety of concerns that have hampered the effective functioning of the democratic government. Consider "Exit from Afghanistan & Iraq"; how might these new, flawed states avoid serious problems of organized crime? In the context of the discussion of corruption in "Indonesia," what factors have contributed to crime and corruption in Mexico's government?

TOPIC 1: REBUILDING HAITI

ISSUE A: How should the U.S. government and the international community provide aid to Haiti? (Select one)

Directly to the Haitian government.	2%
Channel aid through NGOs, with initial pre-screening of NGOs.	43%
Give non-cash aid directly to the Haitian people.	16%
Provide 50% of aid to the government, 50% aid to NGOs.	23%
Other	16%

ISSUE B: As part of its assistance to Haiti, the U.S. should subsidize a program for Haitian expatriates living in the U.S. with appropriate skills to return to Haiti to help with reconstruction.

Agree	75%
Disagree	26%

ISSUE C: Decisions made with respect to rebuilding Haiti should be made by: (Select one)

Haitians should have the right to determine their priorities without external interference. 7%

Haitians should be the primary decisionmakers, with voluntary guidance from a select group of external organizations and individuals. 51%

Given limited government capacity, these decisions should be made jointly with equal veto power between Haitians and external representatives. 35%

Since money and resources will be external, these decisions should primarily be made by a select group of external representatives. 6%

ISSUE D: In the reconstruction of Haiti, what should be the extent of the U.S. role? (Select one)

Given its geographical proximity and U.S. capabilities, the U.S. should take a dominant leadership role with respect to Haiti's rebuilding. 3%

It should be a regional process, but with the U.S. at the helm. The U.S. should have greater decisionmaking authority as the majority contributor of resources. 14%

It should be an extensively regional proceeding, with participation from nations across the hemisphere, and a multilateral decisionmaking process. 42%

Given prior experience with Haiti and nation building, it should be led by the United Nations through its stabilization mission in Haiti, MINUSTAH. 42%

TOPIC 2: NATIONAL SECURITY

ISSUE A: In your opinion, which strategy should shape the future of the U.S. military? (Select one)

Counterinsurgency capability (COIN), which recognizes the additional labor required to engage in "irregular warfare." 15%

Traditionalist strategy, which focuses on sustaining military capability and combined arms warfare. 4%

Both, with emphasis on COIN. 71%

Both, with emphasis on traditionalist strategy. 10%

ISSUE B: In your opinion, which of the following policies should be the Obama Administration's greatest priority? (Select one)

Cuts in defense spending and/or raising taxes	49%
Nuclear abolition	8%
Containment of Iran	10%
Resolution of the Israel-Palestine dispute	15%
Denuclearization of North Korea	4%
Other	16%

ISSUE C: Given that America's fiscal imbalance is potentially the most urgent national security "threat" today, rank the following in terms of their effect on the general fear level in the U.S. (Rank from 1 to 7, with 1 being the greatest and 7 the least)

	1	2	3	4	5	6	7
Spread of nuclear weapons	31%	22%	18%	11%	8%	6%	4%
Cyberspace activity	21%	20%	16%	12%	12%	10%	10%
Homegrown terrorism	30%	21%	14%	10%	9%	8%	7%
Iran	9%	16%	22%	24%	18%	8%	2%
North Korea	3%	9%	16%	23%	24%	20%	6%
Yemen	1%	2%	4%	9%	17%	32%	37%
A disgruntled China	9%	10%	10%	11%	12%	15%	34%

ISSUE D: Which of the following aspects of the intelligence/security bureaucracy presents the most significant hindrance to the successful execution of post-9/11 security? (Select one)

Excessive bureaucracy and jurisdictional disputes, such as those between different agencies and officials, such as Leon Panetta and Dennis Blair's confrontation. 29%

Lack of coordination/cooperation between agencies, such as problems with information sharing. 54%

Outdated strategies from the cold-war era. 13%

Other 4%

TOPIC 3: HORN OF AFRICA

ISSUE A: Would you support future U.S. military involvement as part of an international mission to address governance failures in Somalia?

Yes	15%
No	66%
Not sure	20%

ISSUE B: The U.S. and the international community should stop trying to reconstitute what has proven to be a failed state in the case of Somalia.

Agree strongly	15%
Agree	51%
Disagree	30%
Disagree strongly	4%

ISSUE C: Short of direct recognition, should the U.S. support the greater legitimation of Somaliland and Puntland by supplying direct economic and military aid to these regions?

Yes	23%
No	46%
Not sure	31%

ISSUE D: Rank in order of priority U.S. interests in the region: (1=Highest, 6=Lowest.)

	1	2	3	4	5	6
Preventing al-Qaeda, al-Shabaab and other terrorist groups from establishing a base in Somalia.	33%	21%	16%	15%	13%	2%
Creating the conditions for effective domestic governance in Somalia	16%	17%	24%	22%	20%	1%
Ensuring a stable and peaceful Sudan, regardless of the outcome of the referendum.	7%	17%	21%	30%	25%	1%
Humanitarian and economic aid for some of the poorest countries in the world.	24%	20%	23%	16%	16%	1%
Ensuring safe passage of oil and other goods travelling through the Gulf of Aden and the Bab al-Mandeb strait.	26%	26%	14%	13%	20%	1%
Other	13%	4%	9%	10%	11%	52%

TOPIC 4: FINANCIAL CRISIS

ISSUE A: In situations such as the Icelandic banking crisis, the failing bank's home government should bear the burden of repaying losses incurred by its international investors.

Strongly agree	9%
Agree	44%
Disagree	39%
Strongly disagree	8%

ISSUE B: In your opinion, should there be a concerted effort to reduce the interdependence of governments and banks?

Yes	50%
No	28%
Not sure	22%

ISSUE C: Should the U.S. participate in treaty-based (binding) cross-border financial regulatory regimes?

Yes	54%
No	19%
Not sure	27%
Other, or comment.	1%

ISSUE D: What do you think will happen to the U.S. dollar's role as the international reserve currency in the future? (Select one.)

The dollar will lose its dominant position in the next 10 years. 16%

The dollar will be gradually overtaken in the next 15 years by a mix of other currencies. 26%

The dollar will continue as the reserve currency of choice, due to the lack of any viable alternatives in the midterm and a relatively strong U.S. economic recovery. 58%

TOPIC 5: GERMANY'S ASCENDANY

ISSUE A: The U.S. should promote the leadership of a strong Germany within Europe.

Agree	70%
Disagree	13%
Not sure	17%

ISSUE B: Germany's insistence on austerity measures for crisis-prone countries as well as fiscal conservatism in its own country is, primarily: (Select one)

Ignorant of the needs of the troubled euro-zone economy and detrimental to the recovery of the global economy. 9%

Rational and conducive to a more responsible global economy in the future. 92%

ISSUE C: The impact of Germany's actions to reduce military spending is, for the U.S.: (Select one)

A positive step, lessening the threat of a resurgence of German militarism. 32%

Dangerous, leaving Europe vulnerable in the event of an attack. 32%

No real effect. 37%

ISSUE D: With respect to the U.S. tactical nuclear weapons in Germany and several other European countries, the U.S. should:

Remove any remaining weapons in the interests of nuclear disarmament. 45%

Insist on their continued presence due to military concerns and Europe's reliance on U.S. security guarantees. 31%

Negotiate to transfer weapons to trusted countries that want them on their soil. 25%

ISSUE E: Should U.S. policy focus and prioritize issues of concern to Germany (i.e., climate change and international criminal law) in order to strengthen the political relationship?

Yes	62%
No	18%
Not sure	20%

TOPIC 6: SANCTIONS AND NONPROLIFERATION

ISSUE A: To what degree do you feel that U.S./EU/UN economic sanctions against nuclear proliferators represent an effective policy tool for dealing with "rogue states" that pursue nuclear weapons? (Select one)

They represent the best option available. 12%

They are not necessarily the best choice, but one of the only tools we have. 68%

They have proven ineffective time and again and are a waste of time and political and diplomatic resources. 20%

ISSUE B: To what extent do you feel that the current military engagements in Afghanistan and Iraq are the main factor in discouraging U.S. military action toward Iran? (Select one)

They are absolutely the main reason why we are not at war with Iran. 7%

They are part of the reason, but other independent factors such as the economy and Iranian capabilities also play a role. 69%

They are not really relevant to the discussion on Iran. 24%

ISSUE C: How realistic is the goal of nuclear nonproliferation and containing nuclear weapons to just the nine de facto nuclear nations on the scene today? (UN Security Council permanent members plus India, Pakistan, Israel, North Korea) (Select one)

This is a realistic goal that the U.S. can achieve by working with others in the common interest of global security. 24%

Ideally, this is an achievable goal, but the U.S. has many other more important priorities to address, both at home and abroad. 22%

This is ultimately an unrealistic goal. The temptation for other states to acquire nuclear weapons will prove too strong. 55%

ISSUE D: Which of the following U.S. policies would be most effective in stopping North Korean proliferation? (Select one)

Signing a peace treaty with North Korea ending the Korean War that includes some kind of security guarantee for Pyongyang in exchange for destroying all nuclear weapons and technology. 22%

Continuing to pursue a diplomatic solution through the six-party talks and bilateral talks. 36%

Having frank discussions with China and doing whatever is necessary to convince Beijing to enforce comprehensive sanctions on North Korea and to use its influence to support U.S. interests. 40%

Taking military action, whether it is a targeted strike or something more. 3%

TOPIC 7: CAUCASUS

ISSUE A: U.S. relations with the regional powers, Russia and Turkey, are more important and should have priority over relations with other states in the region.

Strongly agree	19%	Disagree	20%
Agree	59%	Strongly disagree	2%

ISSUE B: Since the Russia-Georgia war in 2008, Tbilisi has been actively seeking access to U.S. arms transfers. Should the U.S. supply arms to Georgia, arguably its strongest local ally, despite Russian objections?

Yes	19%
No	82%

ISSUE C: Rank in order of priority U.S. interests in the Caucasus: (1=Highest, 4=Lowest)

	1	2	3	4
Maintaining stable and productive relations with Russia and Turkey.	72%	18%	7%	3%
Maintaining some influence over Azerbaijan for reasons of energy security (e.g., to ensure that natural gas transit routes are not monopolized by Russia).	10%	41%	35%	15%
Promoting political and economic liberalization in the region.	18%	28%	30%	23%
Resolution of the Nagorno-Karabakh dispute between Armenia and Azerbaijan, and improvement in the relationship between Armenia and Turkey.	4%	12%	26%	58%

ISSUE D: In terms of involvement in the Caucasus region, the U.S. should: (Select one)

Limit its involvement to economic and development interests and leave it to Europe to get involved politically or militarily. 47%

Continue to promote economic and governance reform throughout the region, but not do anything that actively challenges Russia. 35%

Maintain its presence in the Caucasus for strategic and economic reasons, including constraining Russia's attempt to assert a "sphere of influence." 18%

TOPIC 8: MULTILATERALISM

ISSUE A: If the international community only has the time and commitment to cooperate on one of the issues discussed, which issue do you think most critically needs to be addressed at the global level? (1=most, 5=least)

	1	2	3	4	5
Nuclear nonproliferation	41%	23%	14%	10%	12%
Climate change	28%	21%	16%	14%	21%
Global economic coordination	21%	21%	22%	21%	16%
Economic development	11%	16%	22%	29%	23%
Human rights (e.g., R2P)	12%	17%	23%	23%	25%

ISSUE B: Rank the five issues discussed based upon your perception of how difficult they are to solve cooperatively at the global level. (1=most, 5=least)

	1	2	3	4	5
Nuclear nonproliferation	36%	24%	18%	9%	13%
Climate change	30%	25%	17%	12%	16%
Global economic coordination	11%	18%	22%	30%	19%
Economic development	4%	12%	21%	32%	31%
Human rights (e.g., R2P)	21%	21%	21%	16%	20%

ISSUE C: The U.S. must work toward achieving a binding domestic and international agreement on climate change that includes all major carbon-emitting countries, even at the expense of short-term economic growth and jobs in the U.S.

Strongly agree	35%
Agree	43%
Disagree	16%
Strongly disagree	7%

ISSUE D: The lack of enforcement mechanisms or punitive measures in multilateral agreements such as the NPT and Kyoto Protocol make them useless. The U.S. should not waste time pursuing voluntary cooperative agreements that are ultimately up to the signatory states to implement.

Strongly agree	8%
Disagree	46%
Agree	25%
Strongly disagree	20%

TEACHER TRAINING INSTITUTE

Test lesson plans with students in a simulated classroom environment

SINCE 2005, the **Great Decisions Teacher Training Institute** has been organized by the Foreign Policy Association to assemble educators from across the United States to learn about how *Great Decisions* can be used to teach their students about the world. Over 120 teachers have participated in Teacher Training Institutes to date, gaining skills for teaching their students and valuable resources to share with their colleagues.

Hear from experts on the Great Decisions topics

J oin us in New York City in summer 2012 for the eighth annual Teacher Training Institute!

Participate in workshops to integrate Great Decisions into curriculum

The Foreign Policy Association's 2012 Teacher Institute will focus on some of the critical challenges to U.S. policymakers, using the 2012 **Great Decisions** *topics.*

To learn more or to obtain an application, contact the Programming Department at
(212) 481-8100 ext. 250 or **programs@fpa.org**.

Visit us at **www.greatdecisions.org**

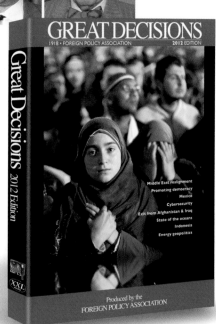

GREAT DECISIONS

ON PBS GOES

BACK TO THE EXPERTS IN 2012

Featuring
After the Arab Spring,
Defense in the Digital Age and Drawdown:
Exiting Iraq and Afghanistan

**Order a DVD of the 2012 television series
online at <u>www.FPA.org</u>**

Headline Series

SINCE 1935, the Foreign Policy Association has published over 3 million issues of the insightful and concise *Headline Series*. The roster of over 330 authors represents a who's who of foreign policy experts and leading journalists. Each issue of the pocket-size *Headline Series* is devoted to a single geographic area or topic of global concern. Recent titles include *India at Sixty: A Positive Balance Sheet, Europe: A Year of Living Dangerously* and *Mexico's Struggle with 'Drugs and Thugs.'*

Available as single copies, on standing order (four consecutive issues) or in bulk at a discount, these inexpensive, succinct and well-researched books demystify the complexities of international affairs. Many provide background for **Great Decisions** topics.

The Persian Gulf:
Tradition and Transformation

by Lawrence G. Potter

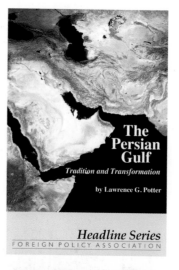

HEADLINE SERIES No. 333-334 (double issue)
Published Fall 2011
$14.99 plus S&H
ISBN# 978-0-87124-234-1; ID# 31610

The Quest for African Unity:
50 Years of Independence and Interdependence

by Robert Nolan

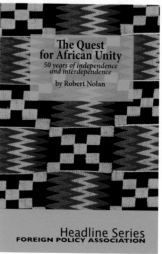

HEADLINE SERIES No. 332
Published Fall 2010
$8.99 plus S&H
ISBN# 978-0-87124-225-7; ID# 31594

It's easy! Order the Headline Series *and any other FPA titles:*
Call toll-free **(800) 477-5836**, 10 am–5 pm EST,
Or visit us online at **www.fpa.org**.

Become a member

Associate—$250

Benefits:
- Free admission to all Associate events (includes member's family)
- Discounted admission for all other guests to Associate events
- Complimentary GREAT DECISIONS briefing book and *Headline Series* subscription

National Associate*—$75

Benefits:
- *Headline Series* subscription
- Complimentary issue of FPA's annual *National Opinion Ballot Report* and GREAT DECISIONS Updates

Residents of New York, New Jersey and Connecticut are not eligible.

Student—$50

Benefits:
- Free admission to all Associate events
- Discounted foreign policy publications
- Complimentary issue of FPA's annual *National Opinion Ballot Report*

Make a donation

Your support helps the* FOREIGN POLICY ASSOCIATION'S *programs dedicated to global affairs education.

Make a fully tax-deductible contribution to FPA's Annual Fund 2012.

To contribute to the Annual Fund 2012, contact an individual-giving specialist by calling the Membership Department at **(800) 628-5754 ext. 232,** or by visiting us online at **www.fpa.org**.

The generosity of donors who contribute $500 or more is acknowledged in FPA's *Annual Report*.

All financial contributions are tax-deductible to the fullest extent of the law under section 501 (c)(3) of the IRS code.

FPA also offers membership at the SPONSOR ASSOCIATE and PATRON ASSOCIATE levels. To learn more, contact the Membership Department at (800) 628-5754, ext. 232.

Return this form by mail to: Foreign Policy Association, 470 Park Avenue South, New York, N.Y. 10016.
Or fax to: (212) 481-9275.

TO ORDER FPA PUBLICATIONS: (800) 477-5836

ORDER ONLINE: WWW.GREATDECISIONS.ORG

FOR MEMBERSHIP CALL (800) 628-5754 EXT. 232

☐ MR.   ☐ MRS.   ☐ MS.   ☐ DR.   ☐ PROF.

NAME _____

ADDRESS _____

_____**APT/FLOOR** _____

CITY _____ **STATE** _____ **ZIP** _____

TEL _____

E-MAIL _____

☐ AMEX   ☐ VISA   ☐ MC   ☐ DISCOVER
☐ CHECK (ENCLOSED)

CHECKS SHOULD BE PAYABLE TO FOREIGN POLICY ASSOCIATION.

CARD NO.

☐☐☐☐ ☐☐☐☐ ☐☐☐☐ ☐☐☐☐

SIGNATURE OF CARDHOLDER

EXP. DATE (MM/YY)

PRODUCT	QTY	PRICE	COST
GREAT DECISIONS 2012 TEACHER'S PACKET (1 Briefing Book, 1 Teacher's Guide & 1 DVD) E-MAIL: (REQUIRED) _____		$65	
GREAT DECISIONS 2012 CLASSROOM PACKET (1 Teacher's Packet & 30 Briefing Books) E-MAIL: (REQUIRED) _____		$460	
GREAT DECISIONS 2012 DVD		$40	
Headline Series Nos. 333-334, THE PERSIAN GULF: TRADITION AND TRANSFORMATION (Double issue)		$14.99	
ASSOCIATE MEMBERSHIP		$250	
NATIONAL ASSOCIATE MEMBERSHIP		$75	
STUDENT MEMBERSHIP		$50	
ANNUAL FUND 2012 (ANY AMOUNT)			

For details and shipping charges, call FPA's Sales Department at (800) 477-5836.

Orders mailed to FPA without the shipping charge will be held.

SUBTOTAL $ _____

plus S & H* $ _____

TOTAL $ _____

It's better under the umbrella℠

Always forward-thinking, Travelers provides innovative, flexible insurance to protect individuals and businesses in this ever-changing, global economy. Choose Travelers for broad coverage, first-class service and the peace of mind that comes from working with a leading insurer.

Learn more at travelers.com

TRAVELERS

travelers.com

From Maya Mihindou FOR eni

energy for development, everywhere in the world

eni.com